IDEAL HOMES?

Until now, the 'home' as a space within which domestic lives are lived out has been largely ignored by sociologists. Yet the 'home' as idea, place and object consumes a large proportion of individuals' incomes, and occupies their dreams and their leisure time while the absence of a physical home presents a major threat to both society and the homeless themselves.

This edited collection provides for the first time an analysis of the space of the 'home' and the experiences of home life by writers from a wide range of disciplines, including sociology, criminology, psychology, social policy and anthropology. It covers a range of subjects, including gender roles, different generations' relationships to home, the changing nature of the family, transition, risk and alternative visions of home.

Ideal Homes? provides a fascinating analysis which reveals how both popular images and experiences of home life can produce vital clues as to how society's members produce and respond to social change.

Tony Chapman is Head of Sociology at the University of Teesside. **Jenny Hockey** is Senior Lecturer in the School of Comparative and Applied Social Sciences, University of Hull.

IDEAL HOMES?

Social change and domestic life

Edited by Tony Chapman
and Jenny Hockey

London and New York

First published 1999
by Routledge
11 New Fetter Lane, London EC4P 4EE

Simultaneously published in the USA and Canada
by Routledge
29 West 35th Street, New York, NY 10001

Routledge is an imprint of the Taylor & Francis Group

© 1999 Selection and editorial matter Tony Chapman
and Jenny Hockey; individual chapters, the contributors

Typeset in Goudy by
BC Typesetting, Bristol
Printed and bound in Great Britain by
TJ International Ltd, Padstow, Cornwall

British Library Cataloguing in Publication Data
A catalogue record for this book is available from the British Library

Library of Congress Cataloging in Publication Data
Ideal homes?: social change and domestic life/edited by Tony
Chapman and Jenny Hockey.
p.   cm.
Includes bibliographical references.
1. Home–Great Britain.   2. Dwellings–Great Britain.   3. Housing–
Great Britain.   4. Family–Great Britain.   I. Chapman, Tony, 1953–
II. Hockey, Jennifer Lorna.
HQ613.I34   1999
304.2'3'0941–dc21   98-54119
                                                                              CIP

ISBN 0–415–17121–0 (hbk)
ISBN 0–415–17122–9 (pbk)

CONTENTS

ILLUSTRATIONS

Figures

Tables

CONTRIBUTORS

Mark Bhatti is senior lecturer in housing in the School of Applied Social Science at the University of Brighton. He has written widely on housing and environmental issues and is currently working on a study of gardening and lay ecological knowledge using the Mass Observation Archive at the University of Sussex.

Tim Brindley is principal lecturer in the Department of Architecture at De Montfort University. He is a sociologist who specialises in architecture and the built environment, and he convenes the study group of the British Sociological Association in this field. His other publications are on aspects of housing and urban planning.

Tony Chapman has taught at the University of Teesside since 1990 across a range of issues including the sociology of consumption, domestic architecture, gender, work and home life, urbanism and sociological theory. He has published widely on women's and men's social mobility, gender and graduate employment, family life and careers; and is currently completing a new book on men and domestic life. He is author of *Men's Work, Women's Work* (Information Education, 1987).

Eileen Fairhurst is senior lecturer in the Department of Health Care Studies at Manchester Metropolitan University. In addition to continuing research on home among older people, she is studying the interface between lay and professional boundaries in health care.

Laura Goldsack is senior lecturer in criminology in the School of Social Science at the University of Teesside. She has undertaken a number of research projects on domestic violence in the North East of England, and is currently writing the final report (with Louise Ridley) on the Zero Tolerance campaign in Middlesbrough.

Mike Hepworth is reader in sociology at the University of Aberdeen. His interests include the sociology of deviance and the sociology of ageing. His current research includes a study of the role of visual and verbal images in constructing 'normal' and 'deviant'.

Jenny Hockey is an anthropologist who teaches health and gender studies at the University of Hull. Her principal research interests are in the anthropology of death, dying and bereavement; she has published widely on this topic, including *Experiences of Death: An Anthropological Account* (Edinburgh University Press, 1990), *Death, Gender and Ethnicity* (Routledge 1997, with David Field and Neil Small) and *Beyond the Body: Death and Social Identity* (Routledge, 1999, with Elizabeth Hallam and Glennys Howarth).

Liz Kenyon is a research fellow in the Department of Sociology and Social Policy, University of Southampton. She was awarded her doctorate in sociology from the University of Lancaster in 1998 and is currently working on an ESRC-funded project on young adults' experiences of living in non-familiar shared households.

Ruth Madigan is senior lecturer in the Department of Sociology, University of Glasgow, where she teaches research methods and urban sociology. Her research interests including housing, domestic architecture and the meaning of home, owner occupation, gender and family. She is currently developing an interest in accessible housing design.

Moira Munro has been professor in the School of Planning and Housing at Heriot Watt University/Edinburgh College of Art since 1995. Her research interests are around issues of housing quality and the use of internal space, access to owner occupation and the behaviour of owners and housing finance. She is editor of *Housing Studies*.

Karen Fog Olwig is senior lecturer in anthropology at the University of Copenhagen and has done fieldwork in the American Virgin Islands and among people from Nevis, the former British West Indies, living in the USA, Europe and the Caribbean. She is currently doing life-story interviews in three global family networks of Caribbean origin.

Martin Wood is assistant director of the Northern Consortium of Housing Associations. At the consortium he has directed and a wide range of projects on social housing. He is currently working on a community study of St Hilda's in Middlesbrough, funded by the Joseph Rowntree Foundation.

PREFACE

Under headings such as social class, work, family and gender, sociology has examined the lives of society's members. When it comes to the homes within which their domestic lives are lived out, the discipline has remained somewhat silent. It is a domain which has been left largely to housing policy, planning, architecture and, to a limited extent, social anthropology. At best, the home appears as a bit-part player within weightier discussions, a site where more 'central' social issues can be addressed. Yet 'home' as idea, place and object consumes a significant proportion of individuals' incomes, preoccupies their day-dreams and their leisure time, and, in its absence, constitutes a major threat both for governments and homeless people themselves.

Though we are dealing with the material objects and spaces which most of us inhabit on a day-to-day basis, it is home-based desires, imaginings and aspirations which we prioritise as key aspects of a wider cultural and social nexus. This is reflected in our foregrounding of qualitative studies and textual and graphic representations which effectively capture the specificity of the experience of domestic life, of home as inhabited. Indeed, as we argue throughout this book, the relative permanence and consistency of popular images and experiences of home life can produce vital clues as to how society's members both produce and respond to social change. The topic of the home as idealised and experienced inevitably confronts the sociologist with the changes in family structure which have resulted from the twentieth century's transformations in femininity and masculinity and their impact upon expectations of love and marriage, intimacy and relationships with children, family, friends and neighbours. At the intersection of the public world of planners and policy makers and the personal world of family, friends and neighbours, the home is a site within which key social and personal values can be examined. It is this task which the contributors to this collection have undertaken. Our starting point is the Ideal Home Exhibition which, since its inception in 1908, has provided a synthesis of society's architectural and domestic aspirations. This is complemented by a wide range of studies – qualitative, literary, archival, historical, quantitative – which afford us views into the homes of particular social categories and individuals, from those in transition from youth to adulthood or from mid-life to old age, to those who are abused and those who are haunted.

The volume therefore begins by tracing the emergence of contemporary ideals of home during the nineteenth century. It goes on to acknowledge that within the *longue durêe* of historical time must be placed the more rapid turn-over of individual lives as the home's occupants grow up and grow old. Further, the volume examines the diversity of ways in which home may be experienced, depending for example upon the gender or ethnic origin of its occupants. Indeed, in its focus on paradox, contradiction and heterogeneity, the volume ends by posing questions about change within the homes of the future.

We hope that readers will be inspired as well as informed by the material which this book comprises. It is our intention that the bricks and mortar which have remained largely invisible within our discipline and perhaps taken-for-granted by our readers will emerge as a rewarding and indeed exciting focus for the sociological gaze. Hallways and dining rooms, front gardens and street layouts, once the spaces within which other agendas were pursued, are 'made strange' in this volume in an endeavour to inspire reflection and further research.

The editors wish to give particular thanks to the following individuals, whose help has proved invaluable: Peter Cross, Elizabeth Hallam, Les Johnston, Jacinta Kilcran, Rosemary J. Lucas, Robert MacDonald, Diane Nutt, George Reid, Steve Taylor and Rosie Wilson.

Tony Chapman, University of Teesside
Jenny Hockey, University of Hull
February 1999

1

THE IDEAL HOME AS IT IS IMAGINED AND AS IT IS LIVED

Tony Chapman and Jenny Hockey

Since 1908, London has hosted the *Daily Mail* sponsored Ideal Home Exhibition. While the exhibition has changed a great deal since its early years, it remains an occasion where people can go along and find out what the latest fashions are in domestic architecture, interior design and house furnishing, and see on display all of the latest labour saving gadgets. From a sociological point of view, the Ideal Home Exhibition provides interesting insights into the way that big companies attempt to persuade show visitors to subscribe to a particular model of the ideal home. As the purpose of this book is to explore the way that the ideal home is imagined, as well as the way that it is actually lived, this exhibition proves a unique model of the home as it has been popularly imaged and idealised in society. Not only does it reflect popular representations of the ideal home, but also it attempts to project the way that it should develop so that people can live ideal lives. By definition, this means that the exhibition organisers need to sow a seed of doubt in the minds of visitors about their quality of life in their current homes. This was achieved at the 1995 Ideal Home Exhibition by the principal feature, entitled 'Yesterday's Homes', which presented to the public a mock-up terrace of four houses which were constructed to depict the changing design of housing across the twentieth century.

Instead of celebrating a nostalgic view image of 'Yesterday's Homes' the exhibition designers went to some lengths to suggest that these houses were fundamentally inadequate for modern living – the antithesis of the ideal home. This process of undermining confidence in existing houses began at the rear of the houses, where the viewing public queued up along a path. The backs of the houses were purposely presented in dingy condition with greying net curtains and stained, flat, white-painted window frames. The back gardens gave further clues about the dismal existence that old-fashioned houses were likely to afford. For example, the back garden of a 1967 dormer bungalow

1

with a steeply pitched roof and large picture windows featured outmoded 'ranch-style' fencing, a rotary washing line and an orange 'space hopper' sitting forlornly on a rank patch of grass. The back garden of the next house, a plainly designed 1944 semi-detached house with white-painted concrete rendering and Crittall style metal window frames, had been dug up to plant white cabbages – that most loathed vegetable among a generation of wartime children. At the end of the garden, an Anderson shelter had been sunk – suggesting that this house was fit only for bombing.

Although the Show Guide (1995: 33) hoped that 'you enjoy it, and that many of you will indulge yourselves in a bit of good, old fashioned nostalgia', it was made plain that the nostalgia that people might feel was to be tempered by the negative aspects of old houses. As visitors were herded into a mock-up of a 1908 terraced house in cohorts of twenty, spotlights picked out in turn each of four rooms: the bathroom, bedroom, kitchen and sitting room. The visual display was accompanied by a pre-recorded narrative read by the late Sir Michael Hordern, together with the supposedly contemporaneous dialogue of the inhabitants performed by actors. In the bathroom of the 1908 house, the narrator drew attention to the cast-iron roll-top bath and single cold tap, while in a dimly gas-lit parlour, the visitors heard the hacking coughs of the inhabitants who complained, morosely, about the state of the guttering.

In the next house, a 1926 semi-detached, the visitors were reminded by the narrator that this was the year that Houdini and Rudolph Valentino died 'and the country was brought to a standstill by the General Strike'. The Show Guide issued stark warnings of the dangers of buying such a house:

> the house's hot pipes and heated water combined with poor insulation means that it loses even more heat than its predecessor, giving George and Daisy higher fuel bills. Also, George doesn't realise, of course, that the clever electric lighting is served by metal conduits which will gradually degrade. Heaven help any future buyer – rewiring the entire house isn't going to be cheap!
>
> (Show Guide 1995: 35)

In the wartime house, visitors were reminded about flying bombs in the same breath as the corroded condition of the metal windows was discussed. As if all this were not enough, the Show Guide sarcastically referred to the inhabitants' taste: 'the *charming* sideboard/drinks cabinet [which] has pride of place in the living room. And the bathroom sports the very latest in sanitaryware – a *fetching* bath, WC and pedestal basin, all finished in *tasteful* green' (Show Guide 1995: 35, original emphases).

Finally, in the 1960s house, the narrator fuelled notions of 1960s decadence by mentioning the Rolling Stones on drug charges, while the visitors surveyed the contents of a late 1960s sitting room with a ceramic tile coffee table,

2

Dansette record player, vinyl-fronted mini bar and the once popular *Blue Lady* print.

> Taste aside, this house isn't without its problems either. The central heating system, some basic insulation and the absence of a chimney flue mean that the house is warmer and cheaper to heat, but it also leads to more condensation caused by poor ventilation. And while building techniques had improved, the materials used were often of poor quality. Untreated timber often led to rotting window frames and the plastic gutters tended to leak badly. The unexpected bonus of a paddling pool of rainwater on the garage's flat roof could also lead to damp penetrating the adjoining house walls.
>
> (Show Guide 1995: 36)

Just in case the visitors missed the point, the Show Guide reminded them of the purpose of the exhibition and the appropriate interpretation:

> Our memory tends to be selective, and we often look back through rose-tinted spectacles. We may remember our first 1920s-built house as being 'solid' and having 'character', while forgetting that it was cold, draughty and cost us an arm and a leg to run! Sunny days spent relaxing in our gardens are more easily remembered than the amount of time we had to put in painting window sills, repairing broken gutters or fixing roof tiles . . . We also forget that we could hear our next door neighbour sneeze because sound-proofing was non-existent at the time, and we may look back fondly at the amount of time it took us to save for a new cooker.
>
> (Show Guide 1995: 34)

As the show visitors left the darkened terrace, they emerged onto the patterned brick drive of a brand new show home – the so-called 'House of Tomorrow'. This was a large 'state of the art' 1990s 'L shaped' executive show home with integral double garage. The house was constructed in brick and tile, rather than a mock up of hardboard and timber as was the case in the terrace of 'Yesterday's Homes', and so provided the public with an extremely favourable impression. Inside the freshly painted and decorated house, visitors viewed a gleaming new hi-tech kitchen, a bathroom with power shower and Jacuzzi, while the rest of the house was furnished with the best new furniture and fabric that British Homes Stores could muster. As the Show Guide stated:

> The reality is that housebuilding has come a long way this century, and the owner of a brand new home will never have to put up with these and the many other easily forgotten problems associated with older properties . . . should a similar feature ever be staged at the

Ideal Home Exhibition in 2095, the equivalent turn-of-the-millennium house's imaginary family won't be prompting memories of cold bathrooms, damp walls, broken gutters and heating bills that break the bank.

(Show Guide 1995: 34)

When analysed in the context of an academic book like this, the strategy of the exhibition designers looks transparently manipulative. But in the context of the Ideal Home Exhibition, it is a subtle marketing technique that implants a notion that the visitors' own homes provide an inadequate level of comfort, security and facility (see Chapman 1999).

The above discussion suggests that manufacturers, advertisers, marketing professionals, retail psychologists and others can persuade people to buy into prescribed images of the ideal home. Indeed, there is much evidence to demonstrate that capital is successful at achieving these ends (see Chapman, Chapter 4 in this book; see also, for example, Lodziak 1995; Kellner 1982, 1989; Corrigan 1997; Falk and Campbell 1997). But capital cannot place desires in people's minds as if it were painting on an empty canvas. As this book will demonstrate, other important cultural, economic and personal experiential factors come into play when we consider the way that people envisage the ideal home. When visitors pour into the exhibition, they bring with them a well-developed if unspoken set of personal aspirations, as well as individual frustrations and fears. It is from this perspective that they consume manufacturers' images.

Before we begin our study of the ideal home as it is *lived*, it is therefore important to explore other factors which shape popular images of the ideal home. As we have seen from the discussion of the Ideal Home Exhibition, images change over time, but these transformations may have less to do with technological factors, as the exhibit suggests, than with changing social relationships between, for example, husbands and wives, parents and children, householders and servants. Transformations in the design of houses also come about in response to changed patterns of urban life, employment, expectations of leisure, privacy, respectability, community, security and the projection of social status. It is beyond the scope of this chapter, and indeed beyond the scope of the book, to explore the cross-cultural variations in the development of models of the ideal home (for a useful cross-cultural analysis, see Rapoport 1969; Kent 1990). Instead, we concentrate on the Western model of the ideal home in general, but emphasise in particular transformations in Britain.

Confining ourselves to the British experience for the moment, we begin by asking to what extent is the model of the ideal home shaped by the needs of the individual in isolation from or in opposition to the cultural prerequisites of society more generally? That tired old adage, 'an Englishman's home is his castle', suggests that while individuals and families might face a lifelong struggle for survival in the hot-house of public life, the private home is a 'haven' or 'retreat' where we are free to express our individualism in whatever way we choose. While there are many possibilities for individuals to do what they want in their home – however creative or terrible the consequences might be for the rest of the people living there – evidence presented in this volume reveals strong social pressures from the public world which constrain that behaviour. That home should be a focus for the sociological gaze is therefore highly appropriate and indeed somewhat overdue. In the second half of this chapter, we turn our attention to the problems people encounter when attempting to realise the dream of the ideal home, but for now we shall concentrate on the way that the 'model' of the ideal home has been shaped.

Beginning with individual options, we can state that most people do not have much choice over the fundamental design characteristics of houses – although there are many variations on a theme – because these characteristics are defined by social and cultural factors. Even the very wealthy need planning permission or the advice of the professional architect and interior designer who, likely as not, will have something to offer in the way of advice on structure, function and aesthetics. For people who cannot afford to buy their own home, the issue of what kind of place they should live in is determined by housing officers, planners, architects, politicians and social philanthropists; the criteria that these professionals use to define an 'appropriate' living space impose a significant constraint on personal choice (see Brindley, Chapter 3). For the rest, the great middle mass of private home owners, now amounting to around 70–75 per cent of households in, for example, the UK, USA and Australia (Balchin 1995: 194), can choose from a range of styles of existing houses or opt for a new home.

In Britain, however, there is relatively little scope for building a new home according to one's personal requirements (see Chapters 4 and 15). In this respect, the British experience is different from that of North America, much of Europe and Australia, for instance, where householders have more control over the design of their homes. This can be explained partly by the restrictions the state has imposed upon new building, such as the establishment of conservation areas, green belts, preservation orders, building regulations and so forth. But more importantly, the range of 'models' of the ideal home is relatively limited in Britain, which is something that has been achieved by the successful identification of 'what people want' by speculative builders. If we take a critical look at our own built environment, we find evidence of 'pattern book' models of the ideal home, a trend which has emerged because speculative builders have identified a popular view of how the ideal home should be constituted. Over time, these ideals have changed and we need, therefore, to examine the way they have been transformed to meet different social expectations.

Changing images of the ideal home

Since the eighteenth century, British speculative builders have been producing homes according to pattern book designs. Rather than asking their potential clients what kind of house they wanted to live in, builders have been prepared to take a gamble – buy some land – and then build houses on it which they hoped people would buy or rent. The eighteenth century witnessed the first large-scale phase of speculative house building in England. The process began with the development of neo-classical terraces, crescents and squares in west London and the spa town of Bath. This pattern of building reflected a signifi- cant shift in the pattern of urban life from what Heer (1990: 46) described as the 'ebullient, raucous and quarrelsome' life of towns in the earlier medieval period to the relatively 'polite' society of the spa and the suburb. Girouard (1990) has described this transformation:

> The eighteenth century evolved in reaction against the seventeenth. Many people felt that the traumas of the latter must be avoided at all costs; the heat had to be taken out of the system . . . Civilisation was the result of [people] learning to act together in society. The polite [person] was essentially social, and as such, distinguished them from arrogant lords, illiterate squires and fanatical puritans.
>
> (Girouard 1990: 76)

Simply put, the creation of elegant terraces with everyone's house looking the same as their neighbours' helped reinforce the image of the new 'polite society' where people learned the art of tolerance and equality, rather than drawing their sword at the slightest insult. It is not that people asked the builders to provide terraces, because that model did not yet exist. Instead it depended upon the entrepreneurial and social vision of speculators like Beau Nash, who cashed in on the opportunities arising from the new social confidence created by the rise of the polite society. The building of houses in a new way, then, arose from changing social attitudes and was realised in real estate as a conse- quence of the foresight of speculators (Borsay 1990; Reed 1984; A. Morris 1994).

By the end of the eighteenth century, most English towns had developed new suburbs of elegant terraces, while existing home owners often concealed the original façades of their houses and refronted them to make them look as if they were built in the new style (Clifton-Taylor 1984). The rise of these new spas and suburban developments was led by the significant growth in the number of merchants, manufacturers and professionals such as lawyers and doctors, a response to rising trade, the developing commercial and industrial economy and the expanded functions of the state (Porter 1990; Hobsbawm 1969; Hill 1969). Architectural historians suggest that this was a society where very wealthy people felt secure enough to move relatively freely between country house and town house; where the emergent middle class gained access to and helped develop polite society by socialising in private domestic drawing rooms and the town assembly rooms, and by taking holidays at the spas (Girouard 1990; Cruickshank and Burton 1990; Borsay 1990). It is dangerous to read too much meaning into the restrained style of the domestic architecture, of course, for the eighteenth-century town remained a lively, debauched and dangerous place. Then, as now, images and external façades concealed ways of life which were at odds with home as idealised. As Porter (1990) puts it:

> Life was raw. Practically all youngsters were thrashed at home, at school, at work – and child labour was universal. Blood sports such as cock-fighting were hailed as manly trials of skills and courage. Felons were publicly whipped, pilloried and hanged, traitors were drawn and quartered. Jacobites' heads were spiked on Temple Bar till 1777. Work-animals were driven relentlessly; England was notoriously 'hell for horses', and cruelty to animals worsened with industrialization and the craving for speed.
>
> (Porter 1990: 17)

Within the houses themselves life was also often far from polite.

> Hardly any houses boasted a bath. Before cottons became cheap, clothes were difficult to wash; children were sometimes sewn into theirs for the winter. Vermin were not just metaphorical; rat-catchers royal and flea catchers royal made good livings. Chamber-pots were provided in dining-room sideboards, to save breaking up post-prandial conversation among the men . . . People had an ingrained tolerance of such inconvenience and squalor, and compensated by aggressive pursuit of pleasures and passions. Emotion was near the surface.
>
> (Porter 1990: 19)

The conditions that led to the development of the polite society of the eighteenth century had changed dramatically by the early nineteenth century as the industrial revolution gathered momentum. By the nineteenth century new factories were built in the towns – a process that was accompanied by a massive influx of industrial workers (Briggs 1968; R. Morris and Rodger 1993; Hobsbawm 1969). The consequence of this was a steady deterioration of the urban scene into a socially disordered, ugly, overcrowded and polluted environment (Engels 1845; Gauldie 1974). As a consequence, speculative builders began to design new kinds of dwellings in new locations for the middle classes. Their models were in keeping with a Victorian preference for the aristocratic styles of previous centuries, a trend which revealed a new and unstable middle class seeking status and respectability through the trappings of upper-class forebears. They built florid Gothic styled detached villas, protected from the outside world in secluded suburban gardens; they filled their rooms with gargantuan solid oak and mahogany furniture and cluttered every available surface with ornaments (see Hepworth, Chapter 2; see also Girouard 1978; Davidoff and Hall 1987; Muthesius 1982).

The Victorian and Edwardian escape from the town into the new suburbs of detached villas was, in turn, despised by Modernist architects and planners in the twentieth century. Intellectuals of the Modern Movement ridiculed the craving for rigidly defined uses of rooms, clutter and the Victorians' preoccupation with the past. Instead, they proposed the building of homes in new materials (concrete, steel and glass), denied the necessity of decoration and devised new streamlined designs. In Le Corbusier's famous pun on Marx, the point was not to 'decorate' the world, but instead to 'change it' (Fishman 1977). Modernist architects and planners had some success in persuading private clients and public housing authorities to subscribe to their aesthetic preferences, but they never won the hearts of the next great cohort of socially mobile private house purchasers in inter-war England (see Brindley, Chapter 3).

To the horror of the Modernist elite, it was the speculative builders who identified what people really wanted and developed vast estates of suburban semi-detached houses (Carey 1992; Oliver et al. 1981). The semi-detached house of the inter-war period had up-to-date features such as a bathroom and indoor lavatory, light and airy rooms, and the convenience of modern appliances run by electricity and gas. The 1930s still provide evocative images of depression epitomised in the political action of the Jarrow marchers, Orwell's *Down and Out in Paris and London* (1933) and Greenwood's *Love on the Dole* (1933). In fact, social mobility into the lower middle classes in the 1930s fuelled the vast expansion of new speculative building. In the 1930s alone, some 2,700,000 houses were built, including a minimum of 200,000 homes a year in the worst years of the depression (Oliver et al. 1981: 13).

While the suburban semi was popularly accepted as the model of the ideal home, it offended the aesthetic sensibilities of the intelligentsia. Critics ridiculed the cavalier manner with which speculative builders mixed and matched a wide variety of architectural adornments on the 'universal plan' of the three bedroom semi. As Eric Bird wrote in the 1946–1947 edition of the *Daily Mail Ideal Home Book*, in a crude attempt to persuade the buyers of such houses to change their ways:

> Public taste is not wholly to blame for the rash of 'Tudor-bethan' semi-detached housing which covered square miles of country on the fringes of towns. The wish to have light, charm and social dignity in the home is praiseworthy. The wrong lay in the fact that people were satisfied with the flashy and snobbish as a substitute for really good design.
>
> (quoted in Sherman 1946: 12)

Bird's rudeness was certainly not uncommon, but seems all the more surprising given that many of the readers of the *Daily Mail Ideal Home Book* actually lived in suburban semis. Intellectual attacks on the suburban vision of the ideal home were the norm, not the exception, up to the end of the 1950s. Much of this was based on an assertion that the new middle class were incapable of knowing what was best for them without the intervention of expert advice. In the high-brow literary magazine *Criterion*, T.S. Eliot dared to assert that the new middle class 'can only appreciate simple and naive emotions, puerile prettiness, above all conventionalities' (quoted in Carey 1992: 53).

But the intellectuals were losing the battle. The new inhabitants of semi-detached suburbia in 1930s Britain wanted to show their family, neighbours and friends that they had 'arrived' in a new social world through the conspicuous display of their affluence. Capital responded quickly to this upsurge in consumer spending and provided a wide range of goods and services to help home owners realise their idea of a dream home (see Chapman, Chapter 4; see also Forty 1986; Faulkner and Arnold 1985). As a Bendix advertisement in the 1946–1947 *Daily Mail Ideal Home Book* stated:

> The Bendix automatic home laundry makes a house an ideal home. No longer any need for red, rough hands, no running taps and splashes on the floor, no more sweated labour in the heavy, steamy washday atmosphere! Bendix is completely automatic, all you do is to put in the wash, add soap and set the dial, then you're off duty and the Bendix takes over . . . you don't even have to be in the house.
>
> (Sherman 1946: 32)

The rush to consume was led not entirely by capital, but also by the social need to gain the respect of family, friends and neighbours. To fall short of neighbourly expectations may have dire consequences for the individual's self-esteem, as Veblen (1934) notes:

> Those neighbours of the community who fall short of [a] somewhat indefinite, normal degree of prowess or of property suffer in the esteem of their fellow-men; and consequently they also suffer in their own esteem, since the usual basis of self-respect is the respect accorded by one's neighbors. Only individuals with an aberrant temperament can in the long run retain their self-esteem in the face of the disesteem of their fellows . . . So soon as the possession of property becomes the basis of popular esteem, it becomes also a requisite to that complacency which we call self-respect.
>
> (quoted in Coser 1977: 268)

While Veblen emphasises the important of 'conspicuous consumption' in maintaining social esteem in a neighbourhood, it has to be recognised that

9

people can lose the esteem of their neighbours by being too ostentatious or flamboyant in the exercise of their wealth. While there are always exceptions, the influence of family, neighbours and friends should not be underestimated when we consider the way that people make decisions about the presentation of their home to the world (see Chapman, Hockey and Wood, Chapter 15).

The ideal home as it is lived

The ideal home has since the nineteenth century afforded the possibility of retreat from public view, and a place for the exercise of private dreams and fantasies, personal foibles and inadequacies, in practice, we argue, it cannot be seen as a space which is beyond the gaze of the public world. However determinedly we police the boundaries of our 'private' space, it is difficult to ignore or exclude the possibility of incursions into that space. The visit of outsiders, whether they are members of our family, friends and colleagues, plumbers and electricians, doctors and midwives, brings into sharp relief the fragility of the boundary between the public world and the private domain. However much effort we expend in keeping areas of our private space from the public gaze, we cannot easily stop ourselves from imagining how 'outsiders' might perceive us if they gained access to these hidden territories. For example, reclusive or isolated older women who are unable to spring-clean may carry within them the disconcerting vision of their cupboards and attics as seen by those others who will enter their homes after their deaths (see Hockey, Chapter 9). Or when our privacy is invaded by an unwanted visitor, like the burglar, we are forced to re-evaluate our long-established relationship with formerly trusted neighbours, our sense of privacy and security and most especially the deeply personal way in which we treasure our property (see Chapman, Chapter 11). We argue, then, that it is our responses to the actual or imagined intrusions of outsiders that help people to conceptualise the ideal home. We know what is expected of us and recognise the limits to individual taste and choice, decency and respectability as soon as they confront us. This is not to say, however, that we can always conform to those expectations, nor that we might always want to. Thus, in addition to identifying and socially locating the ideal or ideals of home, this volume also explores, in considerable detail, the barriers to the achievement of that ideal home. It reveals, for example, that while privacy is a concept that patterns and legitimises the exclusion of outsiders, it may be denied to certain household members. Madigan and Munro (Chapter 5) demonstrate the way that gender influences the social organisation of domestic space. Women, it is shown, have virtually no personal space in the household, unlike children and husbands, who can retreat to individual bedrooms, studies, garages or sheds. Women's experience of home is likely to be shaped to some extent even before they move in, for the architect has already established the spatial layout. Madigan and Munro show that the open-plan design of 1960s housing removes that private space within which women

[handwritten margin note: Household stuff as a filter for social identity]

10

formerly managed tasks such as cooking, sewing, washing and ironing. In the absence of separate kitchens, outhouses, dining rooms and parlours, women experience an additional pressure to maintain the entire ground floor of their homes in a state of order equivalent to that once required only in the secluded space of the front room.

Gender also impacts upon another core characteristic of the ideal home – its safety. Its nineteenth-century representation as a 'haven in a heartless world' as discussed by Hepworth (Chapter 2) finds echoes in late-twentieth-century crime prevention literature which details the security measures necessary to protect this haven from 'break-ins' and to ward off the likelihood of attack out on the street. The notion that home, in an ideal sense, is a place of safety is shown to be highly gendered. It binds women of all ages into the home and fosters their dependence upon male relatives; adolescent girls, women wishing to separate from a male partner and older single women are often advised, either implicitly or explicitly, of the special dangers that face them in public space (see Goldsack, Chapter 10). Yet, paradoxically, the street is the domain where men are most in danger of attack from a stranger, while it is relatively safe for women when compared with the home. It is in domestic space that women are most at risk – from violent attacks by a male partner. If anything, security systems designed to keep danger out actually make the home more dangerous for women under attack, thwarting their efforts to escape a fist, knife or broken bottle. The example of domestic violence therefore shows how the supposedly desirable features of the ideal home can fail to serve the interests of all members of the household.

While we highlight mismatches between the ideal home as imagined and as lived, we also demonstrate that *exclusion* from the relatively private preserve of the home can have serious consequences for those people who are deemed to be incapable of living on their own. Hockey (Chapter 12) describes how the needs of older, dependent adults cannot be accommodated within the ideal home, but instead are managed within institutional 'homes' which bear none of the characteristics of the private home. Though home may provide a touchstone for our sense of self, a treasured space for important objects, secrets and pleasures (see Chapman, Chapter 11), in practice it also houses those more problematic aspects of human embodiment which range from birth to death. If older people cease to exercise the required degree of control over their own bodies, they may be judged unsuitable for continued inclusion in family life – or indeed for an independent life in their own homes. Older people can also find their opportunities for realising their dream of an ideal home constrained by the strictures of professional architects, who make judgements about the appropriate size and facility required of such a home. As Fairhurst (Chapter 8) shows, the designers of 'sheltered' accommodation produce representations of 'home' which, again, fall short of the ideal in that they fail to provide either the social space needed for visitors, a double bed, or the space required to display the memorabilia that symbolise a lifetime.

It is this symbolic merger of 'home' and 'self' which makes the home, in both an ideal and a literal sense, so important as a focus for sociological study. Representing the intersection of the public world of planners and policy makers and the personal world of family, friends and neighbours, the home stands as a materialisation of key social and personal values. Yet paradoxically it is precisely through the seclusion of the self that a capitalist society, grounded in the principle of individualism, reproduces itself. Two of the most stressful experiences which the householder risks are burglary and relocation. While the former may breed a sense of personal violation or pollution (see Chapman, Chapter 11) the second involves entering the unknown space which previously housed the most secret and potentially shocking aspects of a previous occupant's life. The 'Houses of Doom' which Hockey (Chapter 12) describes may be largely fictional, yet they allude to something less fantastic but nonetheless dreadful, proximity to the intimate spaces of an unknown and potentially undesirable other.

Whether in its ideal or material form, the home eludes certain categories of people entirely. Thus the category 'homeless' encompasses both those who live on friends' settees as well as those who own nothing but sheets of cardboard and newspaper. For others, 'home' is something to which they have multiple attachments. These include West Indian people living in Britain for whom the material space within which they eat, sleep and relax may remain a 'home away from home' since the notion of home is tied primarily to the West Indian ethnic and family-defined spaces which provide their social identities (see Olwig, Chapter 6). Similarly the shared living space of young people who are full-time students is experienced as temporally and spatially distant from the family homes they go back to in vacations and the independent homes they look forward to once they have jobs. Being shared, temporary and often uncared for, student accommodation cannot conform to the ideal of home. Their experience is echoed in the domestic lives of gay and lesbian couples whose relationship with one another can often not be made visible within and around the home or be allowed to offend the requirements of hegemonic heterosexuality. Shared sleeping arrangements and visibly intimate behaviour at the exterior of the home – for example mouth-to-mouth kissing on the doorstep when one partner leaves for work – can be problematic.

While this book emphasises social constraint as a constant theme through its discussion of the ideal home as it is imagined and as it is lived, we do not overlook those people who resist convention. Until the 1960s it was accepted wisdom that the home was a woman's domain, a place to which men returned from their 'natural' preserve – the public world of *work*. Yet men's experience of employment has changed dramatically since the late 1970s, as the labour market has been restructured. The idea that men's status derives from being the household 'breadwinner' in a lifelong career has been strongly challenged, particularly since the experience of redundancy, unemployment and temporary work is no longer exceptional. However, the fact that women make up around a half of the labour market does not mean that equality between the sexes in employment or the domestic sphere has been achieved. Indeed, women continue to undertake the majority of domestic labour. Chapman (Chapter 13) questions the extent to which men's low participation in domestic work and childcare can be explained entirely by their own unwillingness to undertake such tasks, or whether it is circumscribed by women's control over the skills and knowledge required to undertake domestic work.

Alternative ways of looking at the home can also be derived from a consideration of the relationship between the home, the private domestic garden and the wider environment. Bhatti (Chapter 14) argues that new ideas and practices are emerging in response to changed environmental attitudes, whereby the garden is not seen as space to be dominated or controlled, but 'managed' in such a way that it can function symbiotically. Bhatti argues that people can experience the garden and gardening, if they have the requisite skills and knowledge, as a 'reconnection' with the environment as a whole and that by studying how gardens are understood and used, we can show how people can learn about nature, and help develop a deeper environmental culture.

Bhatti's study of the garden reveals the possibilities of resistance to the relentless pressure of capital to provide goods and services that meet every aspect of life from the cook-chill meal to the professional laundry service. For some, this tokenistic resistance to the model of the ideal home is not sufficient; as a consequence, radical steps are taken to establish alternative forms of domestic arrangement. Chapman, Hockey and Wood (Chapter 15) argue that those who 'dare to be different' face a difficult task if they attempt to go it alone. To resist convention is to risk social stigmatisation and social isolation. Consequently, most people who develop alternative domestic lifestyles do so in communal circumstances. For those who bind themselves together within a collective belief system – usually based on religion – communal domestic life can be sustained over the centuries. For those who seek to achieve *individuality* through the commune, however, their chances of long-term success are shown to be bleak. As noted earlier, in the United Kingdom there is relatively little scope for building a new home according to one's personal requirements, a situation which might explain the marketability of Michael Pollan's (1997) account of how he built a wood-frame hut 'of his own' in the garden of his family home. We are therefore describing a context where the conventional model of the private home can be seen to hold some potential as a place within which people can realise their dreams. For the majority, the model of the ideal home remains the most popular model of domestic life, we argue, because it affords the opportunity, if not always the realisation, of a sustainable link between the private world and the public, a connection which also divides the routine of home life from that of work.

Part I

CHANGING IMAGES OF THE IDEAL HOME

2

PRIVACY, SECURITY AND RESPECTABILITY

The ideal Victorian home

Mike Hepworth

It is difficult to exaggerate the influence of Victorian images on present-day beliefs about the 'ideal home'. Rapid social and economic changes since the close of the nineteenth century have done little to change the Victorian belief in the home as a private retreat within which a personal life can be enjoyed in peace and security. The term 'Victorian' is, of course, derived from the name of Queen Victoria, who ruled from 1837 to 1902 over what was once an extensive British Empire. But, like the empire she once ruled, 'Victorian' has come to refer to a series of attitudes and values whose influence goes well beyond the shores of Britain and the boundaries of the nineteenth century. As Grier (1988) has noted in her study of culture and comfort in the middle-class North American drawing room or 'parlour', the concept of Victorian can be defined in more global terms as the 'Anglo-American, transatlantic, bourgeois culture of industrialising western civilisation' (Grier 1988: 2).

Grier's definition suggests that, seen as a global feature of industrialising western civilisation, Victorian culture is dauntingly complex. The aim of this chapter, therefore, is to draw attention to only a single yet nevertheless highly significant strand in Victorian thought, namely the contribution that images of the ideal Victorian home have made to the distinctive features of the idea of home in western society. Images, both visual (photographs, paintings, book illustrations etc.) and verbal (novels, poems, biographies, autobiographies, histories etc.), are closely connected with expressions of the ideal because they often give shape to the hopes and fears of people living during a specific historical period. Mundane everyday life can be seen as a constant struggle to give meaning to life in terms of contemporary cultural ideals. As an image, the 'ideal home' is an expression of value: the kind of private life that individuals hope to achieve. As conceived by the Victorians, the image of the ideal home is an essential link between the public and the private domestic

17

world, at once a coveted symbol of success in both these spheres, and of the effort to achieve normality and respectability by its residents.

It is not stretching the argument too far to say that the image of home dominated the Victorian collective vision of a stable and harmonious social environment in the private and public spheres and also in this world and the next. In his study of the roles of hymns and hymn singing in Victorian every-day life, I. Bradley (1997) noted that a constantly recurring image in 'the depiction of heaven in Victorian hymns is that of the happy home, with work over for the day, the table spread and the family gathered together' (1997: 118). If the home in its ideal expression was analogous to heaven, it was also, as Jalland (1996) observed, the place where many people hoped to die. Certainly for the middle and upper classes, the family home was the appropri-ate place to confront and come to terms with the harsh realities of painful terminal illness and death; an essential link between the secular and the sacred. In these social circles 'death bed scenes were private affairs which were usually limited to a relatively small number of members of the immediate family, together with a nurse or a servant, and occasionally a doctor' (Jalland 1996: 26). The home, then, was described not only as a retreat from the not infrequently harsh realities of the Victorian world but also as a secluded place to struggle with those realities such as illness and death which succeeded in breaching the walls.

Two important features of the ideal home as a retreat were particularly significant. The first was the constructed façade – the physical structure of stone, bricks and mortar which helped to conceal the residents from public view – and the second has been neatly described by Marshall and Willox (1986: 57) as the 'home within'. The home within was the social organisation of private life inside the private spaces such as bedrooms, studies and the various forms of specific social interaction that were possible in these rooms. Because the external structure of the houses built during the building booms of the Victorian period were often uniform in external appearance, as is the case today, it was the home within which gave these homes their individual character and which encouraged an increasing fascination of outsiders (news-paper reporters, novelists, gossips) with the lives of those inside.

While the hedges, fences and walls surrounding residents guaranteed some kind of protection against the world outside, it is important to remember that private spaces of the home were not always sacrosanct and were often open to the scrutiny of other members of the family, especially the 'head of the house-hold' and servants. For this reason, as Bailin (1994: 6) has indicated, the sick-room was often especially valued as 'a haven of comfort', order and 'natural affection'. Because behaviour and expressions of emotions normally repressed in polite society were permissible when someone became ill, the sickroom was the one place within the home where an individual could retreat from the demands of family life and be himself/herself. One of the consolations of illness, as Florence Nightingale discovered during the later part of her life, was that the conventions surrounding the sickroom made it possible for the ill person to abandon the highly disciplined rigours and rituals of respectable conduct and to 'express feelings and essential truths about the undisfigured self' (Bailin 1994: 24).

It is important to recognise that the Victorian home was not simply a place for a relaxed presentation of a 'real' self away from the prying eyes of the world but a complex arrangement of spaces for the presentation of a minia-turised array of variable domestic selves. There is therefore an evident tension here between the idealised image of the home as a private haven for the self and the practical everyday activities of family life and relationships. For those who lived in polite society, the home was as much a display cabinet of social virtues as it was a haven for an army of would-be social reclusives. Standards had to be maintained both within and without its confines and the ideal Victorian home is therefore more accurately defined as a kind of battleground: a place of constant struggle to maintain privacy, security and respectability in a dangerous world.

It was also, of course, a gendered place. While historians such as Tosh (1996) have shown how men became increasingly drawn to the rewards of a domesticated life during the Victorian period, the key role for respectably active women was, as George Elgar Hicks' series of three paintings entitled *Woman's Mission* (1863) graphically asserted, the domestic caregiver. Casteras has recorded that *The Times* newspaper described the trilogy as depicting:

> 'woman in three phases of her duties as ministering angel,' . . . Hicks himself believed that woman fulfilled a sacrosanct function as wife and mother and wrote, 'I presume no woman will make up her mind to remain single, it is contrary to nature'.
>
> (Casteras 1987: 51–52)

Ideal and reality: the home life of Charles Darwin

The example of the sickroom reveals that the relationship between the imagined ideal and the lived experience of home is complex and influenced by a number of social variables including gender, ethnicity and social class. But it must also be recognised that the ideal home of the Victorian imagina-tion was not entirely an illusion. The home life of Charles Darwin (1809–1882), the most influential scientist of the period, provides an interesting example of the efforts he and his family made to live out the ideal of the home as a place of privacy and security in a dangerous world.

For reasons which have yet to be completely explained, Darwin was for much of his highly productive intellectual life a chronic invalid. He 'suffered chronic ill-health from the age of thirty until he was sixty' (Bowlby 1990: 6), although during the last decade of his life there was some improvement and he died at the comparatively old age of 73. A wealthy man who had no need to work for a living, he was throughout his married life, as he frequently acknowledged, totally dependent on his wife Emma. Even for a male, socially advantaged Victorian, Darwin was peculiarly home-centred, his highly conventional domestic life – that of the Victorian paterfamilias – being totally at odds with his iconoclastic denial of the divine origins of the human species and his scientific defence of biological evolution through the process of natural selection. Thus Darwin was domestically conventional, his private resources making it possible for him to live out the Victorian ideal of privacy and respectability while his public image, after the publication of *The Origin of Species* in 1859, was highly controversial and stigmatised especially in conventionally religious circles. Indeed, it was the evidence of Darwin's domesticity which ultimately helped the Victorian establishment to reconcile itself to his profoundly subversive theory of evolution and *The Descent of Man* (1871) from lower life forms.

When Darwin died in 1882 preparations were made to bury him in the graveyard of the village of Downe, near London. He had moved there in September 1842 and spent a large part of the remainder of his life there in rural seclusion. The village of Downe as described by Darwin's biographers, Desmond and Moore (1992), represents the Victorian conception of a rural idyll, set at a convenient distance from the big city: 'Two hours out of London, sixteen miles from St Paul's, this was the perfect rural retreat . . . Here he was at a safe distance from society . . . The nearest train station, Sydenham, was eight miles away, and the hilly drive cut Downe off, secured its inhabitants, preserved their past. A parish set in aspic'. This, wrote Darwin to his old servant on the *Beagle* 'will be my direction for the rest of my life' (Desmond and Moore 1992: 302).

In 1882 arrangements to bury Darwin at Downe were cut short by counter-pressures to have him enshrined, following a state funeral, in Westminster Abbey. The man who had been labelled 'the devil's Chaplain' by the religious establishment, and ridiculed in *Punch* as a grotesque ape-like figure, was now eulogised as a national hero. The role of a lifetime's exemplary patriarchal domesticity played no small part in his sanctification.

> The elegies stressed Darwin's exemplary character, his simple 'everyday virtues', and his wealthy respectability. Mr Darwin's was 'an ideal life', according to the *Saturday Review* – a private fortune, a great opportunity capitalized on the *Beagle*, 'immense labours, wisely planned and steadily executed,' amid scenes of 'quiet domestic happiness,' and all crowned by a sweet and gentle nature blossomed into perfection. Many found Darwin's homeliness especially attractive. It was 'difficult to imagine a more beautiful picture of human happiness than that which he presented in his Kentish home, working at those

great books which are acknowledged to have been a priceless gift to humanity, surrounded by a devoted family'.

(Desmond and Moore 1992: 676)

Respectability and social deviance: the ideal home as fortress

The example of the secluded home life of Charles Darwin offers insight into the notion of the Victorian home as a kind of castle or fortress offering protection against the cruel world outside. It is perhaps not surprising that Darwin, who drew from his observations of the natural world the belief that life was an endless and merciless struggle for survival, should find his haven in a conventional home, run by his conventionally religious wife. In this respect he lived out the more general belief in the boundaries of the Victorian home (such as surrounding countryside and grounds, fences, walls, gates and a supporting team of servants who act as gatekeepers) as the lines of moral boundary between respectability and social deviance. Darwin's example may serve as a reminder of one of the central themes in the sociology of deviance, namely the essential interdependence and continuous interplay between concepts of respectability and deviance.

While respectability is defined in terms of images of the protective environment of the respectable home, deviance is located in the relatively unregulated world which lies beyond. Individuals in their own home have a respectable place in society: they can be located and identified as anchored in the normal social world. But the unfortunate individual expelled or threatened with expulsion from the family home stands on the line dividing normality from deviance: the transition is from 'being at home' to 'homelessness'. In her study of images of Victorian women in English art, Casteras (1987) shows how the contrast between the comforts of the well-appointed home and the bleak world outside was a recurring theme for popular painters. She describes a picture by George Smith, *Into the Cold World* (1876), as follows:

> A beautiful young widow, head and posture downcast, has no recourse but to leave her home. Her equally exquisite son, still young enough to sport long Fauntleroy-ish curls, looks back at his faithful dog, but the latter hesitates in following his master into the cold world. The mother and child cast a long shadow on the hall floor; a sprig of holly fallen there not only indicates the season – and the cruel fate of being turned out at Yuletide – but is also an ironic floral allusion to foresight (which the widow's spouse lacked in planning his estate) . . . The inside/outside dichotomy of the safe, warm haven and cold, cruel world reminds viewers that the lady must exchange the hermetic comforts of home for the chilly reception that awaits in the unknown realm beyond the threshold.
>
> (Casteras 1987: 126)

21

According to Jack Douglas (1970) the definition and social production of respectability is possible only in relationship to its opposite. Respectability is in effect unimaginable without its twin 'other', social deviance and crime. In this sense, the security of the respectability of the home is maintained in terms of its opposite, the inhospitable and exploitative world beyond. This analysis of a recurring theme in Victorian popular painting also shows how necessary it is for a society to continually remind its members of the boundaries separating respectability and deviance by reproducing images which stimulate the imagination of social ideals. Deviance thus has an essential 'boundary-maintaining' function to play in the construction of social order: it is possible to understand the meaning of home only through an appreciation of what home is *not*, or non-home. Without dramatic images of the dangers surrounding us on every side we are continually at risk of losing our bearings in what is in reality an ambiguous and morally bewildering world.

For this reason the middle-class Victorian conception of the ideal home represented the front line in the crusade against the socially and personally destabilising effects of crime and deviance. Davidoff and Hall (1987) have observed that during the early nineteenth century the home was understood to be surrounded by an unstable and threatening world:

> Along with continuing political unrest, the exigencies of poverty, brutality, repressing sexuality, disease and death were all too familiar. Against these, people struggled to control their destiny through religious grace and the bulwark of family property and resources. These shields took practical as well as symbolic form in middle class homes and gardens and in the organisation of the immediate environment through behaviour, speech and dress. The sense that individuals, with God's help, were captains of their fate, was daily confronted by material conditions and recalcitrant human beings.
>
> (Davidoff and Hall 1987: 357)

The moral barricades of the Victorian home were much more than the structural defences of walls and fences, doors, locks and keys. The defences against deviance extended into the home itself to include, as was noted earlier with reference to the sickroom, rules governing standards of conduct in different rooms in the house and relationships between the residents.

A great deal of this protective framework was in fact a complex web of interweaving images and rules of interpersonal relationships which were essentially hierarchical in nature and within which gender played a significant part. Prior to his wedding to Emma in 1839, Darwin had drawn up a list of the pros and cons of marriage:

> In Darwin's eyes, the role of 'Emma was to humanise the brute, care for him, take charge of the sofa' (Darwin had written of a 'nice wife

22

on a sofa'). Her role from the first was narrowly circumscribed – the solitary beast did not want an intellectual soul mate. She tried to dip into Lyell's *Elements of Geology* only to be told not to bother. Lyell's treatment of his long-suffering wife was a paradox. Charles sent an account of the couple's visit: 'we talked for half an hour, unsophisticated geology, with poor Mrs Lyell sitting by, a monument of patience – I want practice in ill-treating the female sex.' Another joke of course, but women were spectators in the male preserve of science, as unwanted here as at the Athenaeum.

(Desmond and Moore 1992: 278)

During the early nineteenth century the gradual separation of paid employment from the domestic sphere helped create a new concept of a realm ruled over by women, bringing with it what some social analysts controversially regard as a form of empowerment in the private sphere (see Chapman, Chapter 13). The central contrast between the home and the outside world placed the onus on women to carry out the emotional and moral labour necessary to create and maintain the ideal home: in other words to transform the image into reality. According to Halttunen (1982) it was the main responsibility of women to create a world free from the dissimulations, manipulations and heartlessness of the outside world. 'By definition', she writes, 'the domestic sphere was closed off, hermetically sealed from the poisonous air of the world outside' (Halttunen 1982: 59).

According to this analysis of middle-class domestic culture in America, 1830–1870, the location of a staged meeting point between the external potentially threatening world of strangers and the internal domestic sphere of intimates was the parlour. 'Geographically,' Halttunen observes, the parlour

lay between the urban street where strangers freely mingled and the back regions of the house where only family members were permitted to enter uninvited. According to the cult of domesticity, the parlour provided the woman of the house with a 'cultural podium' from which she was to exert her moral influence.

(Halttunen 1982: 59)

Within this private sphere clear distinctions were made between deviance and respectability. The parlour was the acme of the latter: a purified social arena subject to constant surveillance dictated by the proliferating rules of etiquette. The private world was established as a respectable social space in constant contrast to the dangers and deviations located in the competitive battlefield of the male-dominated public world where the money was made to furnish the 'soft furnishings' of the home.

As the stage on which respectable domestic social performances took place, the parlour was suitably dressed and embellished. Furnishings and decorations were designed and marketed according to complex rules of moral consumption which it was essential for the successful housewife to command as she moved through her prescribed life course from newly married woman to matron:

> The right furniture was thought to ease social intercourse by helping visitors to look their best, and, when correctly arranged, by encouraging circulation. Similarly, the hostess who tastefully arranged potted shrubs, plants, and flowers throughout the room helped 'brighten' and 'enliven' the company by placing them in 'almost a fairy-like scene.' In addition she selected and displayed the 'curiosities, handsome books, photographs, engravings, stereoscopes, medallions, any works of art you may own,' which were the stage properties of polite social intercourse. Such conversation pieces, according to one etiquette manual, were the good hostess's 'armour against stupidity.' The polite Victorian hostess was not simply an actress in the genteel performance; she was also the stage manager, who exercised great responsibility for the performances of everyone who entered her parlour.
>
> (Halttunen 1982: 105)

A key feature of these genteel performances was the careful maintenance of the privacy of the back regions of the house. Household manuals advised that the 'internal machinery of a household' (Halttunen 1982: 105) should be carefully concealed from public view. In these segregated areas could be found members of the family who had not yet been civilised (infants in the nursery) or whose social status was changed in respect of debilitating illnesses, mental or physical (the sickroom) or the decrements of old age (seated before the kitchen fire).

The housewife was entrusted with the discipline of maintaining the decoration of the home and the smooth running of the material mechanisms of family life and also with the maintenance of the healthy physical bodies of members of her family and the support staff. Above all, the Victorian middle-class home was a privatised arena where comfort and etiquette softened the deviant 'angles' and 'defects' of human character' (Grier 1988: 1). As we noted above, the Victorian home was not only a haven from deviance but also a place where it was possible for deviance to occur and which must therefore be an arena for constant vigilance. In her study of the culture of comfort, Grier (1988), like Halttunen, focuses on the parlour as one of the places 'intended to serve as the setting for important social events and to present the civilized facades of its occupants' (Grier 1988: 1). The intention was to convey domesticity through 'comfort' and cosmopolitanism through 'culture'. The term 'comfort' 'designates the presence of the more family-centred, even religious values associated with "home", values emphasising perfect sincerity and moderation in all things. Social commentators claimed comfort to be a distinctively middle-class state of mind' (Grier 1988: 1).

Hearth and home

As an example of the processes which Grier (1988) and Halttunen (1982) regard as central to the construction of the middle-class home, it is useful to refer to McNair Wright's *The Complete Home: An Encyclopaedia of Domestic Life and Affairs* (1881): 'Between the Home set up in Eden, and the Home before us in Eternity, stand the Homes of Earth in a long succession . . . Every home has its influence, for good or evil, upon humanity at large' (quoted in Briggs 1990: 213). The home of Earth thus takes on a mediating function between the secular and the sacred function. The home and home making were dignified as institutions endowed by God as his ideal of human life and (as noted previously) heaven was conceptualised as an ideal home.

Because of its traditional sacred associations, the fireplace played a special role in the symbolic representation of the ideal home. During the nineteenth century the fireplace, writes Litman (1969), was 'an all-pervasive symbol'. 'Homes lacking fireplaces literally and figuratively lack warmth' (Litman 1969: 632). In this sense the hearth, as the place where heat is generated before the invention of central heating, is closely associated with the heart as the organ which gives life and is traditionally regarded as the source of human emotion. To be welcomed at the hearth is to anticipate a closer and more intimate form of human relationship. Images of hearths filled with burning logs at Christmas are only one idealised set of images of hearth and home. The sacred symbolism of the hearth was not confined to the bourgeois drawing room or parlour but was part of the wider Victorian concern with the moral implications of architecture. Litman (1969) shows how the Victorian reading of architectural forms corresponded with the physiognomic or close scrutiny of external appearances of human beings for evidence of their inner moral character which exercised such an influence on Victorian painters (Cowling 1989; Hepworth 1995). Mary Cowling has shown how the interpretation of character types by painters of modern Victorian life was influenced by the physiognomic tradition dating principally from the dominant influence in the latter half of the eighteenth century of the Zwinglian minister, Lavatar. Victorian audiences were well versed in physiognomic codes deriving from his work and Victorian artists were skilled in drawing on these symbols to comply with the demands of popular taste. Painters and public subscribed to what Cowling (1989: 5) describes as 'a shared system of beliefs about human character, and its physiognomic expression' and we should not therefore be surprised that the paintings were 'read so easily'.

The widespread belief in the idea that the moral quality of a person, a place or a building could be determined through a close scrutiny of external appearance and structure inevitably included the home. The pervasive influence of the so-called science of physiognomy was such that significant connections were made between architecture and the visual and literary arts (Tytler 1982). Thus, as Litman (1969: 630) notes, 'The great mid-century American architectural theorist, Andrew Jackson Downing, put it succinctly: "We believe much of the character of every man may be read in his house".'

Homes and gardens: the rural idyll

Although the hearth has a strong claim on symbolic pride of place in all domestic architecture, the fireplace had a special virtue in another highly emotive symbol in Victorian domestic culture, the country cottage. Downing, whose principal work was published in 1851, believed that the countryside was the most appropriate location of the home, because in a rural environment domestic life was free to expand and 'develop itself freely, as a tree expands which is not crowded by neighbours in a forest, but grows in the unrestrained liberty of the open meadow' (quoted in Litman 1969: 631). The most complete expression of the country home was the English cottage: 'the domestic virtues, the love of home, rural beauty, and seclusion, cannot possibly be better expressed than in the English cottage, with its many upward pointing gables . . . and its walls covered with vines and flowering shrubs' (quoted in Litman 1969: 631).

It is the symbolic nature of the home, that 'storehouse of signs' (Csikszentmihalyi and Rochberg-Halton 1981: 139) where the home is 'conceptualised both as a social symbol and an extension of the self' (Barbey 1993: 103), which finds quintessential expression in the cottage in the country. As Clayton-Payne observes,

> The image of the cottage . . . was a potent one in the late nineteenth century. Its popularity can be seen in terms of a reaction against what was perceived as the ugliness of the Industrial Revolution . . . The simplicity and beauty of the past seemed still discoverable in rural villages and footpaths.
>
> (Clayton-Payne 1988: 32)

Associations between the ideal home and the world of nature were expressed in their most contrived form in the Victorian garden, especially the flower garden. If access to a real cottage garden was not possible, a painting or reproduction of a painting could be purchased. The 'development of flower garden painting began in the 1860's with the work of Frederick Walker and Birket Foster, still basically under the influence of picturesque values' (Clayton-Payne 1988: 9). In paintings of flower gardens, human figures tend to derive their character from their physical surroundings. They are not present as identifiable individuals but as anonymous character types whose position in these floral surroundings reinforces the overall moral message of the tranquillity of the garden. In, for example, Francis Wollaston Moody's *In Chelsea Gardens* (1858) an unnamed and unidentifiable Chelsea pensioner offers flowers to a child while the equally anonymous mother looks on fondly (Wood 1978: 670).

Garden and cottage garden paintings reflected an increasing interest in the cultivation of flowers and gardens and a move away from the utilitarian idea of the garden as the provider of staple fare in a subsistence economy. Ironically, it is not the 'useful' vegetable garden which comes to symbolise home in popular images but the 'useless' flower. This in part reflects a greater interest in the cultivation of flowers alongside the staple vegetables which continued to play such an important part in the rural subsistence economy. It is also part-reflection of a longer tradition of floral symbolism as elaborated by the Victorians in paintings, poems and other works of art. By the mid-nineteenth century the better-off cottagers were cultivating bedding plants among their vegetables. For the socially advantaged the accent moved away from material subsistence towards colourful floral displays and the cottage garden was transformed into an aestheticised moral enterprise. In this floral enterprise there was a strong element of nostalgia and longing among an urbanised population, especially the affluent middle classes, for a rural idyll unspoilt by the forces of industrialisation from which their wealth was derived.

The most ornamental and flowery cottage gardens were those created by landowners as a public display of their own taste. By the 1880s the cottage garden had been transformed into an indigenous gardening style. Painters played an important part in promoting what came to be known as the 'cottage garden style' (Clayton-Payne 1988: 63) and there was a slow effacement of the 'distinction between the labourer's cottage and the middle class small house' (1988: 68). Alongside innovations in gardening and botany the Victorians elaborated a rich domesticated iconography of plant life. Grier (1988) cites a chapter in Richard Wells' *Manners, Culture and Dress*, frequently reprinted in the 1890s in the USA, as containing a list of the meanings of 318 flowers and plants: 'A deep rose signalled "bashful love"; an iris signalled "melancholy"' (Grier 1988: 11). The invention of photography and the concern of Pre-Raphaelite painters in Britain with the meticulous reproduction of the details of nature reinforced the symbolic appeal of plant life. Indeed, a preoccupation with accuracy of natural detail was bent to the service of symbolism. 'With all their "botanizing" associations,' writes Bartram (1985: 38), 'the plant images of the period have qualities transcending any scientific purpose', adding in a quotation from a review published in the *Athenaeum* in 1858:

> It is like reading Keats and Tennyson to look at the soft, white, velvet hair of the poisonous, veined nettle-leaves, green and rank, huddling up in a dark guilty mass to hide where the murdered child was buried, while the bee sings round the white diadems of

their beguiling flowers as if nothing was wrong and earth was still a Paradise.

(Bartram 1985: 38)

The symbolic value of the home as rural haven and of the garden as a sub-stitute for a full-blown rural life (homes and gardens) is thus reflected in the complex symbolism of plant life, especially flowers and gardens, evident in Victorian middle-class culture. As testified in the life of Charles Darwin, botany was regarded as one of the virtuous hobbies with close associations with gardening as both a science and an art. If the private Victorian home and garden represented a moral barrier erected against the enemy outside its walls, it also functioned to contain and discipline any enemies that may be found within. The cultivation of the garden as an aestheticised living space required the disciplining of deviant nature (weeding, pruning etc.) according to the tastes of the period reflected in images of ideal homes and gardens. Gardens were therefore part of what has been described as the 'domestic scenery' (Grier 1988: 6) of the home. Alongside architectural design, furnishings and other choice domestic objects, they acted as a constant reminder to residents of the moral quality of their surroundings.

In this expanding and symbolically complex arena of ideal homes and gardens the role of the woman as the quintessential housewife remained crucial. Modern developments in consumer culture, particularly the depart-ment store, reinforced the Victorian ideal of woman as home maker by playing an important part in educating women as modern housewives (Laermans 1993). In the department store the housewife learnt both to indulge what were regarded as typical 'feminine' whims and fancies, expressed in an 'impul-sive' fascination with shopping, yet at the same time to temper her desires with a rational eye to the exigencies of 'good housekeeping'. As Laermans (1993) has observed, the department store reinforced the traditional distinc-tion between the home as woman's realm and work as the male sphere of influence. These developments perpetuated the powerful series of symbolic associations established between mundane objects and broader social and spiritual values which were essential to the Victorian images of the ideal home. Grier (1988: 8–9) observes that 'Sentimental poetry and fiction not only helped to demonstrate the way in which such chains of association worked in connection to objects such as furniture, but they probably also served to perpetuate conventional associations'. She quotes the example of the poem 'The Old Arm-Chair' by Eliza Cook published in Godey's Lady's Book in March 1855. 'The Old Arm Chair' was hallowed because it had belonged to the owner's deceased mother and reminded her of childhood teachings at her mother's knee. She cannot bear to be parted from it because it represents in material form the union between their two souls – a union made, it need scarcely be added – within the sanctity of the home.

Conclusion

This chapter has surveyed what are considered by historians and sociologists to be some of the key characteristics of the ideal Victorian home. It has for the most part been concerned with images, or representations in visual and verbal form, of hopes (and fears) concerning the role of the home in the wider society, a society which was undergoing rapid upheaval and change. The Victorians were, therefore, extremely conscious of the instability of society and the need to establish a basic series of ground-rules for moral conduct – a clear set of boundaries between deviance and respectability. The Victorian home can be seen, in its ideal version, as a controlled private realm within whose walls even more controls had to be established to maintain a desired congruence between appearance and reality. The moral home life not only had to be lived on a daily basis but also had to be seen to be lived. Hence the need to continue to reproduce these images in art, literature and consumer culture. Inevitably these pressures produced conflict and the symbolic richness of the Victorian home, as displayed for example in the increasingly popular collections of Victorian domestic design, must be examined in the context of a continuous struggle to reconcile the demands of the ideal with the exigencies and contingencies of everyday living. All the signs are that just as present-day conceptions of family life have been heavily influenced by Victorian ideas so we can continue to learn from their success, and failures, in making the ideal a practical reality.

3

THE MODERN HOUSE IN ENGLAND

An architecture of exclusion

Tim Brindley

Destruction

1970s ESTATE TO BE RAZED

A Cheshire housing estate built in the spirit of early 1970s public housing and designed by the internationally-acclaimed architect James Stirling, is to be demolished . . . The average annual turnover of tenants was 30 per cent . . . The estate has earned the reputation of being the worst in Cheshire for crime, drugs, and social deprivation . . . The site will be redeveloped with a mixture of private and rented 'conventional housing'.

(*Guardian*, 23 February 1989)

Redemption

THE TASTE CYCLE

the idea of listing an entire council estate from the late seventies, as happened last week, poses some difficult questions. Alexandra Road, a sweeping curved development in Camden, north London, was listed by the government . . . a striking piece of architecture and historically important . . . Alexandra Road's flats – with their sliding partition walls, split-level plans, double-height studio rooms and black-tiled kitchens – represent homes that architects themselves would have chosen to live in.

(*Guardian*, 24 August 1993)

When F. R. S. Yorke published *The Modern House in England* (1944), he acknowledged that the houses in 'the new manner' which he championed were not yet popular, but he believed they represented the architecture of the 'ideal homes' of the future (Yorke 1944). These two quotations reveal the divided fate of the Modern house some fifty years later. On the one hand, as housing to live in, Modern housing has become profoundly unpopular. In some cases it has become such a potent symbol of contemporary social evils that it has been destroyed and replaced with something which it is hoped that people will like. As a major survey of high-rise housing in Britain concluded, 'By the early 1970s, Modern public housing seemed to have lost its validity across the entire spectrum of endeavour, theoretical and practical' (Glendinning and Muthesius 1994: 324). In contrast, its 'cultural value' is being reasserted by the cultural elite as part of the nation's architectural 'heritage'. Individual Modernist houses and even whole council estates are being hailed as great works of twentieth-century art which must be preserved in their original form and condition.

This divided view of the Modern house – both popular disaster and work of artistic and cultural significance – reveals the gulf that exists between the two major discourses of Modern housing. In the discourse of architectural history and theory, Modernism is understood as one of several movements within twentieth-century art and architecture. In this view, the Modern house has to be judged on aesthetic criteria, and opinions are divided. While some critics hold Modern housing in generally high esteem, seeing particular houses and estates as among the greatest architectural achievements of the century (see, for example, Sherwood 1978; Frampton 1985; Scoffham 1984; Glendinning and Muthesius 1994), others are highly critical of Modern design in general and Modern housing in particular (for example, Krier 1978; Knevitt 1985; HRH Prince of Wales 1989; Hackney 1990). Contrary to popular public opinion, the architectural 'establishment' is generally positive towards Modernism and wants to single out the best examples of Modern housing and add them to the canon of great architecture.

In the *social* discourses of housing, however, including accounts of the housing system, housing processes and housing problems, we find an almost unanimous condemnation of Modern housing as a 'failure'. The debate here ranges from attempts to relate anti-social behaviour to Modern architecture (Coleman 1985), to complex analyses of the social, political and administrative processes which have led to the popular rejection of Modern estates (Dunleavy 1981; Power 1987; Forrest and Murie 1988; J. Morris and Winn 1990). In practical terms, its owners – mainly local councils – have either destroyed and replaced them, or else restyled them in a more popular idiom.

This chapter aims to compare and connect these two discourses, the architectural and the social, by looking at the place of Modern housing in contemporary society. Since the two debates are so separate we first have to establish that they are about the same thing: is what architectural theorists consider to be Modern housing the same as the housing which is highlighted as a major social problem? There is compelling evidence that this is the case, and that the Modern house has become the least desirable of contemporary 'ideal homes'. How is it that something so radically ambitious and socially committed as Modern housing has turned out to be so far out of tune with popular sentiment? We shall see that aspects of Modern design have tended to exacerbate the effects of social and economic changes, contributing to the development of housing 'ghettos', and that the attempt to reclaim the Modern estates as architectural monuments risks making things worse.

The Modern house and the Modern Movement

Modern architecture could be defined as the progressive architecture of the middle half of the twentieth century, from the 1920s to the 1970s. Above all else, it was an attempt to develop an appropriate or 'authentic' architecture to express the spirit of 'modern life' in Western, industrial, urban societies. The first manifestations of this 'new' architecture were seen in Art Nouveau and the work of the 'pioneer' Modernists in the early years of the twentieth century. By the 1920s, widely regarded as the 'heroic' period of Modern design, the work of many architects was converging towards an International Style, which they proclaimed as the 'true' architecture of the century. Following the Second World War, this style diversified 'into many tributaries and transformations' and in the process came to dominate many post-war building types. It should be noted, however, that it was not the only twentieth-century style, and it never became universal (Curtis 1987).

Modern architects rejected above all else the highly decorative architecture of the Victorian period and the turn of the century. They saw in the revival of past styles, such as Gothic or Classical, the free use of ornament in the Arts and Crafts style and the elaborate decoration of Art Nouveau, a failure to come to terms with the industrial age. The new architecture was characterised by its rationality, seeking to optimise methods of construction, use of materials and spatial layout by exploiting factory production techniques, synthetic materials and open-plan spaces. It is often described as 'functionalist', and the effective and efficient functioning of buildings was a paramount concern of its exponents. But what was functional for different building types was still open to many different formal, spatial and stylistic interpretations. The International Style, for example, represented a commitment to honesty of expression, of form and materials. It stood for a 'symbolic objectivity', essentially a poetic expression of the application of scientific rationality to design, in new forms of construction and materials, and in the analysis of human needs (see Banham 1960).

The Modern Movement also had moral concerns (Greenhalgh 1990), sharing with Victorian reformers a belief in social progress through material improvements in housing and cities. The Modernists believed that rational types of buildings would be more fitting for modern uses and patterns of living, and would enhance the quality of life in the modern age. The Congrès Internationaux d'Architecture Moderne (CIAM), formed in 1928, saw a strong relationship between Modern architecture and town planning, and housing in particular, became a major focus of Modern architectural theory and application. Modern housing began to be built on a large scale in the 1920s in the Soviet Union, several European countries and even the USA. Often built as apartment blocks for workers, they reflected social democratic governments attempts to tackle social problems through improvements in housing standards and social welfare (Rowe 1993). A key aspect of Modern architecture was 'the expression of a variety of new social visions challenging the status quo and suggesting alternative possibilities for a way of life' (Curtis 1987: 11).

The Modern house in England

Modern architecture and the International Style were first brought to England in the late 1920s by a small number of émigré European architects. With commissions from individual clients with progressive ideas, and working with English followers and collaborators, they built what Yorke described as 'freely planned houses designed for living in rather than to be looked at' (Yorke 1944: 10). These distinctive houses looked quite unlike traditional and established designs, lacking almost all reference to native historical forms and elements and manifesting 'an efficiency style' in place of the contemporary taste for the vernacular and the picturesque. They were mostly built in concrete or finished in render, with plain white-painted surfaces, flat roofs, sun decks and metal railings. They also had novel internal spatial arrangements such as multifunctional, open-plan areas and double height rooms.

The continental architects of these bourgeois villas had previously been leaders in the design of multi-family housing for workers. Yet with very few exceptions, the International Style had little influence on mass housing design and production in England before the war. Only the dramatic Quarry Hill development of 1938, in Leeds, which provided 938 flats and community spaces for 3,000 residents of a former slum clearance area, stands out as precursor of what was to come (Ravetz 1974a). This was modelled on continental socialist housing blocks such as the Karl Marx Hof in Vienna, effectively incorporating a whole neighbourhood in a series of blocks built using a French industrial system. After falling into decline, Quarry Hill was demolished in 1978.

After the Second World War, many European governments faced enormous problems of social and physical reconstruction, and mass housing production was increased substantially. Britain embarked on a major social housing programme and for more than ten years, council housing was the main source of new housing. From the mid-1950s social housing production continued at a high level, but directed mainly to the replacement of the slums. Suburban and new town social housing adopted a popular style of architecture with brick walls, timber windows and shallow-pitched roofs – the so-called 'people's detailing' (Frampton 1985) – in low-density, picturesque layouts. But in the urban areas, high-density housing was called for and Modern housing architecture came into its own. Several good accounts of this housing have been published, which explore its enormous diversity of ideas and forms (e.g. Crawford 1975; Scoffham 1984; Nuttgens 1989), and I shall not attempt a comprehensive review here. But to define the Modern house, and to distinguish it from what I am calling traditional or conventional housing, it is helpful to make some generalisations about its major external and internal characteristics.

First, post-war Modern housing was almost all high density, urban housing. Modern architects started to experiment with new urban concepts for high-density living with the intention that, unlike the tenements and courts of the early industrial city, they would be functional for modern families and communities. In looking for appropriate forms they were strongly influenced by pre-war continental thinking, and in particular by Le Corbusier (1887–1965). Le Corbusier, who changed his name from Charles-Edouard Jeanneret, was a Swiss architect who practised in Paris and became an intellectual leader of the Modern Movement. From 1922, Le Corbusier published visionary proposals for future cities including, in 1925, a plan to demolish the whole of the Right Bank business district in Paris and replace it with skyscrapers, urban motorways and parkland. His most famous plan, *The Radiant City* (Le Corbusier 1967), was published in 1933 and included proposals for huge high-rise apartment blocks called Unités, each containing a complete neighbourhood living in egalitarian, co-operative harmony – 'a high-rise architecture for a new civilisation' (Fishman 1977: 233).

In the late 1940s Le Corbusier eventually realised some of his radical urban and housing concepts from the 1920s in the Unité d'Habitation at Marseilles. Curtis (1987) argues that this twelve-storey apartment block, comprising 337 apartments of twenty-three different types, with its internal streets, rooftop terrace and many shared facilities, provided a collective housing prototype which influenced housing design for the next twenty-five years. It challenged the simplistic forms of the first post-war high-rise blocks, which lacked any clear concept of community life, and led to a search for communal architectural forms which expressed the particular way of life of their occupants in local contexts.

It is the novel communal or collectivised elements in Modern housing architecture which are perhaps its most striking feature. Influenced by prevailing images of urban working-class life, such as Young and Willmott's *Family and Kinship in East London* (1957), and by anti-elitist artistic movements, architects looked for ways to preserve the public and community aspects of the old streets of terraced houses in a Modern setting. As Curtis (1987) has remarked:

It is scarcely surprising that those sectors of the avante garde who sought to crystallise the inner meanings of working class existence should have turned for inspiration to the dense street life of the old slums which either bombs or else bulldozers had done much to destroy.

(Curtis 1987: 317)

For formal models of high-density neighbourhoods, they drew on such diverse sources as the English village, the Mediterranean hill town and the Oriental kasbah. They replaced the old streets with 'streets in the air', both horizontal and vertical, and integrated pubs, shops and social facilities into large housing complexes.

As well as its collectivist aspects, Modern housing took on a radically different external appearance from conventional housing, making extensive use of concrete, sometimes combined with brick. Regular, geometrical shapes were often arranged in complex symmetrical or asymmetrical patterns. The conventional street pattern was often disrupted, with the introduction of semi-public spaces, parking courts and shared access routes to individual dwellings, with a lack of clear differentiation between the 'front' and 'back' of the dwelling. Internally, there was a marked preference for the 'through' living room, lit from opposing sides, and internal circulation was often combined with living areas.

By the late 1960s Modern housing had come under intense criticism and gradually fell completely out of favour. Charles Jencks (1977) has famously specified the precise moment of the end of Modernism as the demolition by dynamite of the Pruitt-Igoe housing complex at 3.32 p.m. on 15 July 1972. Rowe (1993) dates the beginning of the end of Modern housing in Europe and the USA to the late 1960s, accelerating after the 'oil shock' of 1973, and consequent on a new awareness of two main failings. First, that it was too standardised in relation to the cultural heterogeneity of user needs; and second, that it faced 'a crisis of meaning' in the contradiction between technical efficiency and unpopularity with users. In Britain, a marked change in the architectural style of council housing can be seen in the early to mid-1970s, as the unpopularity and technical failings of Modern forms and styles were acknowledged, and very tight cost constraints favoured simpler 'traditional' solutions like the brick-built terrace.

The Modern house today

The Modern house in Britain has thus come to be something quite different from the white villas of the 1930s, but it is remarkably similar in concept and intention to the continental workers' estates of the 1920s. Drawing on the *English House Condition Survey* (Department of the Environment 1994) and other sources, it can be estimated that about 2 million dwellings are of Modern design, equivalent to half the stock of council dwellings and one-tenth of the total stock in England in 1991. The Modern house in the late

1990s is essentially a council flat, maisonette or house, built between 1945 and about 1975.

It is the council tenants who occupy this housing who have had to judge it as 'consumers', in comparison with more traditional dwellings. There are two main sources of evidence on their views: the direct evidence of user studies or surveys of tenant satisfaction, and evidence of the relative popularity of different types and designs through choices made by tenants. User studies have repeatedly found that the tenants of Modern council housing express strong satisfaction with the internal qualities of their homes, but high levels of dissatisfaction with their external appearance (Burnett 1986). Tenant satisfaction seems to show a negative correlation with what might be termed the 'degrees of freedom' in the design. Internally, Modern housing was subject to a high degree of regulation through government standards and design guidance. This dealt with matters like the number, size and types of rooms, and was often based on user research, which tends inevitably to be conservative in its recommendations: what people say they want in a house seems to have remained remarkably constant since the early part of the twentieth century, allowing for changes in kitchens and sanitary facilities (Hole and Attenburrow 1966).

On the other hand, the external properties of the dwelling were much more open to innovation, for two main reasons. First, there have never been any 'reference data' for the external characteristics of dwellings which could be applied in an objective manner. In the absence of objective criteria, professional architects have generally been accepted as the 'authority' on what dwellings should look like. This left them relatively free to invent new external forms and spatial arrangements without having to demonstrate their acceptability, or even their practicality, and in the spirit of Modern design encouraged this search for novelty. In general terms, it is the external spatial innovations such as semi-public spaces and shared access routes which have proved to be the most unpopular features of Modern housing. Second, innovation in the external appearance of dwellings was actively encouraged through the drive to industrialise house building in the 1950s and 1960s (Finnimore 1989). This resulted in the use of new materials and new construction methods which radically changed the appearance of dwellings and limited the range of economic forms. It therefore appears that where Modern architects were tightly regulated against objective criteria, they generally satisfied the end users, but where they were free to innovate in their main sphere of professional competence, the external form and appearance of dwellings, they have not.

The indirect evidence of tenants' preferences and choices is found in research on so-called 'problem estates'. In this work 'Modern' is not a widely recognised analytical category and we have to make some assumptions about the overlap of various architectural types and accept that a fully accurate picture is not yet achievable (Glendinning and Muthesius 1994). However, three distinct trends have been identified: polarisation, residualisation and ghettoisation.

The social *polarisation* of housing tenure categories is a well-established trend, with council housing increasingly becoming the tenure of low income groups and the lowest social classes; the lower their class or socio-economic group (SEG), the more likely someone is to be a council tenant and the less likely to be an owner occupier (Reid 1981). Semi-skilled, unskilled and economically inactive people have become increasingly concentrated in the council sector over the period (Hamnett 1984). As J. Morris and Winn explain,

> as the privately rented sector declined, skilled manual workers, intermediate and junior non manual workers and professionals, employers and managers moved into the owner-occupied sector while the other socio-economic groups (the semi- and unskilled manual workers and the economically inactive – the economically worst off) moved into the public rented sector.
>
> (J. Morris and Winn 1990: 38)

The increase in the proportion of council tenants who are economically inactive and living on state benefits is particularly striking. By 1992 this had reached 62 per cent (*General Household Survey 1992*: Table 10.9). Other social indicators confirm this with the council sector showing an over-representation of those on low incomes, with low educational attainment, no telephone and no car (Forrest and Murie 1988; Kemp 1989). This trend has led to the claim that council housing is becoming a *residual* sector, a 'safety net' for the poor and those who cannot otherwise obtain housing. Whereas at one time being a council tenant commanded a privileged status within the working class, it has become a disadvantaged status for those who are least able to support themselves. This is not a simple consequence of the characteristics of the housing stock, the tenants or even housing policy, but a convergence of changes linked to broader trends in society described as 'marginalisation' (Forrest and Murie 1988: 84) which refers to the progressive polarisation of the economically unproductive population from participation in mainstream production and consumption relationships.

Within the council sector, there is further evidence which suggests that this marginalised population is concentrated in 'unpopular', 'problem' and 'difficult-to-let' estates. This in turn can lead to a process of *ghettoisation*. While the causes of this process are complex and their discussion beyond the scope of this chapter, it is clear that a scale of preferences for different dwelling types and locations is inevitable in the public sector – as is the case in the private sector. For many public housing authorities, this does not just produce estates which are slightly less desirable, but instead, some areas become exceptionally unpopular with prospective tenants – such that only those with no choice will accept them. Two factors in particular have reinforced the trend for the ghettoisation of some estates. First, difficult social conditions on estates are compounded when housing managers adopt allocation policies which (often informally) match 'problem tenants' with the worst accommodation (J. Morris and Winn 1990). Second, the introduction of 'right to buy' policies in the 1980s led to the sale of the best council house stock while, at the same time, new building was reduced to a minimal level. As a consequence the best quality conventional houses with gardens on suburban estates have been lost from the public sector, while hardly any flats have been sold at all (Forrest and Murie 1988).

While ghettoised estates are not all of the same type, and cannot simply be equated with Modern housing, there is a very marked overlap between extreme unpopularity and extreme Modern design. As Forrest and Murie (1988: 167–168) noted, 'stigmatised estates . . . are more likely to be high rise and system built, [and] to consist of flats and maisonettes'. This picture is confirmed by official reports. As far back as 1974, the first survey of the problem by the Department of the Environment (DoE) found that 75 per cent of unpopular post-war estates were flats, and half were less than ten years old (Power 1987). A subsequent DoE investigation found design to be a 'primary issue' in the demise of concrete system-built estates, through a combination of technical deficiencies, unattractive appearance, and 'intense communality' (Burbidge 1981).

Power (1987) reports that the Priority Estates Project (PEP), a national programme of tenant-based projects for problem estates, found particular problems with what she terms 'modern concrete-complex' estates from the 1960s or later. These were characterised by 'Modern architectural features such as decks, high-rise blocks, underground garages and futuristic layouts' (Power 1987: 125). Her list of the design problems of flatted estates puts a strong emphasis on recognisably Modern features:

- oppressive character, resulting from size (the Modern estates were the largest) and density (200 to 400 bed-spaces per acre)
- intense communality of living, with a 'no man's land' of communal external space and ill-used communal internal areas
- unguarded lifts, entrances and garages (in courts or underground areas) and unpoliceable decks and bridges
- industrial building systems, with manifold technical defects
- high-rise blocks (although free-standing point blocks had fewer problems).

The unpopularity of these estates was reflected in letting difficulties, high tenant turnover, high levels of vacancies, vandalism and squatting. Power (1987) considers that none of the estates was a 'total ghetto', but she reports that they housed, 'almost entirely, households from the lowest-income backgrounds, or increasingly unsupported, dependent households' (1987: 157).

The PEP survey showed that by no means all difficult-to-let council housing is Modern, and that pre-war cottage estates and walk-up blocks are distinct categories of potentially unpopular housing. However, it is the Modern housing which stands out as the 'worst', particularly from the point of view of tenants' attitudes to design. These estates seem to be rejected mainly because of their Modern design, even though other factors are involved. They figure very largely in the 'accretion of households with problems on estates with problems' (Forrest and Murie 1988: 168).

Modernism and the fate of the Modern house

The Modern house as realised in England after 1945 stands in the moral tradition of urban reform. It was an attempt to provide a dramatically improved, functional environment which would sustain the way of life of an urban working class, based on families and communities with a strong collective life. Around half of the post-war council housing stock was built in this spirit but has turned out to be among the least popular of all contemporary housing. Consequently, it is now occupied predominantly by a socially marginal population, a disadvantaged minority with no other choice. We have seen that many factors in the operation of the housing market and housing allocation processes have been involved in causing this situation. However, it is important to ask whether Modernism itself as a philosophy of design has contributed to the fate of Modern housing. A sociological analysis suggests that it has.

The house, viewed from a sociological point of view, can be interpreted in terms of Western material culture where its fabric and the artefacts and objects it contains act as both material supports for a particular way of life and as symbols of social relations and social values (see Chapters 2, 4, 10 and 12 in this volume). This view has also been developed by many writers in the field of cultural anthropology, looking at house form and settlement patterns in a variety of pre-industrial and modern societies (see, for example Rapoport 1969; M. Douglas 1973; Lawrence 1987; Miller 1987).

In industrial societies the house stands out particularly as a symbol of social status. As Saunders (1990: 246) put it, 'there can be no doubt that, in Britain at least, housing carries clear symbolic meaning as regards the attribution of status'. There are many dimensions of housing which carry status connotations, but three principal factors can be identified: tenure, locality and dwelling type. The status ranking of housing tenure reflects the social position of those who occupy the different tenures, and hence changes over time. When Rex and Moore (1967) proposed their theory of housing classes, they were able to postulate a rank order of owner occupation, council housing and private renting, with further subsets of each 'class' situation. At that time, it was possible to question how far this was a universal rank order (Couper and Brindley 1975), but today the lowered social status of council renting, even to the extent that it has become a stigmatised tenure, is widely acknowledged (Saunders 1990). Locality and social status are closely linked, and this remains a central factor in explanations of residential mobility and urban social structure (Robson 1969; Johnston 1980; Walmsley and Lewis 1993). Dwelling types also acquire a status rank order, from detached houses to terraced houses (D. Chapman 1955). This is related to the relative size of dwellings, but it also tends to reflect the degree of autonomy and privacy which each type of dwelling provides for its occupiers. The conventional status scale goes from the detached – a house in its own large grounds – down to the most communal – a room or flat with shared facilities.

The Modern house can readily be seen to rank at the bottom of all three of these status scales: it is a council house, occupied by the lowest status tenants; it is typically located in low-status urban areas; and it is built in a dense, collectivist form. There are two further reasons for thinking that the Modern house is inherently open to negative social connotations which would tend to make it unattractive.

First, consider the meaning of collectivist urban forms. When Modern architects started to design for the urban working class, they tried to find built forms which expressed their idea of the nature of working-class life. In the 1950s, there was a rediscovery of the importance of community in the urban working class, largely through the Institute for Community Studies and its research in the East End of London. Architects influenced by Le Corbusier and the post-war New Brutalism movement took it as axiomatic that urban council housing should be collectivist in form, with a high proportion of shared external and internal space and shared facilities. Hence the proliferation of semi-public open spaces, 'streets in the air' and shared laundry rooms in Modern housing complexes. But what this did was to 'freeze' the physical environment for a community which was already changing. As Willmott and Young (1960) went on to show in their studies of migrants to the suburbs, younger, better-educated members of the inner city communities were leaving for suburban homes and better-paid jobs. Community turned out to be a function of shared adversity, something those who were benefiting from the new prosperity of the 1960s chose to escape. Ironically, much of the new housing built for slum clearance did not, therefore, rehouse the whole of the old community. Instead, it came to house residents from a number of clearance areas who could not afford to go to the suburbs or new towns, together with other poor residents including people with high priority on waiting lists and (later) homeless people (Lambert et al. 1978). The communalist philosophy of the new housing projects was, then, undermined from the start.

Second, consider again the radically different physical appearance of Modern housing. Like Modern music or painting, Modern architecture is theoretical, critical and intellectual – some would say 'highbrow'. In all spheres, Modernism has been an elitist movement actively rejecting popular taste. The appearance of Modern housing was so different from the established conventions of English housing that it created a radical disjuncture between two categories, Modern and traditional, with very few points of contact or overlap.

This contrasts markedly with the range of housing prior to the production of 2 million Modern dwellings. In the nineteenth century, a hierarchy of urban housing was created, based on the terrace, in which a degree of similarity connected the grandest with the meanest house (Muthesius 1982). In a very direct way, the form and appearance of housing expressed the social hierarchy of Victorian society. In the early twentieth century, Modernism attempted quite deliberately to refute this hierarchical conception of housing and to replace it with 'socially neutral' functional forms which would provide for objective needs, rather than express and reinforce a rigid social status hierarchy. This was a radical, socialist proposition about how society might be, rather than a response to how it actually was.

Although the status structures of the nineteenth century have gradually broken down, they have not altogether disappeared (Halsey 1978). Modern housing has therefore found its place in the contemporary social structure, with the result that housing intended for a supposedly egalitarian working-class urban community has become the housing of the poorest and most marginalised people in society. Its radical appearance significantly heightens the sense of difference and separation of its residents from the mainstream society.

It could be argued that Modern housing has from its inception run counter to the growth of individualism which has resulted from the differentiation of labour in modern society. Modern architects tried to apply the criteria of mass production to housing in the form of standardisation, uniformity and economies of scale. However, in the sphere of consumption the trends have been towards product diversification, differentiation and choice. In market conditions housing has behaved like other consumption commodities, where products which fundamentally meet the same needs are differentiated to provide consumers with a range of choice and to represent perceived social distinctions – exactly the opposite of the principles applied to Modern housing. The radical disjuncture which the latter now represents puts it outside the 'normal' range of housing choices. If this hypothesis is correct we would expect to see Modern housing either totally rejected or modified to make it more like the norm, and this is exactly what has happened. In some cases, like Pruitt-Igoe, or the Southgates estate in Runcorn, or Hulme in Manchester, Modern housing schemes have been destroyed in an attempt to eliminate what they stand for. In others, where their owners find they have to retain them, Modern schemes have been modified to make them look more like conventional housing. For example, four-storey maisonette blocks have been reduced to two-storey terraces, and conventional cladding materials have been added to hide concrete construction. Where individual owners have purchased Modern council dwellings, they have added 'traditional' doors, porches and windows to make them more like a normal house. All of these are attempts to break down the radical disjuncture between the Modern and the conventional, and to reconnect Modern housing with the mainstream.

Conclusion

The evidence presented here on the fate of the Modern house suggests that it is no longer progressive and liberating but is now contributing to a process of social exclusion. A highly marginalised sector of the population is increasingly identified with a type of housing which is both highly unpopular and radically different in appearance from the mainstream. It is not too much of a simplification to conclude that the 10 per cent of the housing stock which can be classed as Modern has become the refuge of the most marginal 10 per cent of society. While the unpopularity of Modern housing has come about for a variety of reasons, its collectivist design features and its radical appearance have been major contributory factors, and in addition these factors have created a radical discontinuity between Modern and mainstream housing.

It is not the place of this chapter to propose policy solutions, but it could be argued that the reintegration of those people who have been socially marginalised through poverty and unemployment would be helped by breaking their association with a distinctive, unpopular and socially stigmatised form of housing. One way to tackle this is to try to make this housing less unpopular. If more people found it acceptable, then it might become less dominated by the marginal poor. The physical reintegration of Modern housing with conventional housing, together with diversification of ownership, could help this process, by allowing it to be modified by individual occupiers, landlords or owners to make it less radical in appearance and less collectivist in form. This conclusion has been reached by many different commentators, from Alice Coleman (1985) and Anne Power (1987) to housing managers, individual tenants and owners, together with radical critics like John Turner (1976) and Colin Ward (1985). What this chapter has shown is that the social position and social meaning of Modern housing are problems in themselves, which need a response.

Consider, finally, the comments of the architectural critic Deyan Sudjic (1993) on the listing of Camden's Alexandra Road estate, cited at the head of this chapter. Sudjic argues that listing was exactly the wrong response to a Modern estate which was just beginning to be adapted and modified by individual occupiers and notes that:

> in the back gardens you can see the sliding partitions that have been torn out by those tenants who find them a nuisance. The black tiles

have been chipped away. In many flats the plate glass has been replaced with oldie worldie diamond pattern leading, and the flush doors replaced with Edwardian-style panelling. These in fact are evidence that the estate is not a dreadful place in which to live, evidence that there is enough spirit in its residents to take a pride in their homes and to want to make their mark, rather than allow the estate to slip into slovenly squalor, as too much post-war public housing has done. And yet these are precisely the things that the listing process will stop.

(*Guardian*, 24 August 1993)

4

STAGE SETS FOR IDEAL LIVES

Images of home in contemporary show homes

Tony Chapman

On the fringes of most towns in Britain, new houses are currently being constructed by speculative builders for private ownership. On the majority of sites there will be at least one fashionably decorated and fully furnished 'show home' for people to view. Unlike the rest of Europe and the United States, where home owners tend to have more control over the kind of house they intend to live in, most British homes are not built according to the taste and needs of an individual person or family. Instead, new homes are built by a relatively small number of construction companies which adopt a limited range of pattern book designs, so representing a remarkably uniform image of what the 'ideal home' should be. Britain has a long tradition of speculative house building, running back to the early eighteenth century in towns like Bath and in the West End of London (see Chapter 1). Each period has produced its own ideal image of home life as Hepworth and Brindley have shown in Chapters 2 and 3. This chapter is concerned with new homes in Britain and seeks to explore how design reflects and to some extent shapes expectations of home life.

What are the essential features of this new vernacular architecture? First, it is not Modern and progressive in the sense that it projects images of and opportunities for new patterns of domestic life. Instead, it is backward looking, nostalgic and traditional. This is reflected in the re-emergence of the middle-class Victorian preoccupation with shutting out the rest of the world from the domestic sphere. Contrary to the dictates of the Modern Movement, new houses are again feigning the massive fabric of the Victorian house by adding mock beams, high protective roofs, ornate brickwork and glazing. On the one hand, these design features symbolise the imagined folksiness of village life. On the other hand, designers hope to give the impression of a protected environment whose boundaries are clearly marked by garden railings, picket fences or perilously low brick walls. Similarly, new house designers have rediscovered the porch and the portentous front door to reassure buyers that this is not just an important house, but a safe one too (see Chapters 10–12).

Second, there have been important changes to the internal organisation of domestic space in modern show homes. In larger new homes at least, designers have turned their backs on open-plan layouts of the Modern home and replaced these with a nostalgic reinterpretation of Victorian and Edwardian architecture. In this chapter, an analysis of the internal spatial organisation of new houses reveals more than just changing aesthetic fashions; instead, it suggests transformations in the way that idealised families are *expected* to live.

Third, contemporary show homes provide models of domestic life *as lived* by their imaginary dwellers. Quite literally, they 'show' buyers how the ideal home should be lived in. Several features of this lifestyle can be identified. First and most obviously, there is an expectation that buyers will form or have already established themselves as a nuclear family. Virtually all detached show homes provide images of the married couple's quarters – the so-called 'master bedroom' with its en suite bathroom, together with their children's rooms. Second, the interior design and furnishing of the home reflects a strong sense of affluence and well-being, suggesting that one or both of the adults are in well-paid employment and, certainly in larger show homes, that they both have a car. Finally, show homes project images of a leisurely lifestyle. The houses are generally free of the detritus of day-to-day living – except perhaps for a kettle, mugs and jar of coffee in the utility room, which is used by the sales staff. Kitchens are fancifully tidy and well provided for in terms of 'labour saving' appliances, giving the impression that this is a place of leisure rather than work. Similarly, the multiplicity of bathrooms suggests endless opportunity for body celebration. It is not, therefore, the intention of this chapter to explore the realities of domestic life in contemporary Britain, but to analyse the idealised images of home which are constructed by speculative house-building companies.

Consumer behaviour in the home

Since the end of the Second World War, an increasingly large proportion of British people have been able to buy their own homes, rising from only 29 per cent of the population in 1950 to 66 per cent in 1991 (Balchin 1995: 6). This has been made possible by increased affluence, changes in the occupational structure and the growth of social mobility (Payne 1987a; Butler and Savage 1995; R. Brown 1997). This trend reached its height under the long period (between 1979 and 1997) of Conservative government whose ideological commitment to the 'property owning democracy' promoted private ownership for the majority of the population, including council tenants who were encouraged to take a first step onto the property ladder under the 'right to buy' scheme. In 1980 there were 6.5 million local authority dwellings in Britain; by 1991, 1.5 million of these had been sold to their tenants (Balchin 1995: 174). During the same period 1.9 million speculatively built homes were erected (Balchin 1995: 32).

Table 4.1 Size of new houses completed in England 1985–1995[a]

Year	One bedroom	Two bedrooms	Three bedrooms	Four or more bedrooms	N=
1985	6,378	32,252	53,271	25,118	117,019
1990	4,765	26,281	41,187	32,626	104,859
1995	2,320	26,327	43,476	33,949	106,072

Note
[a] Includes houses built by private enterprise only.
Source: Department of Environment (1997: 102, Table 6.7).

There is also some evidence to suggest that the size of new homes is increasing. As Table 4.1 demonstrates, only 20 per cent of new houses completed in England in 1985 had four or more bedrooms; by 1995 this had risen to over 30 per cent. While the former Conservative government encouraged construction companies to build on reclaimed urban land, the so-called 'brown field' sites, the majority of larger new homes are built in green field locations. The new Labour government supports the idea of building on brown field sites, but has also given the go ahead for the building of thousands of new homes on former green belt land and anticipates that around 5 million houses may need to be built by 2020.

While the need for such development is hotly disputed by environmentalists, planners and the people who already live in rural areas (Heatherington and May 1998; Rowan 1998), the demand for executive show homes on green field sites looks likely to remain buoyant for some years to come. This demand arises from changed patterns of consumption and lifestyle within the home since the 1950s. This is partly due to increased affluence among home owners, but more importantly, changing patterns of employment have led to the fragmentation of many aspects of family life. In 1996, 5.9 million women worked full-time and 4.5 million worked part time, and women comprised a half of the working population (*Social Trends* 1997: 73) which has had important impacts on the pattern of domestic life.

Home-based leisure patterns have been transformed. In the middle part of the twentieth century, family entertainment centred initially on listening to the radio and later on watching the television. Families tended to settle in one room for the evening in wintertime due to the cost and inconvenience of heating and lighting. As central heating became more common, fuelled by cheap North Sea Gas, the various rooms of the house were used more fully (Chapman 1996). Teenagers and children, for example, began to expect to have space of their own, which ultimately led to the replication and proliferation of electrical goods like televisions, home computers, hi-fi, musical instruments and so on (see Madigan and Munro, Chapter 5).

46

Patterns of domestic labour have also changed as capital produced new consumer durables. In some cases, manufacturers had to make strong efforts to associate their products with the home. Marketing of the home sewing machine in the nineteenth century, for example, was problematic because people drew a clear distinction between the rationality of the factory and the comfort of the home. Consequently, manufacturers had to illustrate their advertisements with pictures of their highly ornate sewing machines in domestic interiors (Forty 1986). More recently household durables – the so-called 'white goods' like refrigerators, dishwashers and washing machines – are sold on the back of a promise that they provide hygienic protection from dirt and disease and save time and labour. The existence of white goods in the home, shown in Table 4.2, does not necessarily reduce the labour dramatically because of the heightened expectation of cleanliness which has invaded the late modern psyche (M. Douglas 1966). For example, clothes are now washed much more regularly than was the case in the 1940s, and further, the dedication of garments to particular activities, such as leisure wear, work wear, sports club wear and so on, increases the laundry workload substantially (Faulkner and Arnold 1985; Cowan 1989; Deem 1986).

Eating habits have also changed. The main daily meal, for example, which was up until the 1960s something of a family institution in Britain, has become a fragmented activity with different members of the household eating at different times of the day. Furthermore, it is now commonplace for variations in taste and dietary habits among family members to be tolerated, a change which is bolstered by the increasing diversity of easily available ready-made foodstuffs. This represents a substantial shift in attitude from the middle part of the century when the idea of making children eat things they did not like was a sign of virtuous parenting (Mennell 1985; Lupton 1996; Charles and Kerr 1988).

Table 4.2 Percentage of households with consumer durable products in Britain 1972–1996

	1972	1981	1991	1995–1996
Colour television	–	74	95	97
Washing machine	66	78	87	90
Freezer/fridge freezer	–	49	83	89
Video recorder	–	–	69	79
Microwave cooker	–	–	55	70
Tumble drier	–	–	48	51
Dishwasher	–	4	14	20
Central heating	37	59	82	85
Telephone	42	75	88	93
Home computer	–	–	21	25
Compact disc player	–	–	27	52

Source: adapted from *Social Trends* (1997: 112).

A final example of change in patterns of consumption in the home is the shortening lifespan of household goods. In the first quarter of the twentieth century, people bought home furnishings with the intention that they should last a long time (R. Roberts 1973). Furniture was constructed from solid wood with heavy-duty upholstery (which was, in turn, covered at the arms and chairbacks to increase its lifespan). High quality carpets were expected to last for twenty years or more; indeed, it was a common practice to varnish wallpapers to preserve them. At the end of the twentieth century, consumers expect to change their household furnishings much more often. This fashion-led pattern of consumption has been encouraged through the introduction of a wide range of house style magazines, commercial shows like the Ideal Home Exhibition, television series on style and do-it-yourself (DIY) together with regular features in newspapers. The opportunity to change household furnishings has been encouraged partly by the growing numbers of furniture and decorating superstores which can be found at the edge of almost every town, and by the ready availability of 'interest free credit schemes'. The consequences of all these changes is that many families want bigger houses, with more facilities, which are situated in attractive 'high-status' locations and are decorated and furnished with the newest fashions in interior design and furnishing.

Selling the image of the ideal home

While superstores often provide mock-up kitchens, bathrooms and bedrooms to help shoppers to imagine what the goods on sale would look like in their own home, the ultimate method of selling the idea of a dream house is found in the sophisticated marketing strategies of the big-house building companies which provide complete stage sets for ideal living in their fully furnished show homes. In this part of the chapter I shall provide an analysis of the marketing strategies of the builders of show homes to demonstrate how capital projects images of family life as it 'ought to be lived'.

The discussion is based on a content analysis of the marketing brochures from forty executive new home developments in the South East and North Eastern regions of England between 1994 and 1996 and upon the observation of twenty-five fully furnished show homes, built between 1995 and 1997 in the North East of England. It is not possible here to discuss the strategies of builders' marketing ploys in the full range of projects from the first-time buyer's starter home to the custom built home for the very wealthy. Consequently, attention will be concentrated upon the design and marketing of the top end of the new house market, that is, the four or five bedroom detached house built on a green field site, which comprises about 30 per cent of the market.

Making new houses more attractive to buyers than existing properties depends, increasingly, upon the skill of the builder to design a product that fits current fashions and meets the needs of contemporary family life. Since the late 1970s, the architectural style of private domestic houses has changed substantially. For most of the 1960s and 1970s, three or four bedroom houses were built according to a fairly uniform design which adopted an 'L shaped' open plan which connected lounge, dining room and kitchen (see Madigan and Munro, Chapter 5). While this design was not adhered to as rigidly as the so-called 'universal plan' of the 1930s semi-detached house (Oliver *et al.* 1981), there remained relatively little scope for consumer choice in design. Houses on 1980s and 1990s developments are characterised by a wider range of internal floor plans, façades and external decorative features than their counterparts of the 1960s and 1970s, which tended to make a virtue of the similarity of designs rather than difference. The layouts of estates are also planned differently. Long rows of houses are rarely built now, unlike the 1930s and 1960s. Instead, most site plans are emphatically non-geometric with curving roads and culs-de-sac, while houses are built from a range of styles and materials. Houses are situated with differing aspects in order to produce a random, village-like layout.

This 'new vernacular' domestic architecture has parallels with inter-war semi-detached houses in that they attempt to emulate extant architectural forms. In each case, the houses make stylistic reference to more prestigious houses of the past. Houses built in the 1930s and 1990s rarely achieve any degree of accuracy or authenticity in their use of decoration, but it is undoubtedly the case that the motifs adopted suggest traditional design. In the dangerous uncertainty of the 1930s it is not surprising that people sought to buy houses that projected safe images. As Oliver *et al.* (1981) point out:

> The suburban semi was a complex reaction against a number of other house forms: it was opposed to the image of the Victorian terrace, with its 'collective' associations beneath a single roof, and from which many of the lower and middle class had come; it was contrary to the style of the factories with their heartless anonymous, technical efficiency; it was against the style of the Continental Modern Movement, whose 'machines-for-living-in' aesthetic was inimical to the picture of domesticity; and it challenged the style of the municipal housing estate.
>
> (Oliver *et al.* 1981: 157)

This sense of homely identification was strengthened by the architectural adornments on the houses such as mock Tudor beams and oriel windows. It did not please everybody, as John Gloag asked in 1934:

> Why are you, or perhaps your neighbours, living in an imitation Tudor house with stained wooden slats shoved on to the front of it to make it look like what is called a half-timbered house? Those slats

having nothing to do with the construction of the house. They are just applied as ornaments. The house does not look like a real half-timbered house and it never can. It has been built in quite a different way from a real Tudor house. Why do we live in this sort of half-baked pageant, always hiding our ideas in the clothes of another age?

(quoted in Oliver *et al.* 1981: 161)

Gloag's fury with the mock Tudor imagery of inter-war houses was a common reaction among that self-appointed elite of 'experts' on how home life should be lived in the middle part of the twentieth century. As Brindley (Chapter 3) has shown, during the mid-twentieth century architects and architecture critics did not shrink from recommending new styles of housing which were fit for new styles of living, especially for poorer people who could not buy into the more 'popular' traditional styles of private semi-detached houses.

Even private houses became more 'Modern' in the 1960s and 1970s, perhaps reflecting a general sense of optimism for the future during that period. In the 1980s and 1990s, which have been dogged by economic recession and industrial restructuring which have undermined confidence in employment security, it is hardly surprising that, as in the 1930s, there has been a renewed sense of nostalgia for the past. Builders have recognised this trend and attempt to increase potential buyers' sense of security by emphasising the 'traditional' qualities of their houses. This is often reinforced by drawing attention to the heritage of the company itself, in order to provide some kind of architectural and craft lineage. On the inside back page of one company's brochure for a new estate near Northampton, for example, the title caption boasts 'a craft tradition since 1786'. Around the copywriter's text are reproductions of sepia photographs of a bearded 'Young James Lovell (1842–1911) son of James Lovell Minterne Magna, carpenter and church organist'. The short in-fill paragraph states that:

> Lovell is one of Britain's oldest and most respected house building names. The Company pedigree is a clear unbroken *lineage*, stretching back over 200 years to the reign of George III. This Company '*heritage*' remains one of the most durable building traditions in Britain, rooted in the *craft skills* of the English countryside and firmly chronicled in generations of continuous construction excellence.
>
> (Lovell brochure 1995, added emphasis)

Instead of emphasising adventurous style or innovative design features, then, builders are more likely to assure potential buyers that their development is one of considerable substance and durability. This is often achieved by drawing associations between the building site and local historical features. A new development on the Wynyard Estate in Cleveland, north of Stockton on Tees, lends itself to this kind of allusion. The estate is near the landscaped parkland that has as its focus Wynyard Hall, described by Pevsner (1985: 514) as 'the most splendid 19th Century mansion in the county' built by the hugely rich mine-owning family, the Tempests. In spite of the fact that Wynyard Village (as the development is called) is separated from Wynyard Hall, allusions are made to the impressive historical pedigree that potential occupants may inherit:

> From the time that the Crown granted Sir Hugh de Chapell tenancy of the estate in 1230, Wynyard has been a focus of splendour for nearly 800 years. Now, you can be part of the Wynyard experience.
> (Ideal Homes Northern, promotional material 1995)

While the location of Wynyard Village is exceptional, its promotional material is typical of many new developments as it attempts to take advantage of the notion, made popular by the Prince of Wales, that it is possible to develop ready-made communities.

> Nothing evokes the spirit of a traditional English Summer more than the sound of leather on willow. Near the Wellington Monument, cricket has been played in this delightful setting for over a century, where local teams still meet in friendly rivalry in this most English of pastimes . . . Designed on a traditional English Village theme, complete with village green and duckpond, Wynyard Village will offer a unique lifestyle.
> (Ideal Homes Northern, promotional material 1995)

There is, indeed, a duckpond at Wynyard Village – with real ducks – and an operational water pump. But the small village green looks decidedly manufactured as it is festooned with man-hole covers, the verges are not disfigured by muddy tractor wheels and there is no manure on the roads. In fact there is little evidence of working farms in the immediate vicinity because the estate is surrounded by golf courses. While the layout of the houses is pleasingly village-like, with a mixture of house designs built in traditional materials including timber windows and pantile roofs, whether this yet constitutes the ready-made community which is alluded to by the sales brochures is open to question. In fact, Wynyard Village is very quiet during the daytime – almost like an abandoned film set. At the time of study, the estate looked so much like a stage set, a kind of Disney village, that the inhabited houses were almost indistinguishable from the show homes and, as a consequence, had little signs pinned to their front gates to state that fact. Because there are no shops at Wynyard, nor a doctor's surgery, nor a school, access to the outside world is necessarily made by car; as a consequence, only at about 5 p.m. does the village start to spring to life, when the winding roads suddenly become festooned by the residents' apparently obligatory high performance cars.

People cannot be persuaded to buy new homes just on the basis of the currently voguish fashion for traditional-looking houses in villagey environments. In addition such houses incorporate many new features to raise expectations of comfort, utility, safety, privacy and, of course, happiness in the home. This notion of selling a happy home is not new, but it is presented in a radically different way from the 1930s or 1950s in the sense that there has been a shift from the notion that 'collective' family life leads to happiness to one which asserts that 'individual self-fulfilment' for all members of the family is vital within the communion of the family. A number of changes have been made to the fabric of new houses that demonstrate this shift in emphasis. The interior floor plan of the 1990s house reflects, on a much smaller scale, the Edwardian villa. The designers of larger houses have abandoned the 1970s model of a sprawling walk-through living room running from the front to back of the house and featuring huge picture windows and vast sliding patio doors on the garden. Instead, they have reorganised the available space to incorporate a number of smaller rooms including the 'drawing room', 'dining room', 'family room' and 'study'.

Kitchens have also been transformed by removing some tasks from the main kitchen to a utility area for the washing machine and additional sink space. In show homes these spaces are often depicted as 'tradesman' or 'servant' entrances with wicker baskets full of dried flowers, logs or fruit skins, together with huge provisions jars, witch's brooms, green wellington boots and sometimes plaster casts of game birds hanging from hooks. Kitchens themselves have become more public spaces, with big pine tables groaning with baskets of fruit and bread (made from plastic, wax or plaster) providing romantic evocations of farmhouse conviviality. Kitchen furniture and decoration has become an important focus of the home and a crucial status symbol – an artefact of value in itself – instead of the value of the production of wholesome food that it facilitates. While the kitchen is more likely to be separated from the dining room by a door, or perhaps even an additional room in the 1990s house – the breakfast room – the kitchen has by no means reverted to its status of a private back region of the house. As Corrigan (1997) points out:

> There is clearly a collapse of boundaries between the kitchen and other areas. Instead of being a unit compartmentalised into sub-units each with a specific function, the contemporary home turns living, dining and cooking areas into a continuous semi-differentiated space . . . Houseware magazines stress again and again that the kitchen is not somewhere obscured from view, but the most open and important room in the house. In particular, the cook is not isolated from social activity.
>
> (Corrigan 1997: 109)

The extent to which British people actually 'cook' in their showpiece kitchens is open to question; indeed, the evidence suggests that the British are the most enthusiastic consumers of ready-made 'cook-chill' foods in Europe (*Guardian*, 9 October 1997).

The redefinition of other elements of downstairs room space is significant. Take for example, the reintroduction of the study to new homes. This may have something to do with the fact that more people do work from home. But the evidence suggests that the study is used in show homes as a definitive masculine space to raise men's expectation of renewed status in the family and the opportunity of splendid isolation; like Elizabeth Bennet's father, in the BBC television serialisation of *Pride and Prejudice*, ruling benignly over his family from the relatively safe enclave of his room where he could enjoy a good book and sip at a glass of fortified wine. In many show homes, designers use the study to exhibit specifically masculine symbols such as framed architectural drawings, old-looking leather-topped desks with a green banker's lamp and, perhaps, a heavy wooden captain's chair. Often, the study is the only room in the house that has not been festooned with dried flowers, draped curtains and fussy cushions. Instead, it is decorated in a restrained masculine style, adopting gilded striped wallpapers and to give the impression of scholarship and cultural distinction, the positioning of a classical bust, a violin with old sheet music and a few, but not too many, old books. Pedantic observers of show homes may be interested in some of the titles of these books, which have, presumably, been garnered from jumble sales or auction houses. In one show house in Middlesbrough, the study contained the following: *Skin Disease in General Practice*, *The New Phonographic Phrase Book* and *The Dambusters*. This led me to wonder what kind of imaginary person was meant to live in this house.

Upstairs, the floor plans of new show homes have also been transformed to incorporate a larger number of bedrooms and the now obligatory proliferation of bathrooms. It is not unusual now for four or five bedroom houses to have three upstairs bathrooms; these include the 'family bathroom' and two en suites off the guest bedroom and the so-called 'master bedroom'. The introduction of so many bathrooms is significant for a number of reasons. First, it demonstrates the current social cachet to be gained from such a level of opulence: it is a symbol of status, like the double garage in the 1970s or the pretension of servant bells in the reception rooms of larger three bedroom semi-detached houses in the 1920s. Second, and at a deeper level, the doubling or trebling of bathrooms illustrates how the body has taken centre stage in the late modern psyche (Featherstone *et al.* 1991; Falk 1994; Rivers *et al.* 1992). The bathroom is no longer a place to get in and out of as quickly as possible, but a place of self-indulgence and body celebration. Third, the separation of the parents' bathroom from the children's shows how important privacy *within* the family has become. This preoccupation with privacy not only shows that bodily taboo may be increasing, but also demonstrates how the sellers of new homes are promising potential buyers the kinds of sexual opportunities in the marital bedroom that was for several decades available only in hotels.

Sometimes this allusion to sexual gratification is exaggerated by interior designers. In one house studied in Darlington, County Durham, the interior designer decorated the master bedroom of a four bedroom house with a double en suite shower in a particularly sexually provocative way. On the door handle of the shower room, a pink hand towel had been tied into an elaborate knot from which a single silk rose protruded. At the bottom of the bed sat a small chest, upon which an engraved silver tray was set out with two fluted glasses and a bottle of Cinzano Bianco. As is quite common in modern show homes, an entire wall of the bedroom was mirror glazed to conceal the wardrobes (and to make the room look larger) and the bed was, of course, a portentous four poster with drapes and canopies. As if it were possible for the viewers of the show home to have missed the point, the designer added the finishing touch of a slinky claret satin nightdress draped across the bed. It may be a vulgar technique to sell houses on the basis of a fantasy of adult privacy, marital communion and sexual excitement, but this principle has been built into the design of most larger new houses. Because the internal walls of new houses are so thin and impossible to soundproof, the master bedroom tends to be blockaded from other parts of the house by the central landing and the use of wardrobes and bathrooms as baffle boards between the parents' and children's rooms (see Chapman and Lucas 1998).

Providing images of a safe and folksy neighbourhood environment, a well-planned, high-status and functional household helps to sell new homes. But in the process of product development, volume builders also lend support to their buyers by giving guidance on colour co-ordinated and stylistically uniform furnishing and decoration of their home. Builders offer their 'expertise' to take away the attendant risks of making mistakes in decorating decisions, together with the offer of short-term financial inducement for the purchaser.

> To help you choose carpets, curtains and blinds, we have commissioned interior designers to pre-select a top quality range. We have colour selection centres in each of our sales offices so you can see and feel how they will look and see how our suggested colour schemes work. If you choose from our range we are able to supply matching accessories such as bed spreads, valances and lampshades . . . To ease the inevitable expense of moving, the cost of these goods can be added to the basic price of your new home, and may be included in your mortgage.
>
> (Wimpey, promotional material 1995)

In the 1990s, building companies add value to their product by offering 'choice' in the decoration and furnishing, but the range of choice is strictly limited to allow companies to buy in bulk. While the long-term cost is substantial, the short-term advantage for customers is that they can include the cost of decoration and furnishing in the mortgages. For the builder, the advantage comes in increasing the prospect of sales and by adding value to their product by drawing money that might have been spent in the high street or shopping mall into their own coffers.

Conclusion

In this chapter, I have discussed a number of strategies that house-building companies employ to persuade people to buy a new home. While there are undoubtedly many minor variations on the theme of the ideal home which are presented to the house-buying (or house-viewing) public, I argue that there is also striking uniformity in the key elements of the 'dream home'. All of the executive show homes built on green field sites that I have studied were detached from their neighbours, suggesting that the house will provide high-status accommodation, personal privacy and safety from the 'dangerous' environs of the town or city. Their interior design offered spaces for family activities, space for parents to be secluded from their children and space to entertain and impress their friends. For men, the show home promises space to enjoy splendid isolation in their study, while for women, the kitchen and utility room promise all the latest facilities to ease the burden of domestic labour. Like a cook-chill meal, package holiday or an off-the-peg suit, the show home offers its buyers a complete product, where they apparently need do no more than move in and live a happy life.

Some people buy into the dream with such enthusiasm that they buy actual show homes; occasionally, people buy all the furniture and ornamentation that the designer put in place too. Moving into an instant home, even for happy families, can cause some confusion to the people who live there, however, because they find it hard to distinguish their taste, and even their artefacts, from those that seem to belong to the imagination of the show home designer. This point was caught effectively in a BBC television series *Signs of the Times*, first screened in 1996. The aim of the series was to allow householders to explain in their own words how they felt about their homes and the way they had decorated and furnished them. One couple, who had bought a show home lock, stock and barrel, reflected on this:

HUSBAND: It's a strange concept to move in and suddenly [there are] all these ornaments . . . I think it's the ornaments which generally are personal things that you go out and buy for a special occasion. And they are all here, and they haven't got any history attached to them. I mean, in the lounge there's a bust of Mozart. But I wouldn't have bought it . . . but having it here it seems right. I keep saying to Moira 'I didn't know we had this' . . .

WIFE: The children do it all the time [they say] 'Is this ours, mummy, or the house's' which I find astonishing. I say it's all ours, Rachel, it's all ours. There's a lot of dried flowers hung around the oak beams that appeals because it feels very cottagey and country. And I would love to think I'm the sort of person who dried and hung those flowers myself. But I'm not and I'm glad someone else has because I think they look lovely.

But did it make them happy?

WIFE: When we first came in I felt the house was very, very flash. You just felt you were invading a very posh person's house . . . Our friends just think it's out of this world *and they hate us*, and we love it.

HUSBAND: I'd say this is our dream home. We couldn't wish to achieve any more than we have here. It's arriving to me, arriving somewhere we've been travelling to for a long time.

WIFE: I think it's mega. I think it's perfect.

HUSBAND: Perfect for us.

WIFE: For us.

(*Sign of the Times*, BBCTV, 1996)

But can contentment be guaranteed by turning the front door key of a dream home? It is important to conclude the discussion by highlighting potential mismatches between image and reality. Reflecting first on the generation of idealised images, it is not surprising that speculative builders design show homes the way they do – for the sole purpose of their enterprise is to sell houses. A building firm could hardly be expected to pepper the doormat of a show home with facsimile gas, electric and telephone bills and a letter from the building society about a rise in the mortgage rates, just as it would not leave a load of dirty pots piled up in the kitchen sink or laundry all over the central heating radiators. However ingenious companies may be in designing show homes that masquerade as real homes, we must be careful not to over-state their influence; certainly, building companies attempt to shape our needs and wants, but they do so in response to wider social changes which also impact upon people's hopes and dreams. (See Lodziak 1995 for a critical appraisal of the way that capital manipulates people's needs.) In an aspira-tional culture that increasingly demands that people make displays of affluence and well-being through conspicuous consumption, it is likely that show home viewers would prefer not to be reminded of the realities of day-to-day life. If people choose to consume goods in the hope that they will have a better life, they would not want to see medicines on view in the bathroom, terry-nappies soaking in the utility room or a Zimmer frame in the hall. It is from objects such as these that show home viewers wish to escape.

Buying into the dream of the ideal home is expensive in economic terms, and yet it is an expense that is hard to resist because of the popularly accepted association between home ownership and personal success (see Chapter 15). This leads many people to over-stretch themselves financially and for many house buyers, the burden of debt they take on – especially if they become unemployed or suffer from poor health – is too great to manage and they lose their homes as a consequence (Ford *et al.* 1995). Between 1990 and 1995 there were around 50,000 repossessions a year of homes in Britain because people fell back in their mortgage payments. Even if couples can afford to keep up the payments, the sheer effort of juggling paid employment, home care and the personal and financial costs of maintaining a home, together with the associated financial and personal costs of arranging care for children while both parents work, can cast a heavy burden on householders.

It is not possible to gauge, with any degree of confidence, the extent to which unrealistic expectations of a happy home life are fuelled by construction companies, DIY chains, furniture retailers and so on. It is clear, however, that the structure of households in Britain is changing dramatically. An increasing proportion of the population do not marry, more people delay marriage until they reach their thirties than was the case in the 1970s, more people are electing not to have children. Most worrying of all, perhaps, is the high level of marital breakdown: in 1995 there were 155,499 divorces in Britain, that is 13.1 divorces per 1,000 marriages (*Annual Abstract of Statistics* 1997: 23). This is not to suggest a crude causal relationship between domestic consumption and marital breakdown of course; the reasons for divorce and separation are various, ranging from sexual problems, intellectual incompatibility, achievement differentials, stresses created by parenting or childlessness, domestic violence, downward (and sometimes upward) social mobility, economic uncertainty, overwork or unemployment, friction over domestic responsibilities and so on (Hart 1976; Winn 1986; Riessman 1990). It may be the case, however, that the barrage of positive images of lifelong contentment and happiness in the ideal home which capital presents to consumers may help to produce a profound sense of disappointment when the reality of home life manifests itself.

The impact of changed household structures in Britain has not been overlooked by the house-building industry. Estimates of the extent to which households will change in the first two decades of the twenty-first century have been prepared by the Department of the Environment (1995), whose projections to 2016 are presented in Table 4.3. This table demonstrates clearly that there will remain a large market for family homes in Britain up to and beyond 2016, although the number of families will reduce in absolute terms. As a consequence, builders are recognising that their current model of the ideal home which is aimed at married or cohabiting couples with children needs to be reconsidered. If the Department of the Environment projections are about right, there will be a need for over 10 million homes for single people or single parent households by 2016, that is nearly half the total number of households. It is instructive to note that builders recognise that there is more

Table 4.3 Projections on household types 1971–2016 (in millions)

	Married couple household	Cohabiting couple household	Lone parent household	Other multiple occupancy	Single person household	Total
1971	11.249	.204	.378	1.168	2.944	15.943
1981	11.012	.500	.626	1.235	3.932	17.305
1991	10.547	1.222	.981	1.350	5.115	19.215
1996	10.341	1.377	1.122	1.512	5.824	20.176
2006	10.118	1.499	1.243	1.852	7.185	21.897
2016	9.945	1.579	1.257	2.240	8.577	23.598

Source: Department of the Environment (1995: Table 1).

than one model of the ideal home for single persons than is apparently assumed for married people with families. Builders are now erecting or converting properties, especially in large cities, which are aimed at the burgeoning market for flats for the under-35s who are not yet married and perhaps never will, for divorcees who need to scale down their properties as their family home is broken up, or for older people who seek smaller and perhaps supervised private accommodation. As ever, big business seems to be one step ahead of the politicians and the sociologists in gleaning clues about changing social attitudes – while also capitalising, of course, upon these insights.

Part II

BETWIXT AND BETWEEN
Homes in transition

5

'THE MORE WE ARE TOGETHER'

Domestic space, gender and privacy

Ruth Madigan and Moira Munro

Despite significant shifts in patterns of household formation and household composition, the concepts of 'house' and 'home' continue to carry enormous symbolic and, indeed, ideological significance. In this chapter we wish to explore ways in which the physical design of housing reflects dominant conventions about both the conduct of relationships within the household and the relationship of the household to the outside world. These conventions, in turn, reflect idealised notions of 'family' and 'class' which have only a partial relevance to the way in which people actually conduct their lives, and yet representations of these ideas become embedded in the physical design of the house (Ravetz 1995).

In many ways the Garden City Movement set the seal, at least in the English cultural tradition, on the suburban house and garden as representing the epitome of 'domestic bliss'. It appeared to combine the convenience of a 'tame' urbanised environment with the 'safety' of a socially homogeneous, semi-rural landscape (Davidoff et al. 1983). As Thompson (1982) argues, the suburb was presented as providing a healthy and morally superior environment for women and children, segregated from the overcrowding and corruption of the city. It was a secure, controlled environment in which the private family household could be defended, a space of 'individual domesticity and group monitored respectability' (Thompson 1982: 8). These sentiments have contributed to a domestic architecture within the private sector which is conservative, often nostalgic in tone, calling on symbols of past 'community' (the rustic cottage, the urban courtyard) to convey ideas of stability and security (Forty and Moss 1980).

McDowell (1983) has pointed out that for many the process of suburbanisation has created a geographical separation of 'home and work', 'domestic and public', 'female and male', with women trapped in the child-centred world of the suburb, without transport or access to the public facilities of the city. Yet the traditional division of labour in which women were expected to work as full-time housekeepers while men earned the family income has been

61

substantially eroded and the suburbs themselves have changed as shops, offices, factories and leisure facilities have moved to out of town locations. The collapse of manufacturing and the depopulation of the city has opened up city sites to new private housing estates, while gentrification has transformed some older areas of the city.

Saunders (1990) has presented the growth of owner occupation as a re-assertion of a popular commitment to the self-sufficiency of the family house-hold, the domestic virtues of house and garden and the security of ownership. He points out that the house itself is a source of great personal satisfaction for both men and women home makers. Yet we are also aware that the privacy of the family can be a cover for violence and abuse (see Goldsack, Chapter 10) and the idea of the private household, particularly when coupled with private ownership, has been used to promote the superiority of market solutions and individual enterprise over collective or state welfare driven solutions (see Brindley, Chapter 3).

In this chapter we wish to examine the issue of privacy *within* the family household rather than the privacy *of* the household in relation to the outside world. The advantage of this approach is that it allows us to disaggregate the household and begin to look at the different experiences of family life accord-ing to gender and generational differences. By focusing on patterns of behaviour and experience we hope to be able to unravel some of the elements of family ideology from how families and households work in practice. First we need to look some of the dominant patterns of housing design, since privacy within the household has both a social and a spatial dimension. Housing design, as we observed at the beginning, comes to embody dominant assump-tions about family relations which may or may not correspond to the way in which family households actually live. If these assumptions are built into the bricks and mortar then they have some impact on the residents, whatever form of household they occupy.

Conventions of housing design in the private sector

Architectural historians (Muthesius 1982; Worsdall 1979) have drawn atten-tion to the symbolic differentiation of front and back, public and private, as a recurrent feature of nineteenth-century speculative housing. The front of the house represented the 'public' face with a formal entrance and higher quality finish, while the back always had a more utilitarian aspect. The higher the social class status, the greater the distancing from the street, with railings, front gardens and even driveways to create a buffer zone between the public area of the street and the inner sanctum of the house (Daunton 1983a).

The differentiation of front and back has repercussions within the house also. In the 'gentleman's town house', the formal rooms used for public display were located at the front, the more private areas like the kitchen were located at the back. Matrix (1984) have suggested that this created a gendered division of space where the front represented the public, male domain while the back represented the private, domestic sphere – the preserve of subordinates, such as women, children and servants. This form of internal differentiation reached its peak in the bourgeois household where 'back stairs' completed the internal segregation, but it also found echoes in quite modest households. Working-class terraced houses typically maintained a front room or parlour which was kept 'for best' and hardly ever used.

In the twentieth century the design of housing began to change in style; the semi-detached in England (Oliver *et al.* 1981) and to some extent the bungalow in Scotland (McKean 1987) became the favoured form. In many respects the private housing of the inter-war period can be seen as a scaled down version of what had gone before. In particular, the social conventions of 'front' and 'back' remained intact and were indeed enshrined in the basic design of the 'parlour house', which became the dominant form in this period.

From the 1950s onwards a new style of volume built 'estate' houses began to emerge (Hole and Attenburrow 1966; Burnett 1986). In the face of somewhat contradictory trends (the development of a 'modern' aesthetic which favoured a sense of light and space coupled with rising cost of land and shrinking size of building plots) the building industry sought a new solution for the design of standard two and three bedroom houses. In order to maximise the sense of space within the confines of a narrow plot, the parlour was abandoned and replaced with one large lounge/dining room which ran from front to back with windows at either end (see Figure 5.1). The streamlined 'technological' kitchen emerged as strictly functional work space leading directly from the lounge/diner (Matrix 1984).

Although the through lounge/diner has become the dominant layout for modest estate housing built in the second half of the twentieth century, surprisingly little has been written about its social implications or social meanings. The construction of a family house with only one public room raises all sorts of interesting questions (Watson 1986). How do individual members of the household escape from one another? Whose activities take precedence in the one public room? Where can more formal social interactions take place, or have they ceased to exist? With no 'back region' in which to hide domestic clutter, does this mean that the household is permanently on display and tidied up? If so, does this imply higher standards of housekeeping and a greater penetration of consumer 'fashions' and competitive display? How does this coexist with the idea of 'home as haven', a place in which to relax and put your feet up?

Writing about parallel developments in the USA, Fox (1985) has suggested that abandoning the 'parlour' represented a change in family ideology from the overtly patriarchal and hierarchical family, in which the man was acknowledged as head of household, to a more democratic model in which the family is portrayed as a mutually supportive grouping and marriage as a partnership of equals. However, the evidence on how far relationships within

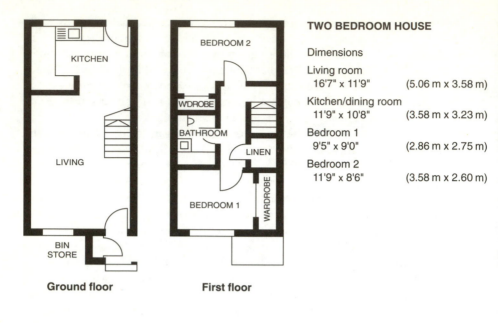

TWO BEDROOM HOUSE

Dimensions

Living room	
16'7" x 11'9"	(5.06 m x 3.58 m)
Kitchen/dining room	
11'9" x 10'8"	(3.58 m x 3.23 m)
Bedroom 1	
9'5" x 9'0"	(2.86 m x 2.75 m)
Bedroom 2	
11'9" x 8'6"	(3.58 m x 2.60 m)

Ground floor   **First floor**

THREE BEDROOM HOUSE

Dimensions

Lounge	
15'8" x 11'6"	(4.78 m x 3.50 m)
Dining	
10'6" x 8'8"	(3.20 m x 2.65 m)
Kitchen	
13'2" x 5'8"	(4.00 m x 1.72 m)
Bedroom 1	
11'8" x 7'5"	(3.55 m x 2.26 m)
Bedroom 2	
12'6" x 8'5"	(3.80 m x 2.56 m)
Bedroom 3	
9'11" x 5'11"	(3.02 m x 1.80 m)

Ground floor   **First floor**

Figure 5.1 Combined living/dining room design 1980s

the two parent family household have actually changed to something more egalitarian or democratic is somewhat contradictory (Gittins 1993). Men do seem to be playing a more active role in childrearing and increasingly can be seen cooking and shopping (see Chapman, Chapter 13). Women are more likely to have paid employment and are perhaps more confident in asserting their preferences. However, the continuities with the past are also marked. Women continue to earn considerably less than men and they still carry the major responsibility for housework and childrearing. The idea of home as a place in which to relax away from the stresses of the outside world is still very much more true for men rather than women (Darke 1996). For women, the home remains a place of work and though modern technology may have lightened some domestic chores, there is evidence that this has been offset by rising expectations (see Chapman, Chapters 4 and 13; Schwartz Cowan 1989).

Privacy and the use of space within the home

Our own research was based on a sample of households living in modest post-war housing in the Glasgow area (see also Munro and Madigan 1993). In selecting these areas we sought to exclude the extreme ends of the housing market by avoiding the upper income executive housing (see Chapman, Chapter 4) and the most stressed and unattractive areas of council housing (see Brindley, Chapter 3). The sample was therefore area-based around a restricted range of house types, in effect the cheaper end of suburban family housing in the Glasgow urban area. Our evidence is based on 382 postal questionnaires and 20 extended interviews. A third of the sample were council tenants and the rest were owner occupiers. Most of the sample were living as couples, with and without children (single adults constituted 15 per cent of the households and single parents 10 per cent). Just over half the households studied can be described as 'manual working class'; this was the case for 80 per cent of council tenants and 40 per cent of owner occupiers.

We chose, for our extended interviews, households from our selected areas with at least three members. This was in order to explore the issues raised when there is a potential conflict over the use of space (which we assumed would not arise so sharply in one or even two person households). The dominant voice in our more qualitative analysis is therefore that of the traditional family unit. The extended interviews were conducted with women, though occasionally men were present, so it is the woman's voice which comes through. We have chosen to concentrate on the issue of privacy for women because home has a particular salience for women both ideologically and in day-to-day routines (see Chapman, Chapter 13; M. Roberts 1991).

Initially many of our respondents were reluctant to discuss privacy within the household. The very idea of individual privacy cuts across dominant ideas about family togetherness and the shared companionate marriage. Responses associated privacy with secrecy and deceit. As one respondent stated: 'There isn't anything private in the house really, I mean we're pretty open with one another, we don't really have a private life as such, I don't think. I hope not' (Mrs W, age 37, owner occupier). As soon as the conversation focused on the specifics of everyday living, however, it became apparent that there is for most people a conflict between the demands of living in a communal household and the desire to pursue and preserve individual autonomy. This is particularly problematic for women who still take on the major responsibility for maintaining the home at both a practical and an emotional level and are often encouraged to subsume their own interests to the point where they cannot or do not distinguish between their own interests and those of the household. At the same time, changes in women's role increasingly expect that women should have a 'public', less familial persona, hence the conflict.

Private space for children

In many ways it was easiest to talk about privacy between adults and children in the household. One of the most striking changes in domestic relationships has been the changing status of children within the household. Smaller families, longer periods of economic dependency and earlier maturity have all contributed to a change in attitudes. The growing importance of the home as a centre of leisure activity and the way in which fears for safety have restricted the outside activities of younger children mean that the demands on domestic space have become increasingly complex. Sending the children outside to play from dawn to dusk is no longer acceptable for many urban households because of the perceived risk of violence from strangers and increased danger from traffic.

Two strategies emerge for maximising privacy within the household – space segregation and time segregation. Privacy *for* children, and for adults *from* children, is in part achieved by designating certain parts of the house for their exclusive use. The idea that every child should have a room of their own was accepted as desirable by almost everyone we spoke to. Children's rooms are generally expected to be multifunctional, combining a sleeping/sitting area with space for clothes storage, study and play; many children's bedrooms are generously equipped with televisions, computers and sound systems. Married couples, however, continue to share a bedroom and very few have their own individual study/workroom or other private space. As Burnett (1986) has pointed out, declining household size has led to a marked improvement in space standards since 1950s, but these gains have been almost entirely given over to improvements for the children in the household. It should be remembered that, though socially approved, not everyone can afford the space necessary for separate rooms. This is particularly true in two bedroom houses and flats, which are very common in Scotland.

Space segregation does not solve all conflicts in use. Younger children are often reluctant to be banished 'upstairs' away from adult activity, and the youngest, who must remain under adult supervision, soon fill even the most strictly regulated living areas with toys and other paraphernalia. Early bed-times and periods away at school or nursery allow adults to reassert their rights over the living room at certain times of day. Teenage children are often only too pleased to be able to 'disappear' to their own rooms, with or without friends. For some women this was a source of regret as it seemed to challenge the integrity of the family and perhaps gave warning how it would be when they would leave home altogether. As one respondent commented:

> Their rooms are their own wee houses, which I don't know is a good idea either. Because I think that's when you lose them, they just do their own thing in their bedroom. Whereas [without their own tele-vision], if they wanted to see the telly they would have had to come down here. I regret them getting television.
>
> (Mrs R, age 45, owner occupier)

Further conflicts arise as children become adults and their friends coming to the house have to be accorded adult status and hospitality. This usually implies offering food and drinks which cannot be done separately where the kitchen is directly off the living room. With grown-up children's adult visitors, it becomes less acceptable to crowd into small bedrooms, with only the bed for sitting space. As children grow up we see the emergence of something akin to a non-family, adult household. The design of the two or three bedroom 'family' house with its one communal space, minimal kitchen and very small bedrooms is peculiarly unsuitable for a household, in which people need a greater degree of independence.

Private space for adults

Though children's and young adults' bedrooms are generally expected to be multifunctional, the parents' bedroom is not. The 'marital' bedroom, or 'master' bedroom as estate agents will insist, remains surprisingly formal in layout and design with few concessions to other uses (see Chapman, Chapter 4). One woman said that if she wanted somewhere quiet to read her book she would go to her son's room when he was out, rather than her own bedroom, because his room had a chair and she did not feel she would make the room untidy. Of course bedrooms in many modern houses are very small and come with fitted cupboards, so there is little room for anything other than a double bed and a small chest of drawers. Despite this, some adults had managed to accom-modate a computer in their bedroom (11 per cent of respondents to our postal questionnaire). With the growth in adult education, and the expansion of white collar work with the possibility of working from home or bringing work home, the need for a study space is a real issue.

Despite the formality of the 'marital bedroom', for some women it was an important means of escape: somewhere to go and sit quietly, listen to music, read a book, study for exams, watch television (in our postal questionnaire 40 per cent had a television in the adult bedroom). It became clear, however, that a private space is not sufficient; women in particular, because of their role in servicing others, need *time* of their own as well as a *place* of their own. When asked where they went for privacy from the rest of the household, we were told, for example:

> The toilet! If I go upstairs to watch the TV, the whole place follows me. If I go upstairs to watch a programme, my son would come up, then my daughter, then he [husband] would come up and say 'What are you all up here for?'
>
> (Mrs H, age 34, owner occupier)

> There isn't really many places in the house you can go. I mean I've tried going in my room . . . it doesn't work because the wee one of three, she's in and out. One's doing the dishes and that, and you know, they'll start arguing and they're in telling me what they are doing and so that doesn't really work. I don't really manage to get any privacy unless they're all out playing and the wee one is sleeping. It's ideal, it's lovely, it's great.
>
> (Mrs V, age 35, council tenant)

Revealingly a number of women cited evenings 'on their own' as one of their greatest luxuries. These examples serve to reinforce the view that women in the domestic setting are vulnerable to others' claims on their time, endlessly fitting in with others' routines. In spite of this, many women said that privacy was not a problem for them because they had the house to themselves for long stretches of the day. This is of course a by-product of the fact that men and women work very different hours. In our sample approximately one-third of women were employed part-time, one-third full-time and one-third were full-time at home. By contrast three-quarters of the men were employed full-time (including quite a lot of shift work) and the rest were unemployed or retired. It was noticeable that women typically entertained their own friends in those periods of the day when the rest of the household was elsewhere. Although much of this entertaining had a casual air – 'popping in for coffee' – in fact, it became clear that it was founded upon a knowledge of often quite elaborate schedules involving children's school hours and husband's shift work as well as the woman's own hours. Women friends would normally call in only when there was no one else to attend to.

We did ask respondents to say what they would do if a friend came to the house wanting to discuss something private at a time when other members of the household were around. People found this difficult to reply to, either because they thought it unlikely to happen, a friend would know the household's routines and come when others were out, or because there was no easy solution. Some women said they would take a close friend up to their bedroom to talk, or children could be asked to go to their rooms. Some thought that husbands or partners would take themselves off to the bedroom, or out of the house altogether, to leave the living room free. Only 29 per cent of the households in our postal sample had a kitchen (a second 'room') which by their own account was big enough to sit down in. Those who did have such a kitchen recognised its importance as a social space.

> I spend most of my time in the kitchen, getting food ready for meals and washing and in fact I've seen me making tea and sitting at the table through there. My sister comes through and we end up blathering rather than sitting in here . . . we do that in her house as well. I say, maybe the men are in or maybe her husband is watching something on TV, there's a football match he's watching that, we'll sit in there [the kitchen] so we can sit and have a blather. We use it quite a lot. My mum's as well, it's the same kind of house as this, we just usually sit in the kitchen there as well.
>
> (Mrs V, age 35, council tenant)

Lack of kitchen space appeared to be one of the most common complaints about modern houses. What was particularly missed was the space to accommodate 'messy' household activities, in particular laundry, but also wet coats, muddy shoes, cleaning materials, storage space, in short a utility room. The lounge/diner or living room is inevitably a multifunctional room. It functions as a 'back region', somewhere for the household to relax away from the world, and where family unity is expressed, and yet without a parlour, the living room also serves as a showcase, a public statement of domestic standards and taste. This dual role results directly in more work for women who strive to maintain the high standards of cleanliness and tidiness required of a public room while making everyone else to feel comfortable and relaxed (Darke 1996).

Since there is nowhere that can be kept free of domestic clutter, the chief response was to maintain a very high standard of tidiness in the main room. There is clearly a conflict for the woman in the household, who is still for the most part charged with responsibility for maintaining standards, and yet wants to create a relaxed 'homely' environment. 'She wants her home to be seen (publicly scrutinised) as clean and tidy, and at the same time she wants it to be experienced (privately appreciated) as free and easy' (Hunt 1989: 69). This dilemma is 'resolved' for many women by internalising very high standards of tidiness. They do not perceive these standards as externally imposed, instead the public and private are perceived to coincide. They see their notions of what is an appropriate standard as something set entirely by themselves, though often inherited from their mothers (Pahl 1984).

Our impression is that women in the home spend a lot of time on what might be termed peripheral domestic activity. Ostensibly they are relaxing, watching television, but actually they are keeping an eye on the dinner cook-ing, remembering someone's packed lunch, waiting for the spin cycle on the washing machine and so on. Most women approved of the modern kitchen design, which is located directly off the living room, just because it allowed them to attend to these 'duties' without being cut off from the conversation taking place in the living room among the rest of the household. When asked what they would do if their husband's friend came round for a private chat, women were much less likely to absent themselves altogether; instead they could use these 'normal' activities (making coffee and sandwiches in the kitchen, seeing to the children upstairs) as a means of creating some 'private' space without anything so pointed as deliberately leaving the room.

Respondents also handled the dilemma posed by the competing demands of the dual function living room by defining the presentational aspects in terms of relatively modest and avowedly 'homely' aspirations. When asked what impression they would like others to have of their home, their replies usually referred to its being clean, tidy and comfortable. As two of our respondents told us: 'That it's welcoming. That it's clean and tidy' (Mrs T, age 47, council tenant); 'I would like to think that it's bright, clean and tidy' (Mrs C, age 30, owner occupier).

Our respondents did not easily engage in discussions of taste and style in the living room and suggested that they did not want to be judged on these grounds, nor would they judge other people in this sense. 'I like the place to be as I like it, and if they don't like it that's too bad' (Mrs G, age 28, owner occupier). However, the explicit responses were somewhat belied by anxieties expressed about their ability to achieve a pleasant visual effect and their response to commercial fashions. Respondents clearly did give considerable thought to the assembling of furniture and choice of decor; many expressed distress at the difficulty they had in 'getting it right' and achieving an effect that was well co-ordinated. Again there was an obvious tension between the view of home as something for private consumption and aspects of public display.

Conclusion

In many respects the gender roles within the households we contacted remain very traditional. Women still carry the major responsibility for maintaining the home in both the practical and the emotional sense (Mason 1989). Only 16 per cent of our postal sample claim to share housework equally. Their servicing role means that women within the domestic setting are still very commonly subordinating their needs to other household members. Yet even within these outwardly fairly 'conventional' households there is a tension between the socially sanctioned goal of family togetherness, sharing, equality and the goal of individual achievement, self identity. No doubt this has always been the case, but the changing role of women, the unwillingness of women to be confined to a familial role and the growing expectation that women should have public persona have heightened these conflicts and forced some re-evaluation and repositioning within the family household. Very often this means women simply shouldering a 'double burden', undertaking both paid and unpaid labour.

The issue of privacy which is posed by the search for home as an expression of both 'family unity and individuality' (Fox 1985) is for most women, in households at this level, solved by time management rather than 'a room of one's own'. The differing routines of members of the household make this possible, though it requires considerable flexibility which generally means a willingness on the part of women to 'fit in' with other people's timetables. Even in those households which would be generally considered overcrowded, with adult children sharing rooms or parents sleeping in the living room, there was often a phlegmatic acceptance that these conditions were temporary; children after all grow up and leave home and the period of greatest pressure, when children are growing into young adults, may be relatively short. Many of our respondents had lived in their houses for a long time and had frequently adapted the use of space within the home to accommodate the changes required by growing, and then declining, families. For many households internal layout and space standards are simply not the top priority in housing. In some areas of council housing, for example, a house located in an area in which people feel safe may more than compensate for other inadequacies. For those on lower incomes, additional space is no advantage if they cannot afford to heat or furnish the extra rooms. Not surprisingly people are inclined to adapt their expectations and aspirations to something close to their own opportunities.

The combination of commercial logic and the preference for large light rooms (Madigan and Munro 1991) has created the modern 'estate' house in which all public and communal space is in a single living room or lounge/diner. Our respondents were quite clear that they did not want to sacrifice this space (reduce its size) in order to accommodate other desirable features. Nonetheless it is clear that this is a design which is firmly focused on a highly communal 'family' household. It is a design which is ill adapted to some family units; it is almost certainly unsuitable for non-family households who want to share with a greater degree of independence.

Since the 1960s there has been very little public debate about housing design. The last major official report on housing standards was in 1961 (Parker Morris 1961). Since then many of the space and design standards have been compromised in the interests of economy, in both public and private sectors. Unfortunately the idea of experimentation in housing design is still blighted by the experience of some of the low quality housing experiments imposed on the public sector in the 1960s and 1970s (see Brindley, Chapter 3). The needs of households and the range of household types have changed dramatically, but the design of mass housing is dominated by a profoundly conservative set of social conventions. Many households eagerly embrace this conservatism, as 'home' occupies a central ideological position, yet it may inhibit the production of flexible housing that will have to meet changing needs and expectations for the next sixty years or even longer.

Acknowledgement

We would particularly wish to acknowledge the work of Hilary Parkey, who conducted the detailed interviews and administered the postal questionnaire. We are also grateful for the support of the Economic and Social Research Council (ESRC) for the costs of the empirical work.

6

TRAVELLING MAKES A HOME

Mobility and identity among West Indians

Karen Fog Olwig

Travel and home are usually regarded as opposites, travel being associated with movement in space, home being related to settling in a particular place, when travel has ended. For many West Indians, however, obtaining and sustaining a 'proper home' has been dependent upon their willingness to travel from their native island and to stay for prolonged periods of time in far-away destinations. Such absence naturally leads West Indians to develop different notions of home, depending on their particular situation. Some continue to regard themselves as temporary sojourners in a foreign place, displaced from their 'real' home, whereas others gradually create a home away from home which may eventually supersede the original home in importance. Nevertheless, even these more settled people usually maintain strong emotional ties with the West Indies.

This chapter analyses the interrelationship between travelling and home making on the basis of life-story interviews with people from the Leeward Island of Nevis. This island, a former British colony, has been part of the independent Caribbean nation-state of St Kitts-Nevis since 1983. The relationship between travel and home making is explored here though a study of Nevisians in Nevis and England. This leads to a consideration of the concept of home among people who, like the Nevisians, have travelled to make a home. The study shows that home is not merely important as a place of habitation and a concrete centre of everyday life. It may be equally significant as a nucleus of social relationships and a point of identification and belonging, whether or not the members of this home are physically present.

A West Indian house

When I began to do fieldwork on Nevis in 1980 I rented a small house in the village where I wanted to concentrate my research. The house was originally built as a two-room wooden cottage with a hip roof and a small gallery in the front – in typical West Indian fashion (Berthelot and Gaumé 1982). A sumptuous flower garden faced the street and behind was a large fruit and vegetable garden, which was somewhat neglected. Several new rooms, including a bathroom with a toilet and shower, had been added in the back of the house, and a kitchen had been attached to the side. The back rooms served as bedrooms; the two front rooms were now a dining room, connected to the kitchen, and a living room which could be entered from the gallery.

Whereas the house had the outward appearance of a traditional West Indian dwelling of the sort which one might photograph to show how the 'natives' live, the living room looked anything but local. It had an upholstered easy chair with a pillow on which was printed a military emblem, a rose and a poem to mother, a niche for a stereo system, a big, stuffed Snoopy placed on a small shelf and, decorating the wall, a framed picture of a snow-clad log cabin next to the inscription 'God Bless Our Home'. All these features reminded one of home furnishings in North America. Indeed, it soon became apparent that a transformer was needed to use the wide range of electrical equipment in the house – iron, record player, toaster, refrigerator – because they all ran on North American rather than local current. The house, in other words, seemed to be West Indian on the outside and North American on the inside.

If it were not for the display in the living room of family photos of people who clearly were of West Indian origin, one might easily be led to conclude that this house had not been home to Nevisians at all, but rather to North American expatriates. Nothing could be further from the truth! The strong presence of western material goods in the house, the expansion and modernisation of the original two-room building, the family members' presence in photographs and their absence in actual life all contributed to making this a very successful West Indian home.

Making a home on Nevis

I fit in to the end of a family of ten children. There were just two boys and eight girls. We were not rich, or even middle class. We had to struggle. I knew myself helping. There were animals to tend to, the land to work. My father was a fisherman and farmer, and my mother raised the family and helped in whichever way she could, being supportive to my father. Work was hard. There was farming, tilling the land, raising the animals. Water supply was not so plentiful, we had to 'head' [that is: balance a pail of water on the head] a lot of water. Times of the year, when the weather was dry, we had to go for miles to 'head' one to two buckets a day. We also had animals to 'head' water to.

Most Nevisians over 40 years of age can identify with this description of growing up on the Nevis: a large family struggling to make ends meet in the small farming economy, where the cultivation of subsistence crops, animal husbandry and fishing provided the main basis of life. Gone were the large-scale plantations which, from the seventeenth century to the early twentieth century, had formed the backbone of the British colonial society. Left behind were the descendants of those African slaves, whose labour power had made the plantation economy possible, and the worn-out land, which was no longer deemed suitable for large-scale cultivation.

Older Nevisians, interviewed in the early 1980s, often regretted the decline in cultivation which had occurred as the fields, once covered with sugar, later cotton, were abandoned to become overgrown with bush and shrub. But these Nevisians did not miss the hard physical labour in the sugar fields or the privileged plantation owners for whom they had to labour. Historical records show how the African-Caribbean population on Nevis, as on other Caribbean islands from the early times of slavery, had attempted to establish their own communities outside the plantation society (Mintz 1974, 1985: Olwig 1993, 1995, 1997). During slavery, they had planted gardens and constructed shelters in the mountainous hillsides of Mount Nevis and the steep and rocky ghuts, or ravines, extending from Mount Nevis to the sea. Here they culti-vated subsistence crops and raised small animals for their own benefit. After the abolition of slavery, the people who had gained their freedom built houses and established their own settlements in these areas as well as in the more marginal plantation areas which were being abandoned by the plantations. Finally, in the course of the twentieth century, they acquired small plots of land and developed their own villages on the large, flat plains where the extensive plantation fields had been located. The African Caribbean popula-tion 'colonised' Nevis from within (Appadurai 1996) and turned the island into their home. This island home, however, was rather impoverished.

As the plantations closed, much of the island's infrastructure declined, and the external marketing system deteriorated. A household-based subsistence economy therefore provided the most reliable, but also the most minimal, means of existence. This economy involved every member of the household, from the smallest child, who was able only to 'head' a pail of water from the water source to the home, to the larger children who were responsible for the care of animals, to the adolescents who might be put in charge of the house-hold while parents were working outside in the field. One Nevisian who grew up in the 1950s recalled:

> We ate things from the land and the animals. Sweet potato mashed into milk. Sometimes we got bread and some kind of relish, cheese or eggs, because we had a lot of fowl. We lived on the ground provisions and the farming milk from the cows and eggs from the fowl . . . because my mother was away working the land from early morning my older sisters and my brother got us ready for school. My brother would plait our hair. All helped, and all went to school.

The 'good' home

The kind of home which could be built and maintained in this subsistence economy was a very basic one. Indeed, from a modern-day, western point of view, the small two-room houses inhabited by large families of ten children or so would be seen to provide a rather inadequate setting for a good home. This is not, however, how Nevisians remembered their childhood home. Most of family life was not confined to the house, which would have been uncomfortably hot during the day. Children often spent their free time on open pastures, where they gathered after school to do sports or just play. When they were at home, they usually stayed in the yard, a fenced-in area surrounding the house, which was a kind of extension of the house itself. This is where many domestic activities, such as caring for small children, cooking on a coal pot or ironing with a flat iron, took place. Actually some of the fondest childhood memories concerned the moonlit nights which the entire family spent together in the yard:

> It was a small house, but we all fit right in. There was no electricity or cable or radio. At nights we would sit outside on a stone in the moon light. They [the adults] told Anansie stories. We [the children] sang and played games.

The family life that did take place within the house was structured in a such a way that it was able to accommodate a great number of children and, at the same time, present a well-functioning and nice-looking home to visitors:

> It was a two-room house. We had the chamber, where there were two beds. There was a curtain separating my mother's and father's beds from the biggest children who were the fortunate ones to sleep on a bed . . . The other room was the hall, where we entertained. It had chairs, table, a china cabinet where my mother kept her things, so that when guests came they did not eat and drink from everyday things. So that she could entertain with something nice to drink and eat out of. That same hall was converted at night into a bedroom. The old clothes and so, what there was, we spread out on the floor and put a big sheet over them to make like a bed. At early morning we would get up and put the clothes outside to sun, so people didn't know that we slept there. In the afternoon we took the clothes in, but we put it under the bed until we were ready to sleep. Even when people were there in the evening, we would wait until they were gone, and then we put out the clothes. We might fall asleep on the bed and then we would move up to the bedding, when the guests had left.

Thus, even in the smallest and seemingly most crowded houses that were maintained largely by a subsistence economy, family life did not simply revolve around the satisfaction of basic human needs. It was organised in such a way that the family was able to maintain a back stage with minimal facility and decoration, and a front stage to display a respectable appearance and some degree of material affluence. Maintaining a proper home was an important mark of social standing in the local community.

The social significance of the home in African-Caribbean society has been linked to the notion of 'respectability' (P. Wilson 1969, 1973, 1974; Abrahams 1983; Olwig 1990, 1993; Besson 1993). Respectability can be seen to be closely associated with certain cultural values concerning family and the home, which were propagated largely by British missionaries and educators working in the West Indies during the nineteenth and early twentieth centuries. According to these values, it was expected that social life would centre on the matrimonial home, with the husband and father functioning as provider and head of household, while the wife and mother nurtured the family and became moral guardian of the home. The material wealth of the home thus is proof of the industry of the father. The moral state of the family, judged by the members' sexual restraint, abstinence from alcohol and dedication to religion, education, hard work and home life, reflects the care bestowed upon the home by the mother (see, for example, Mosse 1985; Shorter 1979; Frykman and Löfgren 1983). It is quite apparent that this notion of respectability had played an important role in the Nevisian homes described in childhood memories. The careful separation of the parents and children when sleeping, the importance attached to the children's education, the attempt to hide the poverty of the family (and hence the limited success of the husband-father as provider) and the maintenance of a room where guests could be received in material comfort can all be regarded as aspects of this ethos of respectability.

Many life stories concerned the conflict between the desire to marry and obtain a respectable home of their own and the difficulty of doing so in an impoverished economy which just barely allowed a family to survive and maintain the appearance of social standing in the community, no matter how hard everybody worked. The expressed desire to establish an independent home, furthermore, was counterbalanced by an equally important urge to help improve the social and economic situation of the parents, who had worked so hard to raise their children. Coming of age was dependent upon two, seemingly irreconcilable conditions: the acquisition of a home of one's own, and the continuation of economic support and help to the parental home. Many Nevisian youngsters sought to reconcile these goals by leaving Nevis for better economic opportunities which would allow them to earn enough to both help their parents and to establish a home of their own.

Travelling

Off-island labour migration has long been practised by Nevisians as a means of solving the social and economic difficulties experienced in an island community with limited resources. Since the emancipation of the slaves in the 1830s, Nevisians, along with other West Indians, have engaged in a great deal of wage labour migration (Thomas-Hope 1978, 1992, 1995; Richardson 1983; Mills 1985; Olwig 1993; Byron 1994). Immediately after emancipation the freed left for destinations in Trinidad and Demerara (later British Guyana). Later they travelled to South America, Central America, Cuba, Santo Domingo and North America. In the period after the Second World War, migration destinations opened up first in the Dutch Antilles, then Great Britain, the British and American Virgin Islands and Canada. Thousands of Nevisians have travelled in search of better opportunities. Most have expected to stay away for only a brief period of time, until they had acquired the necessary funds to return, but ended up staying away for many years. This was partly because their earnings were slimmer than expected, partly because they sent a fair proportion of their meagre funds to their family home on Nevis. Some, furthermore, were held back from returning, because the idea of what would constitute a proper home on Nevis changed, as the material conditions of life (largely underwritten by the absent Nevisians) improved on Nevis. What was meant to be a brief interruption in life therefore became an extended state of being. A closer look at life stories collected among Nevisians in Leeds, England, serves to elucidate how this conundrum influenced the Nevisians' relation to home.

Nevisian sojourners in England

When I left for England I had a son with my future wife . . . We married later, after going to England. Back home you don't marry until you have a home or something that you can call a home. We had nothing, we lived from day to day, and we were too young to get married. I and my future wife were friends from school, and I was 19 when we left for England, leaving our son with her parents, where he had lived. We came to England together. We thought it was easy to save money in England. The exchange rate was 4.82 East Caribbean dollars to a pound, so if we saved, we would get a lot of dollars when we were back home. I thought I would do it in six months. My uncle had been there from 1958, and he had not come back. Still I thought I could do it. I wanted money to go back and do fishing on a bigger scale. But when I came it was not as easy as I thought. The wages were very small, I couldn't save. And I sent money to my mother every month.

This is how a Nevisian explained his move to Leeds, twenty-six years after he had left Nevis for England. To a certain extent his trip to England was a disappointment, because he had not been able to acquire the necessary funds to return soon to Nevis. If this part of the plan had not materialised, however, he had succeeded in fulfilling the goal of obtaining his own home and marrying, largely because having a home in England was not dependent upon owning a house. Though this was not the sort of home he had hoped for, it was socially acceptable in the Nevisian community in England. The temporary nature of the Nevisian sojourn in England meant that it did not make sense to purchase a house in England.

The sense of being temporarily in England made this young couple continue to live in rentals for more than fifteen years, starting with 'bed-sits', moving on to flats and finally, to a council house. Most of these forms of accommodation were disliked intensely. All of them may have been more spacious than the tiny two-room houses where this couple had grown up on Nevis, but they were not perceived in this way. The bed-sits and rented flats involved sharing a common building and yard with strangers; in the case of bed-sits even the kitchen and bathroom were shared. This sort of housing arrangement was completely foreign to the Nevisians, who were used to living in one-family houses with separate fenced yards, which not only extended the living space, but also separated the home from neighbouring houses. Only the rented house was an acceptable solution, both because of the space and privacy it offered, and because it had the appearance of a proper house: 'It was lovely, it had a front and back garden. It was not in bad condition, and my husband decorated it really nice. All thought it was our own house'. Most of the housing available to Nevisians and other West Indians in Leeds was located in Chapeltown, an area where many landlords had converted large one-family terraced houses into a number of smaller rentals, including bed-sits, in order to cash in on the large number of West Indian immigrants. Nevisians, generally speaking, had no choice but to move to Chapeltown, because it was one of the few places where West Indians were not discriminated against when they looked for housing. Though many Nevisians actually preferred to live in areas with other West Indians, they disliked the poor condition of the houses offered to them.

The idea of an early return to Nevis was abandoned as Nevisians realised that their incomes did not allow them to accumulate the funds necessary to build a house and lead an economically secure life on Nevis. Furthermore, some became aware that it would not be easy to transplant their children, born and reared in an English city, to a small, rural, West Indian island. After several years in Leeds, many Nevisians therefore wanted to improve the home environment for their family in England by purchasing a house. This house would also serve as an investment which would help finance an eventual return. At that time a large number of houses could be had at relatively low prices due to the increasingly run-down condition of the West Indian district.

By working overtime and fixing up the houses themselves, many Nevisians were able to finally acquire their own house.

As Nevisians purchased and improved their own houses, they created homes which were very much in accordance with the respectable style, known from Nevis, where visitors were entertained in 'proper' surroundings. In a terraced house with two rooms and a kitchen downstairs it was, for example, not uncommon for one of the rooms to be set aside for special visitors. A young woman, born in Leeds to Nevisian parents, thus noted: 'my mother's front room is dead pretty, it is a typical fancy room. You can tell from the looks of it that she is West Indian. I would have it with more plain things'. Even though the new home owners have renovated and improved upon the neighbourhood, the negative image of Chapeltown has not been overcome, largely because of the social and economic problems which result from racial discrimination.

The family home on Nevis

At the same time as Nevisians were trying to establish a life for themselves in England, they were helping to support their family home on Nevis. Even with the tightest of budgets, which seemed to leave little room for the barest necessities of life, remittances were sent back home:

> I worked at the railway for two years. I made £7 for forty-eight hours a week. After tax, pension, union dues, I only had £6 a week, and out of that I must pay £2 for rent, £2 for food, £1 for sandwich and drink, and that left £1 I could send for my mom. No money was left for clothing or anything.

Substantial sums of money were sent to Nevis, not only from Britain, but also from the United States, Canada, the British and American Virgin Islands and the Dutch West Indies, where many other Nevisians had gone. In 1962, for example, 443,128 Eastern Caribbean dollars, at that time the equivalent of about £92,000, were received in postal money orders from the United States and the United Kingdom. In addition Nevis and St Kitts received a total of 98,211 EC dollars, or the equivalent of about £20,000, from the American Virgin islands (Richardson 1983: 155). The Nevisians who were staying in the nearby Caribbean islands also sent packages of food, household utensils and clothing to their family home on Nevis. Some even shipped refrigerators, electric or gas stoves, various sorts of furniture and television sets to their Nevisian homes.

Those families who received money and material goods were able to make considerable improvements to the home in the form of running water, indoor bathrooms and kitchens, installation of electricity and telephones. Furthermore, many two-room cottages were expanded considerably or even torn down to be replaced by modern, concrete houses. Such improvements of the family home on Nevis have been a source of great satisfaction and pride both for the families left behind and for the relatives abroad who have helped finance them. For the families on Nevis, these material improvements gave the family a higher social status in the local community.

The status identified with modern appliances and furnishings is, to a certain extent, linked to the values of respectability, associated with the former British colonial system. In this value system, a family's affluence reflects upon the success of the husband-father as a provider for the home and thus is indicative of the household's economic autonomy. The source of the material wealth of these Nevisian families is somewhat different, however, because their affluence is almost entirely due to support from absent relatives. Indeed, as a result of this support, and the absence of the younger able-bodied generation which is sending the support, many families on Nevis have stopped cultivating cash crops and minimised subsistence agriculture so that they grow only a few garden crops for the home.

The significance of making an outward appearance of material affluence is also strongly underlined by the cultural values emphasising mutual help and support among relatives, in particular parents and children. A well-kept affluent home, therefore, also evidences a well-functioning family network reflecting the children's filial piety. It is quite clear to every member of the local community that the well-to-do homes are those which receive support from family abroad. Indeed, Nevisians away are quite aware of the fact that they will cast shame on their family on Nevis if they do not send adequate support and thus demonstrate their gratitude to their parents. If they fail in their duties they will hear about this from fellow emigrant Nevisians who, in turn, will have heard about it from their family in the home village (see Philpott 1973).

For the families staying behind, a proper home therefore is a three or four bedroom house, preferably with additions made out of concrete blocks, equipped with all modern conveniences. The living room is decorated with gifts from the relatives abroad, most notably in the form of photographs of children, grandchildren and great-grandchildren taken at special occasions such as graduations from school or university, weddings and baptisms. The house is surrounded by a flower garden, because most of the food for the home, including fruit and vegetables, is purchased in the supermarket or received in canned form from relatives abroad. It is not uncommon to see trees in the garden laden with unpicked, ripe fruit, while members of the family drink canned fruit juice imported from Florida. Some local produce may be grown to provide visiting relatives with 'a taste of home', but the family is not dependent upon this produce for its subsistence. Such a family may include three generations, the elderly parents of those who left for England, one or two of their children who have stayed behind to care for them, and a number of grandchildren, some of whom may be offspring of absent relatives.

Absent relatives who provide well for their childhood home will always receive a royal welcome, when they visit Nevis, but they will also be expected to bring gifts and to display their generosity to friends and relatives in accordance with the supposed affluence of the family. Visiting the childhood home therefore can present quite an economic outlay, involving not only the purchase of expensive plane tickets and a number of gifts, but also the accumulation of a fair amount of spending money to confirm the social standing of the family in the community. As long as their parents are still alive and in the family home, most Nevisians continue to feel strongly attached to that home, even though years may pass between visits to Nevis.

Many Nevisians finally give up the idea of acquiring their own home on Nevis and settle permanently abroad. This is rarely a conscious decision on their part, but one that gradually takes form as they begin to devote more and more of their time, money and energy to a 'home away from home' which eventually becomes their permanent home. They may then solve the problem of their divided loyalties by relocating members of their Nevisian home to their home abroad. When undertaking my fieldwork, I was able to rent a fully furnished home on Nevis because so many members of a family who owned the house had emigrated or died. Indeed, the elderly mother, upon whom this Nevisian home had centred, eventually joined her children in the United States. She had planned to visit Nevis every one to four years to spend some time in her home there, but her visits became more and more infrequent, and finally her house was rented out to visitors like me.

Some Nevisians succeed in making the move back to Nevis. This move is usually made, after thirty to forty years of absence, when they are able to retire; during the past few years, an increasing number of Nevisians have sold their houses in England and built houses in their home village on Nevis. When I studied Nevis in the mid-1990s a number of large concrete houses had been built by returnees from England since my last visit. All home furnishings, ranging from the pink flowered bedspread to the upholstered sofa and the china figurines, had been brought in large containers from England; one of the houses even carried the sign 'Yorkshire Rose'. Some of the returnees missed certain aspects of their former life in England and they had organised a special club for returnees. They longed for their children and grandchildren and found social life on the small island limited. But many were also busy re-establishing their local roots and supplementing their small British pension by growing their own vegetables and fruit trees and keeping a few animals. Some felt that they were the only ones who bothered to cultivate the land on Nevis. Not all of these returnees were able to work the fields, however, for many were visibly worn out after many years of hard physical labour in Britain – working for a home on Nevis.

Conclusion

The concept of homelessness has been used in a number of studies to refer to a prevalent condition of life in the modern, mobile world (for a review and critique see Rapport and Dawson 1999). This study suggests that it may be important to examine carefully the notion of 'home', and its relationship to movement, before designating people as homeless or alienated. In its conventional usage, home has a dual meaning: first, it can refer to a site where everyday life is lived, often surrounded by close family, and second, it can mean a place associated with a notion of belonging, of 'feeling at home'. These two meanings of home are, ideally, expected to coincide, so that one feels at home in the physical site where one lives.

This case study of Nevisians sojourning in Britain exemplifies a situation where physical separation from that which has been defined as home does not necessarily lead to a condition of homelessness. On the contrary, most Nevisians continued to devote themselves, emotionally and economically, to their home on Nevis, while living in another place. Some Nevisians developed multiple attachments to home, and eventually came to feel at home in several places, moving frequently between their several homes. Some returned to Nevis, usually to create a new home based on their multi-local experiences of home. Yet others became emotionally attached to a home abroad and even relocated the family left behind on Nevis to this new home, thus reconstituting their childhood home abroad.

While most Nevisians certainly felt quite far from home during the early stages of their stay in England, none of them expressed a feeling of being homeless. By examining the concept and practice of home among Nevisians, and its relationship to travel, a more fundamental understanding of the idea of home can be gleaned.

7

A HOME FROM HOME

Students' transitional experience of home

Liz Kenyon

It is now widely acknowledged that our conceptions and experiences of 'home' are both complex and dynamic, changing and adapting across the life course and as we come into contact with new social and cultural worlds (Guiliani 1991; Lee 1990; Sixsmith and Sixsmith 1990). In addition to these insights, the discoveries that home can be a source of as well as an expression of our identities and personalities (Cooper 1976; Jin 1993; Rapoport 1981), our cultural and social group tastes and values (Csikszentmihalyi and Rochberg-Halton 1981; Kron 1983; Pratt 1981) and our citizenship (Jones 1995) are of key importance. Together these findings take us one step further towards a recognition that home can be used and perceived by young people as a sign of and a space for developing adulthood. Very often an independent dwelling away from the childhood home is seen to be both a physical manifestation of independence and citizenship, as well as the arena in which other adult emotional and social developments are most likely to occur. Leaving home is therefore viewed as one factor associated with the complex movement from childhood towards full adulthood. Moreover, the physical, emotional and social spaces of a home, and the meanings with which these are endowed, can be of importance in defining if, how, when and why adulthood is reached.

While recent work has discussed and researched structural influences such as class, family form, area and age on the home-leaving patterns and experiences of young adults (Ainley 1991; Jones 1995), little research to date has considered how *home-meanings* alter and adapt during the home-leaving process. A study of young people in such a period of transition is therefore crucial for two reasons; first, to investigate the process via which adult meanings of home evolve, and second, to widen our understandings of the role that home plays in supporting the transition to adulthood. It is the primary purpose of this chapter to explore the experience and meaning of home for a group of individuals undergoing such a transition.

This chapter draws specifically on the experiences and meanings of home for one social group of young people: undergraduate students who have left the parental home to attend university. The proportion of young people in full-time higher education has risen gradually over the post-war period, but most significantly in the 1990s. In the academic year 1994/1995 25.6 per cent of all 19–20 year olds in Britain were full-time students in higher education, compared with only 11 per cent of this age group in the academic year 1980/1981 (Department for Education and Employment 1995). Bearing in mind that over a quarter of all 19–20 year olds in Britain are now in full-time higher education, an analysis of the meaning of home for this sub-group is extremely pertinent for furthering our understanding of the formation of home-meanings during the transition to adulthood. Although not all students decide to leave home to attend university, a significant number are still choosing to do so. Moreover, the very fact that universities continue to build new phases of residential accommodation is evidence that this is still institutionally supported. Using qualitative data taken from doctoral research into the constitution and formation of 'student areas' in Sunderland, a city in the North East of England, this chapter considers the meaning and experience of home for British undergraduate students. During the course of the research, student and non-student interviewees living within four 'student areas' of the city were asked a number of questions about their perceptions and experiences of their home environments. This chapter specifically draws upon data taken from thirty-two interviews conducted with households containing students between the ages of 18 and 23, who had moved away to attend university.

Students who leave the parental home to establish a new home in their city of study often maintain connections with their past homes. Due to the nature of the academic year they typically expect to spend specified times in two dwellings: the parental home in vacations and the term-time home during university terms. This therefore provides one possible explanation for the fact that students could not locate and identify one definitive home-meaning or venue:

INTERVIEWER: What does home mean to you?

DAVID: That's a good question. I don't know. It's somewhere you can come back to and where you want to be. Do you mean home, my parental home or here-home?

(Economics student, age 20)

However, what this does not explain is why students also introduced an as-yet unencountered home into their discussions of what and where home was. For example, Robert told me that 'buying a house, getting married, having kids, having a steady job, paying the mortgage, having a lot of bills and having to take responsibility for other people and stuff' (Technology Management student, age 19) were jointly implicated in the creating of a 'real' adult home. To understand why students spoke of a third, imagined home when discussing home-meanings and experiences therefore requires further analysis. One possible key to unravelling this paradox lies in the recognition that students are undergoing a number of identity and status transitions to adulthood. The introduction of a third, planned, but as-yet unexperienced home environment into students' discussions could thus be explained by the transitional nature of students' lives, and more specifically, their use of their term-time homes as staging posts taking them on to graduate adult lives and homes.

When discussing their homes, the students in the research sample were clear that for a dwelling or social unit to become a real and meaningful home it had to provide for and reflect a number of key elements. Home was seen to exist at four crucial levels: as a personal, a temporal, a social and a physical space. Students illustrated these four broad spheres with a number of sub-ingredients which contributed towards an overall sense of home (see Figure 7.1). These elements interestingly match a number of factors which have previously been found to symbolise and constitute home (see for example Desprès 1993; Hayward 1975; Sixsmith 1986). At first glance these fourteen elements might appear rather inflexible, apparently contradicting the argument that students' identity and status transitions are clearly reflected in their flexible and changing experiences of home. However, as the chapter unfolds it will become clear that although the generic factors associated with 'home' remain stable whichever home is being discussed, the characteristics and quality of each alters depending upon the actual home venue under scrutiny. Thus, for example, students expected 'significant others' to be parents and siblings in the parental home, peers in the term-time home and partners and children in the future home, adaptations which both supported and reflected students' developing independence and adulthood. Using the four categories identified in Figure 7.1 to structure the analysis, the chapter will consider how and why each of students' three existing and imagined dwellings (the parental, term-time and future home) were viewed as homes. In breaking down the home experience in this way, it will be possible to build up an overall picture of the ways in which each venue contributes to the adapting image and experience of home for those in transition and, in turn, supports any identity and status changes that students are experiencing.

The personal home

Figure 7.1 reveals that a house was more likely to become a home for students if a number of personal meanings and experiences were associated with dwelling there. The following analysis discusses which of the three venues that students identified as homes or potential homes (the parental, term-time and future home), provided, or was imagined to provide, these five personal home-making elements.

Despite the fact that the parental home was often coloured by a long history of being a student's sole home venue, my analysis reveals that this home was losing its status as a meaningful home for one main reason: students did not

The personal home

- Home is meaningful
- Home is a sense of independence and freedom
- Home is a personalised space
- Home is a sense of belonging
- Home is memories

The temporal home

- Home is stable and permanent
- Home has the potential to be familiar and lasting

The social home

- Home is made up of significant others
- Home is a supportive atmosphere
- Home is a friendly neighbourhood

The physical home

- Home is made up of meaningful possessions
- Home is a comfortable environment
- Home is a single household dwelling
- Home is a safe haven

Figure 7.1 The elements of home

envisage returning there for any major length of time. As a result it was no longer seen as a home which was worthy of a significant amount of investment. Such short-termism was also central to students' view that their term-time homes could not be meaningful homes, worthy of commitment and investment. This therefore affected the level of emotional investment they were prepared to make in recognising their term-time homes as real next-step homes. Respondents stated that their term-time homes were not treated seriously by their parents, as Peter suggested: 'They [my parents] like to think that home is home. This is just somewhere where you live and work. I get a bit of an ear bashing if I refer to up here as home' (Philosophy student, age 19). Neither do they consider it to be their own home in the full sense of the word. As Claire commented:

> It's not the kind of place that you can really call a home. It's only the kind of place you can put up with when you know it's for a short length of time, so I haven't settled here with the intention of making it my home.
>
> (Historical Studies student, age 19)

In contrast, the home which was believed to have the potential to become a meaningful space, worthy of emotional and financial investment, was highlighted as the future home.

Moving on to the second personal element which affected feelings of home-liness in a dwelling (the availability of personal autonomy and freedom), students felt that their parental homes did not provide the autonomy and independence that they now needed within a home. The first and most com-monly mentioned homely attribute of term-time accommodation was therefore that it provided opportunities and an arena for new levels of autonomy, as Roger commented:

> here you only have to consider yourself, so it means that you have more chance to develop. More decisions to make yourself. That for me is what home is all about. It's far more comfortable when you have room to develop, and it's a more relaxed atmosphere of your own making.
>
> (Technology Management student, age 21)

However, despite the independence and autonomy that term-time homes were seen to afford, they were not viewed seriously as permanent centres of adult autonomy. Opportunities for independence were tempered by the communal nature of these homes, as Matthew described:

> [Home is . . .] Not having to share everything in the same way . . . God I hate that. I wouldn't like to share a place again unless it was with somebody who . . . you know I wouldn't like to share it with a stranger like I am here.
>
> (English student, age 22)

Moreover, as parents frequently provided the financial support for students, respondents stated that they were not in a position to be able to create a truly independent home of their own. As Imogen told me: 'This isn't our house really. I mean our parents are paying for us to live here. We are another one of their assets still' (Biology and Psychology student, age 20). In contrast, students spoke of their future homes as bringing them true autonomy, inde-pendence and freedom. The extra financial bargaining power that an imagined future job would provide was believed to be the facilitator of this change.

The home was expected not only to provide the space in which students' autonomy could develop, but also to reflect and support this growing indepen-dence. As such, home was seen to be a place which could and should reflect students' personalities and needs. This was most often connected with the idea of personalising space through the ordering and decoration of rooms. Students revealed that such freedom had been eroded in their parental homes as younger siblings and lodgers had usurped their space. Although term-time homes were seen to be spaces where students had a level of freedom to order the environment, responses stated that this was tempered by the necessity of negotiating with house-mates and landlords. A really personal home where everything reflected the individual living there was therefore seen to be possible only when the students gained a home of their own. As Jessica said, 'We'll not be prepared to live in student dives after that [graduation]. I suppose we'll all become very consumer oriented and want our own places and to do them in our own way' (Modern Languages student, age 19).

Moving on to the fourth factor associated with the 'personal home', students revealed that a 'sense of belonging' was more likely to be associated with their parental homes. Students spoke of their parental homes being situated in their 'home areas', areas to which felt they had a right to return. However, for those students whose families had recently moved, this sense of belonging had begun to be eroded. In sharp contrast, respondents referred to themselves as outsiders in their term-time neighbourhoods; a perception which was perhaps heightened by the belief that they were not accepted by the locals there.

Finally, turning to the idea of home as a collection of memories, for many students the parental home had provided their only prior home experience, albeit in a variety of dwelling and social forms, as Janet described:

> At the moment I suppose my parental home [is more of a home] . . . Because I spent seventeen years of my life there and I've got a lot of memories. My parents and my brother and sister, and my home friends as well. It's all home: a huge part of your life which you can't just wipe out in eight months.
>
> (Media Studies student, age 18)

In contrast, the short-term nature of their term-time homes meant that few meaningful memories were associated with them, especially when students compared them to the enduring nature of their parental homes. Such memories would not collect again until students were in a stable home setting of the future where they could develop a history within the dwelling.

The temporal home

Two temporal elements were seen by students to be important in defining where and what constituted a real home. The first of these defining elements was that a home should be a permanent and stable base from which life could be conducted. Second, if a home was new, it had to be seen to provide the potential to become a longer-term stable entity. Using these two measures as the basis for an evaluation of home, students revealed that their term-time homes were simply too unstable. The nature of the academic year, with students residing in student accommodation for only around nine months per annum, and often in one house for no longer than a year, meant that this was not viewed as a stable or permanent home.

INTERVIEWER: Do you think that years spent somewhere can help to make it more of a home?

RUTH: I would guess so because you get more used to somewhere, but I think it's more to do with knowing somewhere is permanent. If you know somewhere is permanent and stable from the beginning it can become a home immediately, whereas here we've known it's all very short term . . . we've always been moving or thinking about moving here.

(Environmental Studies student, age 20)

In contrast to the constant fluctuation of students' term-time accommodation, parental homes projected images of stability and permanence. It was this element of continuity which respondents revealed was one of the most important factors responsible for their maintained perception of the parental space as a home. Moreover, while students were in flux between homes, this stability was seen to perform an all important role, as Ruth commented:

It's the only stable thing in my life at the moment. I mean we've changed house three times here, but I always know that home-home will be there and still be the same when I go back.

(Environmental Studies student, age 20)

Moving on to the second element considered here – whether home had the potential to be a familiar and lasting entity – the capacity of both parental homes and term-time homes to become permanent post-graduation homes was limited. Students clearly stated that these homes were not expected, either by themselves or others, to be lasting entities. By citing their future dwellings as having this potential, students indicated that it was more likely that this was where their adult home-life would lie.

The social home

When viewed as a social entity, home was seen by students to be a place which should contain three constituent parts: a living group of significant others, a supportive atmosphere where social and emotional needs were met and a friendly neighbourhood where the individual believed they fitted and belonged. Taking the first of these elements, the main factor which helped to make parental dwellings homely for students was the presence of immediate family members. As Nicola suggested: 'It's the family, the fact that my mum and dad are there, that makes that place home. Their house is automatically home' (Communication Studies student, age 19).

However, having now experienced new social arrangements within their term-time homes, students appeared less likely to remain content with their past home experiences. Friends from university were believed to have taken on new importance as they became the first individuals, other than members of the parental family, with whom students had lived. Respondents stated that living with friends for the first time 'as a family' created a new level of intimacy that old pre-university friends could neither compete with, nor understand. However, this situation was deemed 'homely' only in the most temporary of senses because of its communal peer-group nature. Real homes could, at a pinch, be one-person households, but immediate family members were certainly seen to comprise the most homely social environment. Students therefore stated that close family groupings would eventually form the social units of 'real' future homes. As Mark told me, 'I'll get a job, hopefully, and then I will settle down, you know, probably get married at some point, have a few kids. That's what we all really expect isn't it?' (Applied Biology student, age 20).

The presence of close family or friends within the parental home also meant that students experienced a supportive atmosphere there. However, having experienced the new term-time home social atmosphere, any tensions that existed within the parental home were now deemed to be less tolerable. With increased demands for independence, clashes which occurred with parents were therefore seen to affect the homely atmosphere of the dwelling in an adverse manner. In contrast, respondents stated that their term-time homes fostered good social environments where their needs and lifestyles were fully understood, as Mark pointed out:

> A home is where the heart is and there are seven hearts in this house so that is why it's a home [*laughs*]. Yeah, yeah, you know, it's the environment, and the atmosphere. I mean if I didn't enjoy being here I wouldn't call it home would I?
>
> (Applied Biology student, age 20)

So finally, which of students' three home venues provided for a sense of friendship, neighbourliness and 'social fit'? Students stated that the areas surrounding their parental homes housed close friends whom they had known for years. In their immediate neighbourhoods, neighbours and students' interactions with them were also stated to be important for maintaining a homely atmosphere. These factors were all used by students to stress how their parental homes were deemed more 'normal' and 'real' home environments than their term-time homes. In comparison, the social atmosphere of their term-time neighbourhoods, and the feeling of being 'outsiders' there, contributed towards an overall unhomely atmosphere. A real sense of social fit was seen to be something that a future home would provide again, as Jane said:

> [After graduation] you will have more respect for everything. You will be more choosy about everything. You will be choosy about the type of neighbourhood that you want to live in, and the house you want to live in.
>
> (Technology Management student, age 19)

The physical home

Four elements were seen to comprise the physical environment of home. First, respondents believed the presence of personal belongings in their term-time homes created a sense of continuity and familiarity. As James suggested, 'Yes I think it's your stuff. Wherever your stuff is. I mean you can miss people but you can't take them with you. So when the people aren't here your belongings become more important' (Automotive Design student, age 19). Students used a variety of impermanent techniques to create a sense of belonging and personal space within their term-time homes, as they could not rely on the traditional and more permanent trappings usually associated with home making (such as decorations, furnishings and carpets). Students therefore used their belongings to create a surface veneer of homeliness:

FRANK: Our sort of financial input is posters and little cheap things.
ROGER: We are making it a home in that sense, but we are not at the stage where we can afford more . . . It's more of a visual thing than anything else.
(Environmental Studies students, ages 18 and 21)

However limited the types of personalisation made in the term-time home, they were definitely seen to be more personal than any changes made to parental homes, where parents were the dominant party in decision making. It was therefore in the future home that students believed they would have access to both the conventional home-making tools, plus the autonomy to use them.

Moving on to the second physical factor which affected the homeliness of dwellings, students stated that home should provide a living environment where they could relax and live in comfort. The physical form and comfort of parental dwellings was seen to be a manifestation of all that a home should be. Ruth suggested:

I guess you get to appreciate home more when you have moved away and realise what you had provided for you which you took for granted It's sort of like a treat when you go back there because you can have as many hot baths as you want, and you can walk around in bare feet.
(Environmental Studies student, age 20)

In contrast, the major negative point raised about students' term-time homes, was the fact that they were uncomfortable and basic. Responses indicated that term-time homes lacked aesthetically pleasing and comfortable decor and furnishings, were too dirty to be real homes and had facilities of a standard that would normally be unacceptable, as Mark commented:

[The carpet has] got that sort of pub-carpet type of lacklustre appearance really. I long for a carpet you can walk on in your bare feet like at home. This one's so disgusting you have to wear shoes at all times.

(Applied Biology student, age 20)

Moreover, the means of heating in student dwellings were also deemed insufficient, affecting the amount of time that students could comfortably spend in their dwellings, as Claire described:

If you're sat in your room studying and it's really cold then you are just not motivated to work, which is what happens at the moment really. We come in here [the lounge] to keep warm because it's the warmest room in the house.

(Historical Studies student, age 19)

Students spoke of replicating the comfortable and warm spaces that they had experienced in their parental homes in the future. The creation of a space which would be clean, welcoming and aesthetically pleasant was thus stressed as an essential part of the future home.

As well as deeming the semi-permanent fittings, heating and decorations of their term-time homes 'uncomfortable', students stated that they did not contain the spatial qualities of a real home. Halls of residence were too institutional and student houses often did not have lounges (to maximise the number of tenants). This meant that students had to perform all activities in the private space of their own rooms, as Andrew commented:

There's nowhere to eat in the kitchen as well as no lounge, so I have to eat on my knee in my room. I mean call me fussy, but it would be nice to eat at a table, or even in a communal room. It's been very difficult to get to know people in the house because there is no neutral communal ground.

(Fine Art student, age 20)

To avoid this unhomely spatial organisation, respondents stated that in the future their homes would be single family dwellings. Moreover, the majority of students directly stated that they expected to own their own property eventually. Ruth said: 'I suppose to start off with I would be happy to rent, but I think I would actually like to . . . own somewhere once I was in a proper job' (Environmental Studies student, age 20).

Moving on finally to consider the last physical element constitutive of home (home as a safe haven), students stated that a key unhomely attribute of their term-time homes was their failure to provide total security. Often landlords did not ensure that their rented properties were suitably secure. Moreover, the safety of the actual dwelling and its facilities were also seen as inadequate. Cookers were found to be old and broken; one student group had two gas fires removed by British Gas as they were deemed dangerous and repairs done by landlords were perceived to be neither safe nor adequate. Student houses were additionally believed to be hazardous to students' health, with mouldy and damp rooms, gas leaks, leaking roofs, infestations and dry rot, as Greg described:

> [The bathroom] is the bit that we have had most problems with . . . in the winter we used to have a carpet in there which was soggy the whole time. There was no ventilation, and insufficient heating. It was just a horrible place to be in generally. We've had slugs in there for ages. The shower curtain's covered in mould and the shower doesn't actually work anymore.
>
> (Communication Studies student, age 19)

In comparison, parental homes were hailed as safe havens where students felt free from the dual threats of burglary and unsafe, unhealthy housing facilities. It was indicated that this safety would again be replicated in any future homes that the student dwelt within.

Conclusion

Students' inability to locate one home could at first glance be explained by the fact that they were fluctuating between two home venues during the academic year. However, the helpfulness of this approach is limited by the fact that it cannot explain two factors: first, why students did not see their term-time home simply as a functional alternative which was interchangeable with their parental home, and second, why students introduced a third as-yet unencountered home into their discussions. Responses revealed that the term-time home was more of a temporary stepping-stone leading onto as-yet uncharted waters, rather than a functional alternative in its own right. As a result students were not prepared to compromise on their needs and wishes, nor hinder their transition to adulthood by accepting one of their existing venues as a long-term future home. Beyond the immediate post-graduation year, during which it might prove financially necessary to return to the parental home, respondents spoke of creating a third home which would signify that the leaving home process was at or near completion.

What this provides is clear evidence for the idea that in addition to the here and now, less tangible aspects of our lives and selves (our imaginations, hopes and ideals) are important influences on the development of home meanings and experiences. The future home (although still merely an imagined next step) was already perceived by students as a home which would provide for all their developing adult needs. Although there was no guarantee that such homes would in fact develop, it is interesting to reflect upon students' expectations and hopes that they would, as these helped to fuel their growing dissatisfaction with their past and present homes. This also helps to explain the paradox of why, for these individuals, the elements which were identified as creating a home (Figure 7.1) contained and encompassed a variety of experiences which could at first glance appear mutually exclusive. For instance, the 'significant others' which in part comprised the social environment of home were seen to differ in their expected and desired form in each of the homes that students identified: parents and siblings within the parental home; peers within the term-time home; and a spouse and children within the future home.

Students were clearly moving between statuses and identities. The home, widely acknowledged as a reflector and base for such developments and displays, was used by students as a means by which these changes and adaptations were operationalised, displayed and manifested. Moreover, in providing different 'home' structures and opportunities, students' new home venues in part instigated and expedited their changing needs. A recognition of such multiple home experiences and meanings during the leaving-home period therefore appears crucial to an understanding of how conceptions and meanings of home adapt and evolve for young people on the verge of adult life. In understanding that during this transitional period sustaining a number of homes may be necessary until a 'real' future home can support and provide for all of students' needs, we can additionally understand why, for students, the meaning and experience of home become diverse, complex and fragmented.

8

FITTING A QUART INTO A PINT POT

Making space for older people in sheltered housing

Eileen Fairhurst

Sheltered housing is a firmly established form of housing for older people. In England, for example, there are around 465,000 sheltered houses. Less than 10 per cent are privately owned, about 300,000 are owned by local authorities and 120,000 by housing associations (Balchin 1995: 264). While there is an extensive literature on the social policy aspects of sheltered housing (for instance, Butler *et al.* 1983; Oldman 1986; Tinker 1984) and the experiences of people who live in it (Byetheway 1982; Middleton 1983), little attention has been directed to the sometimes competing perspectives of those who design it and those who are to live in it. This chapter attempts to redress that balance through an examination of sheltered housing in terms of the category of space and specifically how it is bounded and utilised.

In everyday life we view home as both a physical location and a location in space. When the idea of home is considered as a physical location, this involves a conceptualisation of a structure bounded by a perimeter such as a wall or garden. The fabric of the home, its walls and boundaries serve as a marker between home and non-home. If the home is examined as a location in space, it is necessary to explore ideas about a building in the context of the built or natural environment. While the home as a physical location is a place which carries meaning because of the events that occur within its walls, as a location in space it is part of something else and is defined in terms of its relationship to its surroundings.

Older people and architects conceptualise the idea of the sheltered home according to these two perspectives, but in different ways. Architects and designers aim to create homes by manipulating space internally and externally, but they do so from a technical viewpoint. While older people are also concerned about internal and external features, their account of what makes a home is more personal, as it necessarily takes into account features of their previous homes. It is often the case that older people's former homes are larger than sheltered houses, and as a consequence, they have many more material objects – furniture, pictures, books and domestic equipment – than there is space for. While sheltered housing comes in different sizes and with different levels of support according to need (for definitions of different official categories of sheltered housing, see Lund 1996: 169; Balchin 1995), there exists in the minds of architects and designers a notion that the extent of space required by an older person is less than that in the home from which they came. Conflicting perspectives arise on how much space is required. The architect concentrates principally on the form and structure of space according to a 'rational' model of the utilisation of space and upon a preconceived set of aesthetic principles. For architects, then, the manipulation of space is a logical process, dependent upon technical and standardised notions of the amount of space needed to place possessions. For older people, though, this relationship is reversed; their possessions predate the space created by the architect so that objects are logically prior to space.

Because architects construct stereotypes about the needs of older people which centre upon the functioning of the domestic space, they tend not to emphasise the importance that older people attach to their possessions. But as Chapman demonstrates (Chapter 11), objects carry enormous significance for people in that they act as essential cues between a person's past, present and future.

In focusing on this neglected area of how architects' and older people's views on domestic space differ, this chapter will draw upon three sources of data. To assess the attitudes of older adults to the design of sheltered housing, interviews were undertaken with a number of people who were on the waiting list for a new sheltered housing development belonging to a voluntary housing association in a northern English city which comprised twelve specially designed units. The data reported here come from sixteen tape-recorded interviews with men and women who had been notified that accommodation had been reserved for them. Of those who had applied directly to the housing association, one was a widow, one man and one woman living alone and three couples. The local authority nominations to the housing association were three couples and one widow. Couples were interviewed simultaneously by myself and Rachel Welsh. Finally, the chapter draws upon evidence drawn from an interview with the architect of that development.

In order to make sense of the architect's perspective, a textual analysis of professional literature on the design of sheltered housing is put forward. In the 1960s central government standards for local authority housing were published under the title of Design Bulletins and assumed an authoritative status. This analysis will be supplemented by an examination of Valins' (1988) *Housing for Elderly People*. On publication, it was claimed that this text would supplement previous Design Bulletins by pinpointing 'activity led design factors'. As will become apparent though, this discourse represents more a variation on a theme than a fundamentally different view of how space is used. It is to a more thorough analysis of this professional discourse that I now turn.

Designers, space and old people: a view from the 1960s

In the 1960s policy makers, architects and housing professionals produced a spate of publications on the design and function of sheltered accommodation for older people (compiled in Design Bulletins 1974). Their tone was set in *Design Bulletin no. 1: Some Aspects of Designing for Old People*. This report used a patronising language to present a stereotypical account of the needs and abilities of older people, as, for example, in the following guidance on the physical attributes of older people: '[they] tend to get slower in their movements and to get out of breath and tired more quickly: their hearing, smell and sight are apt to become less acute' (Design Bulletins 1974: 3).

While not advocating an overtly medical model of old age, the physical degeneration of older adults was assumed, a sufficient condition to alert the designer to the special needs of this population. In particular, old age was an adversity to be overcome as physical decline predisposes such individuals to become vulnerable to accidents within the home. In other words, the home was considered to be a significant source of danger to older people. By attending to 'comfort, convenience and safety', therefore, it was anticipated that improved housing design may reduce, if not remove such danger. The remit of designers, then, was to use space to pursue these three goals: 'comfort, convenience and safety' for older people. This was to be achieved by the application of anthropometric techniques which measure the human body and its movements. Organising and using space became a technical matter. For example, a subsequent Design Bulletin, *Housing Standards for the Elderly*, not only listed the amount of furniture that would be needed by older people but also defined its dimensions and its ergonomically most appropriate layout (Design Bulletins 1974). The appropriateness of such uniform definitions, it will be shown later in this chapter, can be disputed when the attitudes and needs of individuals and couples are considered.

Through an analysis of the recommendations made in Design Bulletins about the type and range of furniture which would fit into the available space, it is possible to tease out the kinds of impressions that designers had about the lifestyle of residents in sheltered housing. An assertion was made, for example, that a smaller than average cooker would be needed in such accommodation because residents were unlikely to cook a meal for more than three people. By designing a kitchen this way, patterns of eating or entertaining were inevitably restricted as a social activity. That designers were not unaware of the social dimensions of food and eating is suggested by an implied distinction between 'formal' and 'casual' meals. Thus, when noting the extent of space required in a kitchen, reference was made to the 'desirability' of at least two people being able to eat a 'casual' meal in it. Designers, therefore, seemed to have some notion of different socially significant kinds of eating, requiring different amounts of space. Yet arguably, the social dimension of food was minimised overall in that their principal concern was with the kitchen and food preparation as a hazardous activity; as a consequence, attention was concentrated in the 'safe' design features of cookers.

There is some evidence to suggest, then, that designers had preconceived ideas about how many visitors residents might entertain for a meal at any one time. The arrangement of space available for seating in the principal reception rooms suggests that older people did not need to entertain guests in their home: according to the seating specifications of sheltered housing, no surplus chairs were available for visitors.

Being able to invite a visitor to 'sit down' is central to the social process of welcoming a person and, further, suggests that they may engage in social interaction over a period of time. In fact, the Design Bulletin's seating specification contains implicit assumptions about the type of social interaction that was likely to take place within the private domain of the sheltered house. It was not that older people were expected to live completely sedentary or isolated lives; rather, it was assumed that they would congregate or meet family or friends in the communal lounges which were provided in the sheltered housing complex.

Another consistent theme in writings of the time was the importance of window size. This consideration of window size was not so much to do with the provision of sufficient light, but was intended to give residents a view of the outside – to watch the world go by. In the private sphere of the home, therefore, social interaction was envisaged as the passive pastime of a disengaged population.

Designers, space and older people: a view from the 1980s

So far, the discussion has centred on the way that architects' and designers' professional literature on the use of space for older people invoked particular stereotypes of their physical capabilities and their patterns of social interaction. Simply put, it was assumed that older people led a restrictive social life which did not involve inviting others to their new home, either for a general social visit, or to share a meal with them. Moreover, older people were seen as the passive recipients of the 'advice' and 'expertise' of the designer in that they would wish to bring with them only a specified amount of furniture, to be arranged according to the designer's definition of an appropriate layout.

In general terms, these stereotypes relate to the conception of home as a physical location within which space is used in a prescribed way. Intrinsic to such stereotypes is the notion of older adults as a vulnerable social group who require the protection of others. That older people were seen as requiring protection relates to the conceptualisation of the home as a 'location in space' discussed earlier in this chapter. That is, the sheltered home was designed in the context of factors which were external to the site. As Butler *et al.* (1983) point out, the first government reference to sheltered housing referred to the importance of maintaining a proximity to shops and churches, together with giving assurances that the site was properly located to enable the building to be kept warm. These practical considerations were underscored by other meanings, however:

> This meteorological and geographical concept has, with the passage of time, taken on its current social meaning. Sheltered is now taken to imply that the individual is protected, somewhat from the storms of everyday life, rather than the perils of the weather.
>
> (Butler *et al.* 1983: 53)

As well as needing protection and a communal social life, older people were seen to require accommodation which allowed them to maintain their independence in safety. Valins' (1988) focus on housing for the older adults not only echoed earlier government emphases on independence, but also extended it by stressing the importance of privacy to the residents. I want to show how privacy links to a further stereotype of old people which is tied up with the notion of home as a location in space. According to Valins (1988), housing design for older people should move away from a restrictive concern with the specification of particular facilities offered in building types. This initial approach was underpinned by the distinctions drawn by producing different categories of sheltered housing. These categories were defined as follows:

- Category 1: accommodation designed specifically for fitter, more active elderly people, which may contain a common room, laundry or guest room
- Category 1.5: similar to category 1 but must have warden support and alarm system
- Category 2: designed for less active elderly people and must have warden support, an alarm system and communal facilities
- Category 2.5: designed for frail elderly people and can contain additional support facilities such as meals, extra wardens and sluice rooms

(in Lund 1996: 168–169)

Valins (1988) argued that sheltered housing design should move towards an 'umbrella term' which embraces accommodation 'which offers varying degrees of protection and support and aims to retain for them [the elderly] as far as possible a degree of independence and privacy' (Valins 1988: 2). This emphasis on housing as a source of independence and privacy contrasts, as far as Valins was concerned, with the government view which was encapsulated in Design Bulletins on housing for older people. It can be argued, however, that while Valins challenged contemporary wisdom about the sheltered housing needs of older people, he merely reinforced an existing stereotype of these people as a vulnerable group within professional discourse.

What Valins achieved, then, was to put the case for special housing for older people in the context of demographic factors and economic circumstances. In addition, he introduced the notion of 'housing unsuitability'. In constructing this category of housing unsuitability, Valins relied upon the separate notions of home as a physical location and as a location in space. As a physical entity, housing became unsuitable as people moved through the life course because it was, for example, too large once the family had moved away. Similarly, housing became unsuitable because as physical degeneration accompanies old age, so the home itself becomes a hazardous environment.

Valins' conceptualisation of home as a location in space becomes apparent in his consideration of the activity-based design criteria to be used in private living spaces. The characteristic feature of a home, as opposed to an institution, is that 'one has control over what one does within it. It can be a place of refuge from the worries and uncertainties of the outside world' (Valins 1988: 100). Home is depicted, then, as a 'fortress' where what goes on outside must be kept at bay. Implicitly, he states that elderly people are characterised as a particularly vulnerable group who must gain society's protection from the dangers of the world outside.

While Valins' major concern was with sheltered accommodation as a location in space, he did not ignore the importance of personal objects in making a home. For instance, furniture from previous homes was identified 'as a great source of comfort and helps with the identification of a resident's immediate environment' (Valins 1988: 102). Referring to objects in this way should not lead automatically to the assertion that Valins is adopting a stereotypical view of older people – for, as shown elsewhere in this volume, the location of personal objects is essential to the making of any home (see Hepworth and Chapman, Chapters 2 and 11). However, his somewhat patronising account of objects as providing 'a great source of comfort' seems to suggest that older people may be vulnerable to feelings of disorientation. Arguably, almost any person, no matter how old they are, feels disoriented upon moving home, or if they are permanently deprived of access to treasured objects. That objects could have significance in terms of constructing an individual's biography was not, then, articulated fully in Valins' (1988) professional discourse.

The architect of the sheltered housing scheme studied here recognised the traumatic nature of moving from larger to smaller accommodation in old age. While acknowledging that this entailed a 'dramatic change' for new residents, he continued:

> Moving furniture etc., moving from a big house is an insurmountable problem. It's something that they'll [older people] have to like it or lump it. It sounds cruel but it's an inevitability and to be quite

honest if they found any other modern house in the private sector, the standard's even lower than the Parker Morris [1961] standards . . . The actual usable space [in sheltered housing] is considerable but for all intents and purpose there is a net loss of space. That's the hardest thing [older people] have to come to terms with but they have to if they want that accommodation.

For the architect, then, the standard of accommodation offered by sheltered housing requires potential new residents to make a choice between keeping all of their possessions or taking a new sheltered home. Moreover, it is implied that discarding personal possession is a price well worth paying. Because the new sheltered accommodation was to be built in an inner city area, like many such developments, the architect was particularly concerned about the residents' security:

we are tending to construct sheltered housing schemes in inner city areas. There are, therefore, other factors that come into play. The greatest of these is probably security. We're not dealing with leafy suburbs. I imagine there are security problems there. We are dealing with mindless vandalism and that sort of problem and it's essential that tenants are made to feel secure. Therefore, the controlled entry system is absolutely vital. We also adopt a kind of defensiveness about the planning of the building so that the living room windows which tend to be the largest are protected from passers by, by the distance or planting or fencing.

Just as we saw earlier, older people's vulnerability is typically seen as such that they require protection from threats located in the outside world and this is evident in the criteria relating to security which the architect adopt at the design stage. It is interesting to note that in the 1960s, this emphasis on security derived primarily from expectations of vulnerability arising from the ownership of an ageing body. That focus on physical degeneration and the consequent restriction on social life underpinned designers' emphasis on reduced living space and its ergonomic usage in order to make life 'as easy as possible'. In the 1990s this conception of vulnerability continues to exist, although additional external threats are perceived. In the example provided above, problems of vandalism are highlighted by the architect, concerns which can be set alongside the unscrupulous con-artists or burglars who prey on older people.

Perspectives of older people on space

In the previous section, it was shown that designers may conceptualise the needs of older people in a stereotypical way, and as a consequence, quite literally build a number of restrictions into their designs to meet this perception of need. That is not to say that there is a complete mismatch between older people's perceptions of housing need and those of the architects. For example, a number of the older people interviewed for this study *did* state that their existing housing was unsuitable because it was too big for one person and difficult to maintain, especially if the health of their partner was declining.

Similarly, prospective residents were concerned about the interior planning of their homes and the potential problems or opportunities that arise from shared spaces and the link with the external environment. In making assessments about the external environment, however, the people who were seeking sheltered accommodation tended to emphasise social factors rather than physical ones. In particular, the respondents were concerned about the 'kinds of neighbours' they might find themselves living near. Assessments of the suitability of potential neighbours tended also, in turn, to engender a re-evaluation of the suitability of their existing home as an appropriate place to live. 'Noisy' neighbours, barking dogs or individuals perceived as unsociable, such as drug addicts, for example, rendered their current neighbourhood as unacceptable and was given as a possible reason for moving into sheltered accommodation.

Respondents' accounts of their current home as being in some sense 'unsuitable' could be very much more complex than suggested in the discussion of Valins' account. One of the respondents, Mrs Ray, provided an assessment of her existing home which was far from clear cut. She had enjoyed living in her home:

> except for it being on the gable end. You get all the children in the garden, playing football on the wall. They break the fence and you get abuse, knowing that you're on your own. You get egg and tomatoes thrown.

Yet she was ambivalent about moving:

> I am in a way [looking forward to moving] and in a way I'm not. My friends are here. I've lived in this close since 1971, an awful long time to move away. I know it's only ten minutes away by bus but I've got some good friends and neighbours. One young couple get my prescriptions. They're very good neighbours. There's good and bad with it – there are two ways of looking at it. I'm hoping my health will benefit. I know it won't get any better but I hope it will benefit from moving to a warmer house on the ground. By the same rule, I'm leaving my friends behind and my daughter . . . I won't be able to walk from the flat to the precinct.

Her ambivalence about moving to sheltered housing remained after visiting the development's show flat.

> There is only one thing. At first I was alarmed by the patio doors – if anyone breaks in. Anne [her daughter] told me the glass was too thick to break . . . I wouldn't say I'm not keen [on moving] but I'm frightened more of the glass patio door, otherwise it's beautiful. It's a bit upsetting, I've lived in the close for nineteen years. Although I only know about half a dozen people – I'm not one for mixing or what have you – I've got good neighbours. I've got some really good friends around here. It's a big upheaval. I hope I'll settle.

It is clear that various kinds of neighbours' activities may lead to an assessment of a neighbourhood as being both suitable and unsuitable. On the one hand, the position of her home on a gable end unfortunately gave children the opportunity to construct makeshift 'goals' to play football against. Yet on the other, 'helpful', 'kind' and 'neighbourly' actions contribute to a favourable evaluation. It is noteworthy, too, that whereas the scheme's architect saw patio windows as a source of light and as a window on the world, for Mrs Ray it was a potential threat to her safety.

Issues of safety and security were considered as of paramount importance both by Mrs Ray and the scheme's architect. Yet the structure of the sheltered homes may, itself, become a source of anxiety. Mrs Knight, though considering her existing home as unsuitable because of her neighbours, nevertheless saw it as offering her a safe and secure environment.

> When I first came to this house I knew I was going to get it and I didn't feel strange in it. As soon as I walked in I knew. I can walk round this house even in the middle of the night and I'm not afraid. In the night – I can't sleep well, I've been ill myself – if I hear a noise or go to the toilet I can walk in the dark and I'm not afraid. Now what I'm going to do down there I don't know. It will be smaller and they'll have the alarms on.

Mrs Knight pinpointed those features of night-time happenings which conventionally are treated as potential threats to a person's safety. The very familiarity of her environment transcended such fears and enabled her to feel safe and almost immune to danger. Paradoxically the presence of 'alarms' threatened her feeling of security for, by implication, she would need to be alert to them in case she set them off herself.

Mrs Silver's account of her decision to move to sheltered housing reflects, on one level, designers' categorisation of housing 'unsuitability'. Talking about what she was looking forward to on moving, she said:

Well a smaller place to keep clean really and to heat. I think that's the main problem, the heating and the cleaning of it, because you've no sooner finished one part of this than you've to start again. You know what I mean? It's a circle going round. I don't know really. I don't know. Mainly it's for my husband so that he won't have to climb stairs. As I say I don't really want to move. It's a case of having to but it would have to be with adequate space . . . I don't know why they keep building them [sheltered housing] so small. I was having a laugh with one of my sons last night and I said to him, 'Well I know you shrink as you get older but we're not going to be dwarfs'. Oh dear, I don't know. But to me it would be lowering my standard to live there . . . So I thought, well if I've to get rid of everything that I've got, I'd feel as though I was living in somebody else's house. It wouldn't feel like home to me.

When Mrs Silver reflected upon how she might use the space in the house, she drew on unique features of her biography to make those judgements. The point is that in such circumstances old people bring their past to bear on appraising an architect's work. The latter's activity rests upon predicting the former's future actions and this orientation to the future is embodied in design, resulting in a clash between designer's notion of the future and older people's recollections of the past.

The chapter's explication of the utilisation of space hinges on the evaluation of objects placed in the physical location of home. Such processes inextricably connect to aspects of an individual's biography. Earlier we saw that in detailing the size and extent of furniture to be found in sheltered housing, designers pictured residents as unlikely to entertain socially. Mrs Silver recognised the inadequacy of this stereotype for accurately predicting social interaction.

At the moment the grandchildren stay. I know that will be out of the question wherever we went if only we had one bedroom. One of them said, 'But Nana when we come to see you where will we sit?' I just don't know because I mean I don't care how old you are, if you have a family or just friends you're bound to have visitors at some time. Where would they sit? . . . It's got an eat-in kitchen. There's no way I can fit my dining room table into the kitchen. So I should imagine in the kitchen you'd have one of these fold down tables and a chair each. As I say I was so disappointed. I just glanced in at the kitchen and thought well that's not bad. The bathroom's adequate. And where the bathroom is they've made a cupboard. I said to my husband, 'What's that for?' He said, 'That's probably for cleaning materials and brooms.' Well to me that's just wasted space. They could've added that onto the bedroom and made it much bigger. I can't really see an elderly couple having that much cleaning material. What you need nowadays, it's only a Hoover really and a mop and bucket and a brush. You could quite adequately put them in the corner of the kitchen. That's just wasted space.

That designers and old people charge objects with differential significance arguably resides in them being evaluated as memories by their owners (Fairhurst 1997). This matter came to the fore when old people articulated the dilemma of 'fitting a quart into a pint pot' in relation to which objects should be discarded upon the move to sheltered housing.

> They [sheltered housing] might be all right for one but for a couple, I mean they're so inadequate. What are you going to do with all your things? The things I've got over the years. They're not just material possessions. They're memories. My sister went to live next door. She's died. I've got things she bought me, what the children have bought over the years. My collection of Toby jugs which has taken me years. What am I going to do with those things? Things I've brought back from holiday as souvenirs. I can't throw memories away.

For Mrs Silver, memories had a dual sense: they were not only things in themselves but also elaborated in things. For designers, objects are things, no more and no less. It is not surprising to note then that in professional discourses of the home, their value is minimised. This is explicable, of course, because the memories attached to objects are uniquely personal and are, therefore, not accessible to designers.

While it is the case for many respondents that 'fitting a quart into a pint pot' necessarily involved painful decisions about parting with objects, it should be recognised that for others, moving home could be seen as an opportunity to throw them away and replace them with new items. Again memories informed their decision making, but in this case they carried less pleasant cues. Mrs Knight, who referred to herself as 'second-hand Rose', outlined which things she would be glad to be rid of.

> Some things I've had for donkey's years. I want everything new. I've ordered a bed settee and two reclining chairs for our legs. I don't know what else I want. The old furniture I've had for years and years. I want everything away, everything new and I'm going to have it if it kills me. I just want the remaining time we've got to have a bit of comfort which we've never had. I've had my home, thank God for that. We've never gone hungry but I've always had to work hard so I want a bit of peace now.

Mrs Knight had retained many of her possessions through necessity rather than out of choice. They reminded her of a life characterised by economic constraint in which buying material goods was beyond her reach. She wanted to buy everything new – not just to achieve a break from the past, but also to gain a new life of comfort.

Conclusion

In this chapter on the utilisation of space, I have examined the differing perspectives of the designers of sheltered housing and of prospective residents. I have indicated that these different orientations reflect the notions of home as both a physical location and a location in space. I have demonstrated that architects' work necessarily involves the making of judgements about the future experience of potential residents, something which can lead to the generation of stereotypical images of the needs and wants of older people – for example, privacy, security and a small and easily maintainable living space, in the context of declining health. Since designers do not have access to knowledge of the unique features of potential residents' lives, design can be informed only by abstract knowledge. A consequence of this is that assumptions about space and its utilisation remain at a generalised level. By contrast, prospective residents, when undertaking this same process, bring aspects of their own biographies to bear. During this time they make value judgements about the favourability or otherwise of the features of sheltered accommodation in the context of their current living arrangements – a process from which designers are inevitably excluded.

THE IDEAL OF HOME

Domesticating the institutional space of old age and death

Jenny Hockey

Family photograph albums are described by Spence and Holland (1991: 7) as idealised representations of family life in which 'sickness, disease and disability are barely visible'. In this chapter I examine the notion of 'home' as another edited representation of idealised domestic life in which positively perceived beliefs, ideals and values are highlighted – companionship, security, freedom, expressiveness and privacy (Allan and Crow 1989). Less acceptable within this idealised concept of 'home' are aspects of family life such as disease and disability and it is these 'exclusions' which can tell us much about our notions of social identity and family life. By looking at what is included and what is missing from conceptions of 'house and home' we learn about more than just bricks and mortar for, as Gullestad (1993: 129) argues, 'in many cultures the house can be seen as a microcosm of important cognitive categories'.

The exclusions which provide a primary focus here are old age, death and dying. In 1966, Blauner was already describing death as 'increasingly a phenomenon of the old' (quoted in Clark 1993: 7). By the year 2001, it is predicted that there will be 4 million people over the age of 75 in Britain (Bond et al. 1993: 4). What this chapter argues is that some manifestations of the ageing process, and many deaths, are irreconcilable with contemporary notions of 'home'. As a result, family members may at some stage in their lives be admitted to another kind of 'home', the 'residential' or 'nursing' home. While such institutions share the title of 'home', there are many contrasts; for example, rather than a small domestic unit which houses the members of more than one generation, residential homes have traditionally accommodated large groups of people of the same age who are given care by professionals in exchange for pay rather than family members out of love or duty. Furthermore, in an account of the domestication of institutional settings, Higgins (1989: 171) notes that 'although the physical features of the domestic environment are important in creating a "homely" atmosphere [in the institution] they are insufficient, on their own, to provide a true sense of home'. In summary, life in a residential 'home' is at odds with the ideal of home. It is a setting in which we find aspects of human life such as chronic illness, mental and physical degeneration. Many of these do not conform to the requirements of western personhood. It is the tensions associated with the mismatch between the concept of 'home' and the processes of ageing and dying which this chapter unravels.

Living/dying spaces

Tensions between the concept of home and the material reality of human deterioration are by no means universal. In other societies we find examples of homes where domestic space is allocated for death and dying. The Berber house has a lower part which is designated as 'the place of objects that are moist, green or raw . . . . wood and green fodder – natural place also of beings – oxen and cows . . . – and place of natural activities – sleep, the sexual act, giving birth – and the place also of death' (Bourdieu 1973: 99). In a traditional Northumbrian miner's home there are similarly spaces set apart for different domains of life (Dawson 1990). At the front of the house is a neat garden and polished front step which provides access to the front room for outsiders such as doctors, colliery managers and strangers. This is the only admissible route by which the undertaker can collect a body which has been laid out for display in the front room. Culturally and symbolically crucial, this practice can raise practical difficulties. In an example from inter-war Coventry, Adams (1993) also describes the formal display of the prepared body in the front room or parlour, citing older people's recollections that it was 'not very pleasant in them days, 'cos if you'd got no hall entrance you had to come in that way' (Adams 1993: 161). Dawson (1990) recounts the social disruption which resulted when these rules of ritual practice were flouted in 1980s Northumberland. A family laid out the body of one of its elderly members in the kitchen rather than the front room, because they felt that the front room was too cramped and the hearse would have difficulty in pulling up on the unmade road at the front of the house. In angry response, elderly male members of the community 'hijacked' the event by blocking the back entrance to the home with a parked car, thereby forcing the removal of the body via the front door. By restoring an appropriate symbolic use of domestic space, proper respect for a key member of their community was ensured.

In contemporary British society, however, exclusion rather than segregation is the predominant cultural strategy for managing aspects of old age, death and dying which disrupt the use of domestic space. While only 5 per cent of the population over 65 live in institutional care, Bond and Coleman (1990: 161–162) point out that 'a significant proportion will experience institutional living at some time during their later life, particularly people who attain at least 80 years of age'. At the 1991 Census, 9.7 per cent of people over 75 and 23.7 per cent of people over 85 were living in an institution (Bond *et al.* 1993:

215). Though most deaths did take place within domestic space until well into the twentieth century, by the mid-1960s over 60 per cent of all deaths in the UK occurred in hospitals and nursing homes. In 1989 this figure had risen to 71 per cent (Clark 1993: 8). Gore's (1993) work on East Kent undertakers shows this pattern echoed by funeral directors who modified their premises after the Second World War, turning stables or carpenter's workshops into viewing rooms for the dead. By the 1990s, therefore, the presence of dying and dead bodies within the home was no longer customary.

While factors ranging from secularisation to the effects of central heating on a corpse have been used to explain this shift in practice, changing notions of home are an important consideration. Aries (1981) points out that the nineteenth-century stigmatising of visible dirt within the home – particularly organic substances associated with bodily processes – made the domestic management of death increasingly problematic. Thus the 'home' as imagined and idealised within the twentieth century has come to embody privacy, cleanliness and order as its defining characteristics. Access to vacuum cleaners, dishwashers and washing machines has led to a raising of standards of cleanliness within the home, rather than a reduction in the time spent on domestic work (Wajcman 1992).

Contrasts and contradictions

We are now arguably in a position where some aspects of the life course are incompatible with the ideal of home. Although planning regulations require ramps to give disabled people access to public buildings, private homes are exempt. The materials and colour schemes ideally selected for home decoration are highly vulnerable to the 'dirt' produced by young children, older people and indeed pets, even though neither children's nappies, potties, drinks, food and shoes, nor pets' damage to furniture, clothes and slippers are stigmatised. However, to exclude people who cannot adequately participate in the performance of home as idealised is to undermine a view of home as a 'sanctuary' or 'place of secure retreat' where vulnerability can be accommodated – the home as 'castle' (Moore 1984, cited in Allan and Crow 1989: 7).

By contrast, the physical environment of the residential home is entirely compatible with bodily deterioration. There are extensive laundry facilities and removable carpet tiles in anticipation of double incontinence. There are also spaces specifically dedicated to illness and death, the 'sickbay' and the 'morgue'. However, just as the exclusion of very elderly family members from the domestic home undermines the ideal of home as sanctuary, so the accommodation of deterioration within the residential 'home' must be carried out discreetly, if the premises are to be viewed as a living space rather than a charnel house. What this chapter argues is that attempts are made to bring the institutional setting into line with figurative or mythical representations of the ideal home. However, like the literal 'ideal' private home, these attempts are vulnerable to the unpredictable decay of the human body. As Willcocks *et al.* (1987: 1) argue, 'In reality, the ideal of providing a "homely" setting is a genteel facade behind which institutional patterns, not domestic ones, persist'. The example to follow shows how these contradictions were addressed in one local authority residential home.

Highfield House

Forty-five older people who could no longer live independently or in the homes of younger family members occupied Highfield House, the local authority residential home where this study took place (see Hockey 1990). Most had their own single bed-sitting rooms. These were carpet-tiled, with teak bedside furniture, wardrobe, built-in wash-hand basin and mirror. They overlooked lawns, trees and flower beds at the periphery of the city. Residents had brought in favourite ornaments, family photographs, crucifixes and other religious icons. Some had an armchair, rug or small table and together with pot plants these valued possessions filled the light sunny bed-sitting rooms. To an extent domestic home was thereby re-created, on an individual basis, within the context of the residential home. Small lounges and alcoves were available for residents to sit together and watch television; meals were waitress-served at small tables in a dining room with floor to ceiling windows giving onto gardens.

These material circumstances helped re-create an attractive image of home-liness, security and independence. However, the mental and physical decay visible within an elderly population living at close quarters to one another provided unequivocal evidence of bodily processes not customarily featured in idealised images of 'home'. In a society where life and death usually occur in separate spaces, where the domestic home is the place of life and institutions are the places of death, this 'home' was quite evidently a dying space, concerned primarily with the slow process of deterioration. Among the forty-five older people living in the home during the period of the study there were ten who could walk only with a Zimmer frame, seven who had difficulty in communicating, and a further twelve who could neither communicate nor walk with ease. By the end of the nine month study, approximately one-quarter of the home's residents had died, in most cases within the home itself.

To show how the inevitable processes of dying were reconciled with aspirations of homeliness, cleanliness and order we need to focus on the role of Officer-in-Charge, or Matron, and her relationship with her care staff. It was she who orchestrated the illusion of a 'homely' environment despite the undermining evidence of loss and decay. Her position of authority parallels that of the traditional male household head, while care staff played the part of the adult female members of a domestic household. In many respects, therefore, the organisation of institutional life resembled the domestic home where

111

women have traditionally created and maintained the notion of 'home' by fulfilling a male partner's explicit or implicit expectations about the way it should be organised. Skilful domestic work involves not just the cleaning up of literal dirt but also the management of figurative 'dirt' by keeping children, sick or older people in order. As Mary Douglas (1966: 48) has argued, 'If we can abstract pathogenicity and hygiene from our notion of dirt, we are left with the old definition of dirt as matter out of place'. By this she refers to any-thing, or anyone, who falls betwixt and between the fixed points of social structure. Should women fail to manage older family members in ways which keep them quietly on the fringes of home life, both the women's domestic competence and indeed the inclusion of a frail older person within the house-hold may be called into question.

While the traditional 'housewife' manages domestic space, care staff under-take 'care' work – that is, cleaning and toileting incontinent residents, 'walk-ing' immobile or demented residents from place to place and nursing sick and dying residents. Both the housewife and the care assistant undertake tasks which have a symbolic as well as practical importance. Both are concerned to marginalise evidence of deterioration and death. Both operate in relation to the power inscribed in either a male household head or, in the case of the residential home, the figure of the Matron. Peripherally located in her office, the Matron admitted older people to the home, thereby gaining possession of medical, social and financial information about the individual and determin-ing which clothes, ornaments and items of furniture they brought in.

Although physically set apart, the Matron's name was constantly invoked when residents were persuaded to be compliant. They in turn threatened to report one another to the Matron. Such was the Matron's power that Mary, the assistant Matron, jokingly told her to put a sack over her head when she went out in order to retain the illusion of her powerful presence within the home. Like children told to 'just you wait 'til your father gets home!', the residents were disciplined merely by the mention of a name.

Managing death: homely strategies

As forty-five older people edged towards death in Highfield House, the Matron removed herself from most practical tasks while simultaneously effecting critical shifts of meaning within the older people's immediate environment. In this sense, the Matron provided an interpretative framework for everything which took place within the home. The literal meaning of daily life within the residential home was that forty-five people had deteriorated to the extent that they were unable or unwilling to live either alone or with friends or family. Seen by many as a 'last resort', the residential home readily took on powerful associations of deterioration and death. Separated from their past lives and previous identities, residents were undergoing bodily changes that could lead only to their deaths. Within this setting, however, the Matron transformed these realities and replaced them with a representation of the institution as a setting in which older people could continue to live independently.

Located at the periphery she was well placed to make interventions in the way in which the events of institutional space were interpreted. In this condensed world of ageing and dying, she introduced distances of all kinds. Channels of communication between staff were tenuous. Innovation, flexibility and spontaneity were quashed by an unyielding round of bedtimes, bath-times and mealtimes. Thus the rigid organisation of institutional time and space was a necessary precondition for the continuous misreading of what was actually going on. Without the Matron's interventions the transitory, mortal nature of life would be brought home, quite literally and painfully. The following four case examples exemplify the ways in which idealised notions of 'home' were superimposed on the realities of everyday illness and death.

The name of the home

While the Matron described Highfield House as the residents' 'home' within which they should be free to live as they pleased, the word 'home' was excluded from its title, Highfield House. The same is true when private houses are given names – Dunroamin, Derryvale, Rookery Nook. However, the exclusion of the word 'home' from the title of Highfield House also masks its negatively perceived, institutional character. When the word 'home' is prefaced with the name of a dependent social category – 'old folks', 'children' or 'dogs' – its meaning is inverted. Notions of hearth and home give way to images of a rule-bound space into which the individual is 'put away'. In its place therefore, we find the word 'house' and its associations with grand properties owned by wealthy families, with the dignified and the stately. Out of forty-one institutions for older people in this region of the North East, the word 'home' appeared only once at the time of the study. Preferred were titles such as 'Palatine House', 'Gladstone Hall', 'Greenfields House', 'Bydale Lodge', 'Grove Park', 'The Lawns' and 'Moorcroft'.

Rather than being 'put away into an old folks' home' or 'admitted to care', therefore, the older person 'becomes a resident in Metcalfe House'. Dependency and impending death are thus transformed, becoming less perceptible to those facing exclusion from the domestic home and admission to institutional space.

The guidebook for prospective residents

Local social services offered a guide to older people contemplating admission to Highfield House. Carefully phrased, it subtly transformed a rule-bound lifestyle into an idealised conception of domestic order achieved through a loving consensus. Potential residents entered a fictional world of home in which a gentle hand guided them through mutually beneficial forms of social organisation.

The guide opened with an apparently individualised 'message to you from the Director of Social Services'. It went on to acknowledge prospective residents' fears. For example, 'many people are apprehensive about applying for a place in a home'. The frightening implications of lost autonomy were however submerged in the guidebook's representation of the home as:

> well furnished, everything possible having been done to make it as homely and comfortable as possible . . . varied and interesting menus are provided . . . a range of activities are arranged within the home which may include concerts, socials, table games and a library service.

Offered in the hope that 'it will serve to allay some of the worries you may have', it softened its stipulations in subtly persuasive language such as:

> . . . you will be encouraged to . . .
> . . . you are expected to . . .
> . . . it is common practice for . . .
> . . . in the interests of your safety . . .
> . . . you are strongly advised . . .
> . . . you are asked to remember that . . .

This euphemistic guidebook language diffuses the literal reality of giving up one's tenancy or home ownership; most of one's furniture; control over money, valuables, pension book and medicines; freedom to choose when to receive visitors; and freedom to smoke and drink at will. Within this context, the shedding of possessions, freedoms and responsibilities carries obvious implications: death is the impending reality which undermines any idealised notions of 'home'.

This representation of the 'homely and comfortable' environment is persuasive only outside or at the home's periphery. Inside we find the loving consensus disrupted by residents who refuse their pills, smoke and drink in their rooms and stash gin and whisky bottles in their wardrobes. Some residents refused to get up in the morning, some began extended journeys to lavatories when meals were served, one urinated in her coffee cup, some ran away while threatening suicide. By behaving in these ways, residents unmasked the institutional world which lay at the heart of the 'homely environment'. In controlling residents' 'deviance', the Matron and her care staff had no choice but to reveal their positions of authority. However, all those residents who conformed to the institution's required uses of time and social space, on some level subscribed to the fiction of the homely environment, thereby upholding the guidebook's representation of the institution.

The Valentine card

The ideal of home is often realised only when visitors are expected. It is then that attempts to eradicate both literal and symbolic forms of 'dirt' and disorder are likely to occur. Not only are visits preceded by 'cleaning' and 'tidying', but also while outsiders are present, deviations from the customary uses of space may be suspended. Thus meals are eaten at a dining table rather than around the television or in a kitchen. Similarly, parlours and best china come into play as high-status visitors are entertained or calendrical and life course rituals celebrated.

In Highfield House a small group of middle-aged visitors, the 'Friends', both provided as well as stimulated the performance of 'home' within the residential setting. On St Valentine's Day, with its associations of romantic love between individuals, the Friends addressed a poem to everyone who fell within the institutional category 'resident'. Carefully purchasing a card which contained no sexual reference, the Friends typed a verse on the back and pinned it up by the dining room so that the card's printed message for the individual was obscured. It read as follows:

> We love to be among you
> To share in all you do
> The residents of this home are dear to us, 'tis true
> So upon this special day
> We are pleased to write these lines
> To the friends of Highfield House – you all are Valentines.

This card was addressed to those who had no choice but to live among other old and dependent people. Accommodated as one of a group, they were excluded from individualising opportunities to 'love', to 'share in', to be 'dear to', to experience a 'special day' and, indeed, to be 'a Valentine'. Thus an expressive form from the private, familial area of life was being used to address those socially categorised as unavailable for romantic love. Only dependency and age had brought them together, the very conditions that had led to their exclusion from domestic space. So flimsy was the illusion that Valentine cards with any sexual content were dismissed, lest reference to a more literal expression of romantic love should evoke the literal reality of ageing bodies, culturally perceived to be beyond lovemaking.

The Friends of Highfield House were close associates of the Matron. They shared with her a peripheral position from which they were able to construct this somewhat tenuous representation of 'home' within institutional space.

The Open Day

Just as the visits of friends evoke a performance of home-as-idealised rather than home-as-lived, so the separation of public and private space within

Highfield House occurred only on the occasion of the Open Day. Normally staff claimed free, unannounced access to residents' bedrooms, bathrooms and toilets. However, during this public event a congruence was achieved between the domestic home and the nursing home in that aspects of life, ageing and human deterioration, which find no easy place within idealised notions of 'home' were made invisible. Held in summer, the Open Day is staged outside or on the periphery of the home. While teas were served in the dining hall, the bed-sitting rooms, sickbays and corridors where residents lived and died were not 'open' to visitors. By dividing public and privates space when visitors are present, 'home' is performed in a literal enactment of that which customarily remains figurative. While a few fitter residents ran stalls, and a selection of infirm residents were blanketed in wheelchairs, with one care assistant per chair to attend to them, the majority of residents could only be glimpsed as they watched from upstairs windows. The jazz band, the fortune teller, the rummage stalls and the teas served by staff and Friends predominated. The ostensive purpose of the event was fund-raising, but the vitality and sociality of the tea shop and the fairground, in briefly supplanting an everyday atmosphere of boredom, isolation and weariness, offered an effective literal representation of the guidebook's figurative description – of a homely, comfortable environment where varied and interesting menus, concerts, socials and table games are provided.

Implications for policy

Community care policies have required the return of decision making about admission to residential care to older people themselves. Rather than relatives', social workers' and general practitioners' concerns about an older person's 'insanitary' practices or 'eccentric' uses of time and space, older people's priorities are upheld. What is overlooked is that they themselves may adhere to a model of home management which is characterised by 'hygiene', 'fresh air' and 'regular' mealtimes (Allen *et al.* 1992). A decision to enter residential care may therefore reflect deep-seated personal concerns about failure to maintain a domestic environment in a culturally appropriate manner.

Furthermore, older people who choose to age within the 'ideal' homes of younger families members can still find themselves excluded through boundaries which are internal rather than external to the home. In an article entitled 'Solitary confinement in a suburban semi' (*Guardian*, 30 March 1994), Jane Chichester, a representative of a voluntary organisation, describes how her client, Mrs Allen, lived for seven years in social isolation in a self-contained flat within her son's home. Provided with only a kettle, Mrs Allen received brief, occasional visits from her son and the silent delivery of a daily meal tray by her daughter-in-law. Neither contact with her grandchildren nor participation in her children's wider social life were made available to her. Only after her death was her body found during a meal tray delivery, a body which, one imagines, would not subsequently be incorporated within her children's home for display purposes.

Another strategy for the management of ageing 'at home' is to devolve care tasks to a paid worker, a strategy which involves accommodating a 'stranger' within the domestic home and so rupturing the elision of the concepts of 'home' and 'family'.

Issues of power

This chapter not only describes the management of tensions between the ideal of home and the material reality of human deterioration, but also shows how age or gender-based social differentiation can limit access to resources, both material and symbolic, for members of particular social categories. There is an association between culturally specific ideals of 'home', and an unequal distribution of social power. Alongside the exclusion of older people we can place the experience of working-class children who have traditionally been expected to 'play out' for adult fear that they might 'dirty' domestic space and disrupt the domestic time of housework. While older children 'played out' at a distance from the home, younger children might be confined to back alleys, babies being secured within the back yard (James 1983). As a marginalised social category, children share the experiences of dependent older people. In *Under Milk Wood*, Dylan Thomas links babies and old men, both of them cleaned and wheeled out to the yard in their 'broken prams'. Positioned under the drying underwear in hidden external space, the very young and the very old demand feeding bottle and pipe from the adult woman within the home (Thomas 1954: 36). While these practices are now less common, some exclusions persist. For example, a woman's friends will stop visiting during the day if her male partner stays at home because of unemployment (McKee and Bell 1983).

The exclusion from 'home' of those unable or unwilling to inhabit the dominant social category 'adult', whose presence disrupts notions of 'home' in an idealised sense, is a problematic response to later life, death and dying. These are categories of experience which can be distanced spatially, but not temporally. Those approaching death represent the future for those currently occupying more powerful social positions. Structurally weak, they are nonetheless endowed with other forms of power. As Victor Turner (1974) argues, they are in a position to criticise or undermine the values of the dominant social structure.

Thus, centre page coverage in a national newspaper was granted to lonely Mrs Allen, whose 'home' within her children's house did not live up to idealised notions of familial sociality and home cooking (*Guardian*, 30 March 1994). Under the caption 'solitary confinement', parallels were drawn between the situation of this 'tiny woman with sparse lavender hair' and a 'creaky voice' and that of a criminal. It is the structural weakness of her marginal position which, when discovered, allowed Mrs Allen to make a powerful if proxy public statement.

Conclusion

This chapter has argued that while the pursuit of the ideal home can require the exclusion of frail older people, it remains necessary to figuratively transform, to somehow domesticate the conditions of those who are literally pushed to the margins. In representing institutional care as a 'home from home', two very different social spaces are merged in the imagination. Allen *et al.* (1992: 158–159) described the words of a doctor to an older person recovering in hospital after a fall: 'Would you like to go to a place very similar but like a home from home?' Similarly, in the adverts for private residential homes, certain phrases recur: 'home from home atmosphere', 'home cooking', 'beautiful warm home', 'warm and homely atmosphere', 'comfortable family atmosphere', 'the home of good care', 'make our home your home'.

Lakoff and Johnson (1980: 157) argue that 'people in power get to impose their metaphors'. The study of Highfield House showed how the Matron used her position at the periphery of the residential home to give literal form to images or metaphors of the domestic home, via its name, its organisation of time and space, its internal interpersonal relationships and its atmosphere. These four case examples showed how the notion of 'home' can be extended so that aspects of life which cannot be accommodated within the domestic home are nonetheless domesticated, if only on a symbolic level. To include them within the home in a literal sense would be profoundly disruptive in that, as visible manifestations of human mortality, their presence within that setting transgresses the boundaries through which life and death are customarily kept apart.

Part III

ANXIETIES AND RISKS
Homes in danger

10

A HAVEN IN A HEARTLESS WORLD?

Women and domestic violence

Laura Goldsack

Traditionally, the home and the activities that take place within it have been viewed as a private affair; it is the cornerstone of the private sphere, secondary and separate to the mainstream world of work and politics (see Chapters 1, 2, 5 and 11). The home is identified, then, as a place of respite and retreat, its territory being the locus of childhood, family and marriage. The differentiation between the 'public' and the 'private' helps to highlight other dualisms: the political and the personal, work and leisure, male and female. According to Allan and Crow (1989) the private sphere has traditionally been characterised by three features: privacy; security, control and freedom; and creativity and expression. The home as the arena of privacy, in particular, has pervaded social as well as political thinking. Holme's (1985) study of *Housing and Young Families in East London* suggested that people sought privacy over all else, for 'somewhere to be on their own' (cited in Allan and Crow 1989: 3). Being in a private space is a central part of being 'at home' and is viewed as a valuable and important feature of family life. Privacy acts as a shield against public scrutiny, and is generally believed to be important for the maintenance of private dignity and intimacy. However, to be private can signify deprivation as well as advantage. For women in the home, privacy can mean confinement, captivity and isolation. In such circumstances the home is less of a castle, and more of a cage (Oakley 1974a; M. Roberts 1991; Darke 1996; Wekerle *et al.* 1980).

The extent of domestic violence

Since the early 1970s, studies have revealed other aspects of the private sphere, particularly the persistence of violence and the sexual abuse of women and children. Most research acknowledges the difficulty in accurately defining the extent of abuse (Edwards 1986; Hough and Mayhew 1983; Dobash and

121

Dobash 1992). Domestic violence is steeped in shame and secrecy, and as a consequence, most victims do not report the crime to the police or other agencies (Dobash and Dobash 1980). Taking place within the private space of the home and the ongoing time of family life, domestic violence is a crime for which women require a remedy other than 'tougher' sentencing. Women who have experienced domestic violence are also reluctant to report such crimes in victimisation surveys (Hough and Mayhew 1983; Maguire 1994) and the recording practices of many agencies are problematic (Edwards 1986). In addition, there has been no national or large-scale prevalence survey undertaken on domestic violence. However, the evidence available from police and other agency statistics and more substantively from feminist and localised research suggests that the home is frequently the site of persistent violence and abuse.

One survey suggests that three out of every ten women have been injured by their partners during their lifetime, while only one in five of those women reported that assault to the police (Mooney 1993). Mooney also reported that 6 per cent of women had been forced to have sex with their partners in the previous twelve months, while 10 per cent had experienced violence from their partners over the past year. Painter (1991) came to similar conclusions. In a sample of 1,000 women, a reported 14 per cent had been raped by their husbands at some point during their marriage (cited in Maguire 1994: 268). Dobash and Dobash (1980) suggest that 25 per cent of all violent crime reported to the police is domestic violence. In a study of South Tyneside, researched between May 1989 and April 1992, a total of 6,166 domestic violence incidents were reported to the police alone (Walker and McNicol [née Goldsack] 1994: 30).

Crime statistics also point to the frequency and severity of this crime. Nearly half of all murder victims in Britain since 1982 were women. In cases where a suspect was identified, it was in 47.5 per cent of cases, the woman's husband, male cohabitant, boyfriend or former spouse or cohabitant (Edwards 1989: 138). Figures also suggest that many victims were not living with their aggressor at the time of the homicide. The South Tyneside survey suggested that 66 per cent of women were divorced or separated at the time of seeking police assistance. It is clear that women leaving violent men – what many judges, magistrates, police officers and commentators urge them to do – is often not sufficient to afford them safety or protection. The prevalence of domestic violence is not isolated to particular age groups, race or classes. Mooney's (1993) survey reported that 25 per cent of professional women had experienced domestic violence, 29 per cent of lower-middle-class women and 30 per cent of working-class women.

Violence against women in the home crosses both national and cultural boundaries. Indeed, there is evidence of the pervasive nature of this crime in virtually all cultures. A World Bank report suggested that violence against women in the home is the most endemic form of harm committed against women (Heise et al. 1994). This ground-breaking report reviewed thirty-five studies from around the world and showed that in many countries, one-quarter to more than one-half of women report having been physically abused by a present or former partner. To illustrate this point, the World Bank report showed that in one study in New Zealand, 20 per cent of 2,000 women surveyed reported being hit and physically abused by a male partner, 58 per cent of whom suggested that the violence was repeated. In Kenya, of a sample of 3,272 urban women and 2,118 rural women taking part in a national random sample survey, 20 per cent reported that they had experienced physical abuse from a partner while 10 per cent said they had been raped. In the United States, of 6,000 women surveyed in Texas, 39 per cent reported that they had experienced abuse from a male partner during their adult lifetime. The World Bank report pointed out that while the reports are not strictly comparable, due to differences in sampling, research design and definitions employed, these studies speak of a common experience of violence in the home, the shared pressure to remain silent and hidden; and the fear of recrimination, impacts on women's health, their sense of well-being and participation in the world (Heise *et al.* 1994).

Nationally and internationally, women face more danger in their own homes from men they know than they do from strangers in public (Stanko 1985; Heise *et al.* 1994). They are more likely to be raped, assaulted and even killed within this arena than in any other place. The violence experienced in the home is more dangerous than public violence and is more likely to result in internal injuries and unconsciousness; domestic violence is also often accompanied by long-term mental abuse and increases in frequency and intensity over time (Heise *et al.* 1994; Dobash and Dobash 1980). The different risks facing men and women in the private sphere compared with the public world are striking. Men face risk of violence from strangers in public places, while for women, the risks are from men they know in private places (Hough 1985; Mirlees-Black *et al.* 1996).

There is also some evidence to show that men suffer domestic violence from women they know in the home, although the extent of this abuse, or the accuracy of existing evidence, is contentious. Repeated surveys from the United States (Straus and Gelles 1986) suggest that there may be a symmetry of violence in the domestic sphere, with male and female equally liable to both aggressor and victim status. However, this research has been criticised in its use of the 'conflict tactics scale' methodology which 'counts' individual violent acts regardless of motive, context or outcome (see Dobash and Dobash 1992). While this issue has been exposed by journalists and television documentaries in the United Kingdom, there is as yet a paucity of academic research into the female abuse of adult males. Anecdotal evidence, available to me from agencies dealing with marital violence, would suggest, however, that the abuse of men by women is not comparable in prevalence or severity to the abuse of women by men.

The South Tyneside study

Central to the analysis of domestic violence is a consideration of privacy. Indeed, privacy is as central to the constitution of the violent home as it is to the notion of the harmonious ideal home. Privacy serves to mask the nature and extent of crimes against women as well as justify the lack of public and official intervention. The private nature of domestic life has clear repercussions for women living with violent men. This is clearly documented in the research findings from the South Tyneside study (Walker and McNicol 1994). In this study the role of the Police Domestic Violence Unit in South Tyneside was examined between 1990 and 1993. The research combined the use of a postal questionnaire to women who had sought police assistance, together with in-depth interviews with a smaller sample of respondents to highlight the experience of women seeking police help.

The findings of this study suggest strongly that the private nature of the home seriously worsened the likelihood and severity of domestic violence. Indeed, many women spoke at length of their partner's attempts to enforce privacy and maintain the secrecy of the abuse.

As one woman stated, 'I wasn't allowed to talk to anybody, male or female, he didn't like it. Mainly I was frightened to talk to people so I used to walk around with my head down.' Other women felt ashamed that they had suffered from marital violence and chose to keep this information from others. As one woman said,

> I never had violence in my life before, that's why I hid it, I couldn't understand it. It was such a shock to my system, like 'this can't be happening to me' and you're ashamed, you are ashamed for their actions.

The experience of shame was common among our respondents. But these feelings of shame were compounded by their partner's attempts to conceal the abuse. This concealment of violence often involved men developing a premeditated approach to the method of abuse. As one woman told us, 'He used to do it where people couldn't see – the tops of your legs, the tops of your arms, inside your mouth by squeezing your jaw and pounding your head until you just can't think at all'.

Many women feared that their disclosure of the intimidation and violence they were suffering would result in public humiliation. Perhaps even more alarmingly for those woman who were willing to tell friends, family, neighbours and public agencies of their plight found that they displayed a reluctance to intervene. This strongly suggests that people who had a close relationship with victims and even some agencies exhibited a degree of tolerance to the incidence of domestic violence. In other cases, outsiders chose not to get involved, even if they witnessed violence against women. As one woman informed us, 'He banged my head off the glass door and gave us a good hiding in the street. Well everybody seen it and nobody came over to help'.

While for women, the experience of domestic violence brought a sense of shame, the men who committed this abuse typically maintained public respectability. Victims found this extremely frustrating, for it demonstrated that other people were either not taking the issues seriously, or worse, did not believe them at all. One woman from our study commented that:

> I wanted his name put in the papers because nobody believes me. This is such a nice man who wouldn't do anything, he would do anything for anybody, he's so nice. I even have that now where it's been said 'Are you sure?'

Women's fear of crime

In spite of the well-publicised evidence of the danger that women face in the privacy of the home, crime surveys reveal that fear of public spaces is widespread among women. Indeed, it is the image of the solitary, vulnerable woman which epitomises the threat of an urban environment in the popular imagination. This is borne out in the Edinburgh Crime Survey (S. Anderson *et al.* 1990) which reported large numbers of women feeling unsafe in their local area, as well as within their own homes. In central Edinburgh for example, 36.9 per cent of women said they felt very or a little unsafe going out alone after dark in their area, compared to 18.5 per cent of men. The fact that women are generally more fearful of the threat of violence in the public world than men is underscored by the popular notion that the home is a haven in a heartless world. As Darke (1996) has argued, this may affect women according to their personal biographies.

> The home as haven may be particularly important for those who face hostility in the public sphere: for example, women members of ethnic minority communities, disabled women or lesbians. They are seen as having less claim over the public realm than able-bodied, white, heterosexual women, and are thus denied the chance of an authentic selfhood in settings other than the home.
>
> (Darke 1996: 70)

This extract suggests that the home is a place of ultimate safety or sanctuary. Indeed, Darke's chapter is entitled 'The Englishwoman's castle, or, don't you just love being in control?' Darke's implicit assumption that the home is a haven is not extraordinary. Indeed, it is commonly assumed in the academic literature that the home is familial, a protected place where its inhabitants experience a sense of comfort, warmth and security. According to Heller

(1984), expressions such as '"Going home" should mean returning to that firm position which we know, to which we are accustomed, where we feel safe and where our emotional relationships are at their most intense' (quoted in Allan and Crow 1989: 7). While Allan and Crow (1989) recognise some of the contradictions inherent in the ideal of absolute freedom characterised by Heller, and cite the regulation of children by parents as evidence of this, the general tone of their inquiry emphasises harmony rather than distress. This is not to say that there do not exist popular images of the home as a deeply discredited and dangerous place, as Hockey (Chapter 12) demonstrates through her exploration of 'Houses of Doom'.

While much of the sociological literature on home emphasises characteristics of harmony and personal control over their environment, there is now much evidence to demonstrate that the home is a gendered environment where women's options can be seriously restricted. These constraints can include social isolation (Tivers 1988; Roberts 1991), economic dependence (Barker and Allen 1976; Gamarnikow et al. 1983; Finch 1983) and inequalities in the exercise of domestic labour (see Chapters 5 and 13). Similarly, in the case of women who are abused by men whom they know, the home is a place over which they have little control. Consequently, women develop strategies for self-protection which involve attempts to predict and adapt to what is essentially an unpredictable environment. While Allan and Crow's (1989) assertion that the home may be a creative and fulfilling arena – a place for the expression of domestic creativity and style – this image does not sit comfortably with the evidence of intimidation, persecution and fear which pervades many households. The realities of domestic violence contradict the ideals of home and family. Furthermore, they do not sit easily with the political and social views on crime and the dangers to personal safety. The home is the most common site of assault, its very fixtures, fabrics and furnishings – the desired items of consumption – which in reality are the most frequent weapons utilised in the violence (Walker and McNicol 1994). This research reports that kitchen knives, crockery, glasses, household and garden tools as well as items of furniture are among those used.

If we turn to crime prevention literature and strategies developed in Britain since the 1970s, however, home emerges, not as a place of danger, but as a space vulnerable to predatory invasion. Its protection is ensured via a range of practical and personal measures which amount to the fortification of the home. The more that home is constructed as space vulnerable to incursions from a threatening external world – where even the people delivering the milk and post or the health visitor may be villainous imposters – the less evident the interpersonal dangers within domestic space become. What therefore emerges is fortified city, where the public space is disciplined to an unprecedented degree, monitored by video and private security firms, private police guarding the entry to private roadways and gated sections of the city. In the United States, some homes become 'high tech castles' in the search for 'absolute security'. Here the boundary between architecture and law enforcement is eroded. Mike Davis suggests that few buildings are constructed in 'downtown' Los Angeles without the advice and guidance of the Los Angeles Police Department (*Times Literary Supplement*, 30 April 1993). The result is a 'seamless continuity of surveillance' over daily life, the home monitored by cameras, the body guarded by personal panic buttons and the public space watched by private forces and video cameras (Davis 1990, 1992b).

Similar developments can be traced in Britain (Oc and Tiesdell 1997). As in the United States, the construction of public space as a source of external threat opens up a market to be filled by private security companies. While a demoralised police force has retreated both practically and psychologically from the public sphere, there is a proliferation of community self-help groups, private security firms and even vigilante groups (L. Johnston 1992). The growth of such groups and organisations, coupled with inflated anxiety over the danger of public spaces could prompt the development of 'walled cities' in the UK; according to one newspaper report, 'there are already gates across some roads in affluent parts of London which were previously open to everyone' (*Guardian*, 3 September 1994). According to Currie (1988: 284) these developments are an expression of a loss of faith in more 'social' programmes of crime prevention which attempted to alter criminal behaviour or the conditions which underpin it, a legacy of the 'nothing works' era of the 1970s. Crime prevention has become 'situational' (Heal and Laycock 1988), emphasising the responsibilities of the victim in opportunity reduction and risk management (see Chapman, Chapter 11).

A new emphasis on the private individual taking responsibility for domestic and personal safety is evidenced in the proliferation of personal safety literature and advice which has emanated from the Home Office since the mid-1980s, as well as individual police forces and campaigning groups. Women in particular have been the focus of much of this advice, as it is the female home and spaces of the community which are often portrayed as a place of implicit order under threat from outsiders. The view of crime perpetuated in literature directed towards women emphasises danger in the public realm, committed by strangers against the person or property. The advice recommends a series of strategies and behaviours which afford real and perceived safety. Making people 'feel better' about crime is central. Assumptions about what constitutes 'crime' may not however be grounded in women's experiences.

The Home Office pamphlet, *Practical Ways to Crack Crime* (1991), is now in its fourth edition and its format is duplicated in numerous other mainstream and local crime prevention literature. *Practical Ways to Crack Crime* aims to inform the public about the nature of crime as well as empower people to do something about crime against themselves, their property and their community. The booklet acknowledges the existence of high levels of fear of crime, particularly among women, and begins by suggesting that most crime is against property, not people. In so doing, it attempts to reassure the public, particularly women, that their risk of physical assault is low, and that they can reduce that risk still further by taking sensible precautions. The following precautions are suggested to women.

- Strengthen the security of houses and flats
- Draw curtains to discourage peeping Toms
- Use only a surname in the phone directory
- Keep all external doors locked and keep a phone in the bedroom
- Don't show people around the house while alone.

(Home Office 1991)

The booklet also contains advice on how to behave while in public including

- Avoid all dimly-lit short cuts
- Walk facing the traffic
- Scream and run away if a car approaches
- Don't hitch hike or accept lifts from strangers
- Cover up expensive looking jewellery
- Buy a screech alarm
- Run to a public place if you suspect you are being followed
- Phone the police – but not from a call box due to the danger of entrapment
- Always vary your jogging route and join self-defence classes.

(Home Office 1991)

The third and fourth editions of the booklet includes a section on how 'Men can help too', primarily by taking care not to 'frighten women and make them feel safer'. Thus, they should keep a distance from women in the street, not sit too near lone women on trains and remember 'that a woman on her own may feel threatened by what you think are admiring looks' (Home Office 1991: 5). Many similar self-help booklets are dedicated to women's safety such as the government produced *Violent Crime: Police Advice for Women on How to Reduce the Risks* (Home Office 1987) and *A Guide to Safer Travel* written by the Suzy Lamplugh Trust (no date). These echo the advice given in *Practical Ways to Crack Crime* and focus on the reduction of women's fears through the improvement of home security and behaviour in public places.

Local booklets have also been produced by Safer Cities Projects. Middlesbrough's booklet *Your Safety: A Matter of Our Concern* is typical in its attempt to advise on strategies of protection. This again echoes much of the Home Office advice with a few novel additions:

Every woman should take these simple precautions to improve security. Get into the habit of 'walking your beat' before you leave home. Lock every outside door and window – one lapse could put you at risk.

(Middlesbrough Safer Cities, no date: 8)

In addition women are urged to keep hands out of pockets while walking in public, to remember 'safety before style' and that 'a full skirt and sensible shoes enable you to run or defend yourself more easily. A tight skirt and stiletto heels are very restrictive' (ibid.). Unlike the Home Office publications, by page 15 Middlesbrough's booklet does acknowledge the existence of crimes such as domestic violence. However, in direct contrast to the wealth of prescriptive advice contained in other sections, here women are simply informed of the local police concern afforded to this crime. There is no mention of any strategy of protection.

Typically these booklets are littered with graphics of anxious women alone in shadowy public spaces. When the home does appear it is in the context of improved home security, fitted with additional locks, bolts and alarms. While this advice may be of some use, paradoxically, it contains a host of contradictions and may have serious unintended consequences. As Stanko (1990: 180) points out, while this information may be intended to reassure women as to their own competence in handling violence, it fails to provide any real information about prevention and adequate protection. There are numerous reasons for this. First, the booklets rely on a distorted picture of the risks facing women, the place and nature of the danger facing women both in public and private settings. As detailed earlier, women are at comparatively little risk from strangers in public spaces, compared with a higher risk of assault and violence in the private sphere. Yet there is a silence on the risk from the men they may know, and an absence of prescriptive advice for protection against this danger. In reinforcing the image of women as vulnerable from external danger, attention is entirely deflected from evidence that those most at risk are young men under 30 years of age who drink heavily and who are most likely to assault others (Zedner 1994). Furthermore, those who are at greatest risk from violence in public spaces, young men, are given no advice at all on strategies of self-preservation (Stanko 1990).

Most crucially, the emphasis on increased home security and target hardening can actually endanger the lives of women and children. Walklate (1991) suggests that the fortification of property has led to some individuals embracing the policy so effectively as to entrap themselves in their homes in the event of fire. Similarly, the findings from the South Tyneside study highlight how arsenals of home security, particularly the use of numerous locks and bolts on windows and doors, hamper swift and easy escape for women when under assault from violent partners. For women in these circumstances, it is the street rather than the home which offers a place of safety. For example, one respondent reported to us that she increased the level of home security in response to advice she had gained from a crime prevention officer after a burglary. Later she found that this increased her confinement and hampered escape when she was held at knife point by her husband. The women suffered rape and wounding inside her heavily protected front door.

Zero Tolerance campaigns

A crime prevention initiative which attempts to move beyond these contradictions is Zero Tolerance. Launched in Edinburgh in 1992, the campaign has since been adopted by many local authorities in the United Kingdom. Unlike other crime prevention campaigns, Zero Tolerance aims to raise public awareness about the nature and extent of violence against women and children. The Cleveland campaign, which was established in 1996, for example, directly challenges ideas and preconceptions about this abuse rather than prescribing advice on how to reduce what might otherwise be considered as an inevitable risk. The campaign targets the public through the use of large advertising sites on billboards, buses, bus shelters (adshels), council vans as well as distributing leaflets via doctors' surgeries, colleges, community centres and other public buildings. The campaign promotes criminalisation and non-tolerance of violence against women and children while in the long term seeks to highlight the need for both support and intervention and adequate services for victims of violence.

The Cleveland Zero Tolerance campaign has been the focus of an evaluation (Goldsack and Ridley 1998). Unlike personal safety advice which tends to conform to convention, the Zero Tolerance campaign consciously utilises images which subvert stereotypes of both the female victim and the nature of violence against women. As such, the images challenge notions of class, respectability, age and race. Significantly, the campaign often draws upon images of the 'ideal home' and uses them in stark contrast with harrowing text which explicitly details abuse and violence. For example, one poster depicts a middle-class home, ordered, respectable and comfortable, where a woman is seated in a room. The image is the cornerstone of the advertiser's trade, the home and the woman are attractive and speak of success and comfort. In seeking an understanding of the public response to this poster, one of our respondents said that 'it looks a very cosy and relaxed sort of household, with the coffee and the paper on the floor'. But the text reveals a different story. It reads as follows: 'She lives with a successful businessman. Last week he hospitalised her'.

Results from the evaluation of this campaign suggest that the contradictory messages of the image and the text, home-sweet-home and violent attack, were irreconcilable for some respondents. They could not dislodge their preconceptions of the typical victim:

She looks so happy, it's all ordered, she's calm and everything is in place. To me it looks like an advert for fires or furniture. To make me notice it would need to be more graphic, perhaps with a picture of her in hospital I mean, it says he hospitalised her last week but you can't see any marks. What exactly did he do to her? The picture doesn't relate to the message at all.

(male aged 25–44)

Seems a bit incongruous, if that's the right word [that] somebody from such a background should get beaten up.

(retired male professional)

Many resisted the message through a preoccupation with the issue of respectability and blame. One younger male assumed that 'she's been naughty' while another stated:

look how innocent and that she is sitting there, what an ideal woman, but like you say, what's the background on that, what's behind the picture?

(male aged 25–44)

For some members of the public, then, the Zero Tolerance campaign is successful in confronting established stereotypes, though these were mainly women. However, for others, the juxtaposition of the 'normal home' with domestic violence serves to reinforce deeply entrenched ideas about the home, crime and gender relationships.

Conclusion

Popular notions of home and personal security, like ideal images of the home, are fraught with contradictions. This chapter explores a crime prevention literature which actually masks the evidence that for men the greatest risk of violence exists in public spaces, while for women, the risk is in the private domain of the home. As shown, both ideal images and crime prevention policy reinforce the insulation of the private sphere of the home in a way which endangers the lives of its occupants. While the advice given is well meaning, it rests upon distortions about the most likely risks which both men and women encounter. In not acknowledging the wider risks facing women, detailed by various studies, this crime prevention advice insinuates that a change in feelings and attitudes is comparable to offering women real protection from crime.

In sum, there is evidence that the advice women are given increases their vulnerability to attack. For Hanmer and Saunders (1983: 43) the emphasis on public crime undoubtedly increases anxiety about the public sphere, forcing a retreat to the home to seek safety. This in turn encourages a dependence on individual men for protection and an isolation from other people. This fear of public abuse can lead to a loss and restriction of public participation and ironically, a greater dependency on those men they know who may be the greatest source of danger. Attempts to shed light on the private sphere through such campaigns as Zero Tolerance reveal the deep-rootedness of images of the 'ideal home' and the secure life lived within it. For some the displacement of the ideal with the real is long overdue, while for others, public declarations as to the violent and abusive nature of many homes cannot be believed without graphic images of bruises and blame.

11

SPOILED HOME IDENTITIES
The experience of burglary

Tony Chapman

'Home' is one of the most evocative and comforting words in the English language. It produces, at least in its idealised form, notions of safety, comfort, privacy, individuality and communion with a family. However, as shown by Fairhurst and Hockey (Chapters 8 and 9), the supposed permanence or autonomous control over home is undermined in old age as family members and professionals progressively impose definitions of an appropriate way for a person to live. Goldsack (Chapter 10) has shown that for many people, the home can represent quite the opposite of this: instead of a haven, it is a site of intimidation and violence. Indeed, Hockey (Chapter 12) explores the notion of the house as the focus of imagined or supernatural terrors.

This chapter develops our understanding of the meaning of home by considering the importance of the spatial boundaries around the home and the importance of the artefacts that we accumulate within it. Making observations about the importance of space and things can sometimes lead to anodyne or platitudinous celebration of the home. One of the reasons for this is that the sheer familiarity of home makes it difficult for people to recognise the depth of meaning it represents. The event of burglary, however, reveals the crucial importance of objects and boundaries for the way in which people construct an image of 'home' and their own sense of self identity. By exploring the impact of the intrusive act of the burglar, it is possible to demonstrate the fragility of the notions of permanence, safety and privacy that are central to the construction of home.

The home and the presentation of self

There is much debate among philosophers, psychologists and sociologists around the concept of self identity (A. Cohen 1994; Giddens 1991; Goffman 1969; Jenkins 1996). In these studies much attention is given to the behaviour of individuals in the public world where people project their identities through the style of their clothes, the exercise of cultural know-how, their deportment and form of talk. But often, theorists neglect the importance of 'houses' and the 'objects' within them for people's conception and projection of their 'selves'. At risk of stating the obvious, it is argued here that people's investment in their homes is extremely significant for the projection and realisation of self identity. One important reason why people make such an investment in their home is simply stated: because they hope to create a sphere where they have control over their environment – to mould it to their own needs of comfort and security, style and personal morality. As Hepworth (Chapter 2) demonstrated, people's need to control their environment derives from their perception that the world 'outside' is unstable, insecure and beyond an individual's control; a view that is socially and historically specific.

While the home may be regarded as a private place, a retreat from the confusion and dangers that lie without, there exist common patterns of domestic organisation, gendered expectations of roles, broad fashions in decoration and furnishing, and so on. Consequently, most people carefully organise their homes to give a favourable and predictable impression of themselves to significant people in their lives who may come to visit. While it is the case that people feel constrained to present appropriate images of themselves to the world through the home, householders enjoy a degree of control over the way that images are projected in order to preserve their privacy and security. As Goffman argued in *The Presentation of Self in Everyday Life* (1969), householders can present positive images of themselves in carefully orchestrated performances. This performance may require it of the householder to conceal certain aspects of everyday behaviour by establishing a carefully contrived stage set which may involve the bringing out of the best tea set, presenting an image of excessive tidiness, and by encouraging children to behave more politely than might normally be expected. Goffman makes it clear that the same space can take on an entirely different character, depending on the kind of performance that is taking place:

> of a Sunday morning, a whole household can use the wall around its domestic establishment to conceal a relaxing slovenliness in dress and civil endeavour, extending to all rooms the informality that is usually restricted to the kitchen and bedrooms.
>
> (Goffman 1969: 128)

Goffman defines this as 'backstage' behaviour, which is free from the scrutiny of significant others, while the former example of the tea party clearly represents 'front stage' performance. In both cases, householders use practised forms of behaviour and symbols to project or protect themselves much in the same way that clothes can be used as a form of display as well as a shield for the person wearing them (E. Wilson 1985). While many people are deeply concerned about upsetting their families, friends and neighbours by being too far out of the ordinary (see Chapter 15), it is the case that every householder wishes to mark out their 'territory' to some extent with objects or patterns of decoration that reflect their 'personality'.

For example, people mark their territory with cultural symbols of ownership, such as the low garden wall, picket fence or wrought iron gateway. These symbolic markers of personal space are easy enough to traverse physically, but serve to represent meaningful cultural boundaries that are expected to deter strangers. The threshold of the house serves a similar purpose, with the often powerful imagery of cast-iron door 'furniture' that provides a message of strength and impenetrability. In a similar fashion, an elaborate, personalised nameplate gives messages about ownership – that this is a private, not a public place (B. Brown and Altman 1983).

Within the household, cultural boundaries are carefully preserved. Some are marked off by doors to delineate the 'front region' from the private 'back regions' of the house where people prepare themselves for view in the public front space, or food is prepared for serving in the public rooms. Most people are strongly affected by the social pressures imposed upon them by the attitudes and tastes of their family, neighbours and friends. Other influences also come into play, especially in the way we project the organisation of the household to comply with the perceived expectations of professionals who come into our houses including doctors, social workers, health visitors and midwives. The expectations of others often bring people into line with wider social expectations – albeit temporarily.

At another level of analysis, we must consider the importance of the many objects in the household that collectively represent images of our affluence, our cultural and social position in society and our taste. Some writers have gone as far as to say that these objects actually constitute a representation of the 'self'.

> The objects of the household represent, at least potentially, the endogenous being of the owner. Although one has little control over the things encountered out-side the home, household objects are chosen and could be freely discarded if they produced too much conflict within the self. Thus household objects constitute an ecology of signs that reflects as well as *shapes* the pattern of the owner's self.
>
> (Csikszentmihalyi and Rochberg-Halton 1981: 17)

Indeed, attempts to analytically separate the *object* from the *person* can, on occasions, border on the ridiculous.

> A slogan of the gun lobby is; 'Guns don't kill people, people do.' The neutrality of the object is assumed; people's intentions will be carried out independently of the things they use. Needless to say, our position implies the opposite conclusion. There are no 'people' in the abstract, people are what they attend to, what they cherish and use.

> A person who has a gun in his or her house is by that fact different
> from the one who does not.
>
> (Csikszentmihalyi and Rochberg-Halton 1981: 16)

However, objects may not be valued in the same way by different people in a household and the meanings that individuals attach to objects can change over time. An old-fashioned typewriter may be a beautiful ornament to one person, or an irritating dust-trap to another. Much negotiation between family members revolves around the purchase, placement and retention of objects between family members. These negotiations are coloured by the taste, functionality, priority and cost of goods among other things – and in married couples, agreeing entirely on all of these factors would be an unlikely prospect. Similarly, people are constrained to hold onto objects they dislike because it may hurt the feelings of the gift giver, although they may put disliked gifts on display only for the duration of the giver's visit. In every household, there must be something which is on relatively prominent display which at least one member of the household wholeheartedly despises and is constantly injured by whenever it comes into view.

In a similar vein, artefacts may be hidden away when they no longer have any immediate practical purpose. Korosec-Serfaty (1984), following the work of Bachelard (1958), explores the way that people move objects around the house. Attics, lofts and cellars are the depositories for articles such as prams, baby walkers, cots, play houses and baby toys, all of which lose their usefulness as householders move through the life course. Things may also be moved out of the way because they have become unfashionable and give out the wrong messages to ourselves and our family and friends. For people who are highly conscious of style, taste can become a kind of tyranny, as they try to keep ahead of the rest rather than just following on with the crowd (see also Bourdieu 1986; Dittmar 1992).

Moving beyond Korosec-Serfaty, it may be the case that artefacts are also moved around for less practical or aesthetic reasons, because they embody secret meanings. Take for example a special gift received from a lover. When love is new, a gift is a crucial representation of that fondness. It is a visual and evocative symbol of the intense chemistry of a relationship and as a consequence it is likely to take pride of place on the mantelpiece for the whole world to see. When that love is lost, and replaced with the love of another, the artefact can suddenly become an awkward cue, albeit a secret one. So it is moved somewhere less central, perhaps out of the principal room, or maybe behind a curtain. The sense of hurt or injustice which the artefact reproduces might ultimately lead to its removal to the loft. Out of sight, it is a less threatening symbol, but too valuable in some way to completely discard. Years later, when long-time married and up in the loft seeking out some other object, a box is opened and out comes that gift together with a whole raft of memories. Feelings of love for the person who gave it may not now exist, but it might, all the same, be a good time to bring it downstairs again, and put it back on the mantelpiece, not just because it is attractive, but because is it a reminder of the time when *other* people loved us – a secret symbol of the possibility of someone else's love. (For more analysis on the significance of gifts, see Cheal 1987; Bell and Newby 1976; Mauss 1954.)

In summary, it is clear that the space that we call home, its physical and cultural boundaries and the objects that lie within it are all important signifiers of self. The home, taken as a whole, can be used as a social 'front', that is, a medium through which we project images of ourselves. As Goffman (1969) shows, the home is a place where people establish a stage set for social encounters with the express intention of letting other people see them in their best light. This is not to say that people can be certain that the way they present themselves and their homes to others will necessarily give the impression and elicit the response they want to achieve. Whether they achieve it or not is not the point; instead, the central idea being stated here is that the process of presenting an image demonstrates that people make strong personal investment in domestic space. It has also been shown in the first section of this chapter that *things* are crucial in shaping the meanings of home because they embody and reflect the householder's self. It is a position which, therefore, puts people at risk.

Thus, people's association with their own space and the objects within it can be disrupted in a number of ways. Marriage and divorce, the arrival of intolerable neighbours, the death of a partner, serious subsidence or the digging of an open-cast mine in the locality – all represent important life events or disturbances that force a renegotiation of spatial use and a reconsideration of the value of the house and its objects. All of these examples of disruption deserve full discussion in their own right, but given the constraints of space, just one example will be given – the experience of burglary – which, through its shocking and sudden character, causes an immediate re-evaluation of the meaning of things and space and, of course, the transformation of the image of home from one of private sanctity to deep insecurity.

The incidence and impact of burglary

Burglary is a common way in which the household is disrupted by an external force. As Table 11.1 suggests, the incidence of burglary has increased substantially in England and Wales between 1981 and 1995, as have the numbers of other property crimes, although the levels have dropped in Scotland and Northern Ireland. This rise in the level of burglary must contribute to the high levels of fear of crime reported in Table 11.2. Public fear of crime may be compounded by the low clear-up rate for burglaries. In England and Wales the clear-up rate was 30 per cent, but this had dropped to only 21 per cent in

Table 11.1 Crimes against property in the UK 1981 and 1995 (thousands)

	England and Wales		Scotland		Northern Ireland	
	1981	1995	1981	1995	1981	1995
Burglary	718	1,239	92	74	20	16
Criminal damage	387	914	62	87	5	4
Theft[a]	1,603	2,542	201	222	25	33
Theft of cars	333	508	33	38	5	8
Theft from cars	380	813	–	71	7	7

Note:
[a] All theft and handling of stolen goods including car crime.
Source: Social Trends (1995: 155, Table 9.4).

1995. The pattern of sentencing for convicted burglars may also contribute to public perceptions of the risk of crime. In Britain, 38 per cent of the 36,000 convicted burglars gained custodial sentences in 1995, while 43 per cent obtained community service orders and 7 per cent were fined (*Social Trends* 1997: 161).

According to the International Crime Victimisation Survey, England and Wales are the most security-conscious countries in the industrialised world with more than three-quarters of homes with burglar alarms, special door locks or grilles on doors and windows. This compares with less than 42 per cent of homes in Sweden, Austria, Northern Ireland, Switzerland and Finland with one or more of these three security devices. Public awareness of this risk has been extensively researched and it has been shown that more than 9 per cent of people in England and Wales believed that a break-in was very probable in the next year; comparable figures for the United States and France are 4.4 per cent and 5.0 per cent respectively (*Guardian*, 17 May 1997).

Burglary has a sudden and dramatic impact on people's perception of the meaning of home and its contents and their sense of security. Furthermore, the crime leads to a re-evaluation of their relationship with strangers, neighbours and the outside world in general. Research demonstrates that

Table 11.2 Fear of property crime in Britain 1996 (percentages)

	Men				Women			
	16–29	30–59	60+	All	16–29	30–59	60+	All
Theft of car	28	23	19	23	30	26	22	26
Theft from car	26	20	16	20	22	21	16	20
Burglary	18	18	18	18	27	26	25	26

Source: Social Trends (1997: 157, Table 9.9).

much of this emotional disturbance derives from the common belief among people that their house will not be burgled. Korosec-Serfaty (1986) has demonstrated that the occurrence of burglary is necessarily unexpected, because people commonly believe that it will not happen to them. The surprise factor takes on a number of forms. The first surprise is that most burglaries take place during the day, not at night as is commonly expected, and they occur on 'ordinary' days not after a weekend away or a holiday. The evidence suggest that the vast majority of burglaries are 'opportunistic' events rather than a calculated and rational criminal act (Cromwell et al. 1991; Maguire 1982). Although there is no space here to explore the motivations of burglars (see Wright and Decker 1994), it is clear that they engage in a process of risk assessment while targeting a house. Consequently, most prefer to break into empty houses or take advantage of open doors or windows rather than making forced entries. There is indeed considerable evidence to suggest that most burglaries are opportunistic and come as a result of the carelessness of the householder.

Another surprise for the victim is that neighbours may have seen the burglars, but did not suspect them because they looked like ordinary people. The children's story book character, Burglar Bill, under the cover of darkness in striped shirt, mask and beret, with a swag bag over his back (Ahlberg and Ahlberg 1977), is a comical but enduring image that has a strong presence in the adult psyche. But as Cromwell et al. (1991) have shown, burglars make strong efforts to look as normal as possible by, for instance, wearing jogging gear, pretending to be house hunters and so on. In their study, they report on one burglar who took her 2 year old child with her to people's front doors to ask for a glass of water, and would commit a theft while they were in the kitchen. Experienced burglars may adopt complex social performances to conceal their real intention.

> The more experienced burglars stated that it was important to fit into a neighbourhood or situation. They attempted to make their presence in a neighbourhood seem normal and natural. The most professional of the burglars in our study, Robert, always drove a car that fit the neighbourhood's socioeconomic level or a van disguised as a delivery vehicle. He dressed befitting the circumstances as a plumber, deliveryman, or businessman. He would walk to the door of a potential target residence, open the screen door, and unobtrusively hold it open with his foot while he pantomimed a conversation with a non-existent person inside . . . if the door was locked, he pantomimed a conversation that appeared to instruct him to go around to the backyard . . . To possible onlookers, he had knocked on the door, talked with the owner, and, following instructions, had gone to the rear of the house on some legitimate errand.
>
> (Cromwell et al. 1991: 36)

As Korosec-Serfaty (1986: 333) shows, when the notion that burglary happens only to other people is contradicted by reality, 'the question "why us?" arises. It is then an enquiry about oneself, about what, in one's home, might be coveted by others, about one's image and the messages of vulnerability emitted by the house itself'. The fact that the burglar is unlikely to be caught and is inevitably unknown (in spite of our suspicions!) also has an important impact not only on people's confidence in security but also in their reconstruction of the crime and the criminal.

> While some continued to envisage a frightening stranger (typically employing terms such as 'rough', scruffy', or 'unemployed' when asked to describe their mental picture of him), on reflection more than half came to suspect that the burglar was 'somebody local' who knew them, or was familiar with their habits. On the whole, the latter conclusion was more likely to prolong the worry caused by the incident. Victims tended to re-interpret small events in the past – arguments with neighbours, visits to the house, prying questions, etc.
>
> (Maguire 1982: 126)

Korosec-Serfaty (1986) also shows that many of her respondents wish to believe that the crime was committed by opportunist youngsters rather than by a professional thief in order to relieve themselves of the possibility of having been specifically targeted or at risk of repeat victimisation.

Also in the process of building an image of the burglar, the victim assesses both what has and what has not been stolen. Korosec-Serfaty shows that respondents are surprised when articles that *they* value are not valued by the burglar. This makes the crime seem 'gratuitous' and presents an image of the burglar as neither 'greedy' nor 'brutal' and therefore, perversely, 'enigmatic' (Korosec-Serfaty 1986: 334). When vandalism has occurred, the sense of a personal act of aggression is so great that victims prefer to make sense of this crime in terms of a stereotypical view of burglars in general rather than the actual thief who carried out the act.

The sense of mistrust that burglary victims may project onto their neighbours and outsiders can subsequently be redirected back onto themselves by the representatives and procedures of insurance companies, to whom they must demonstrate proper resistance to criminal penetration and verify their losses. As one of Korosec-Serfaty's (1986: 335) respondents stated, 'It's almost as if, in the eyes of the insurance companies, you're no more than a thief yourself'. Parents also feel weakened by the action of burglary, because it has been demonstrated that the boundaries of the home which they have promised were secure are not safe. Parents are, then, revealed as 'victims' rather than 'guardians' in the eyes of their own children.

Reconsideration of the safety and security of the home

The shock of burglary, it has been shown, leads to a fundamental reconsideration of the safety of the boundaries of home. Just as importantly, the order of the household is disrupted and its contents polluted by the attention of a stranger. A child of one of Korosec-Serfaty's respondents worried that the burglar may have lain down on her bed: that the security and privacy of her bed had been spoiled by his presence. The disruption also throws into sharp relief the value of those objects whose meanings have been overlooked or underestimated over time. The full extent of the impact of this disorder may take a long time to manifest itself as the victim discovers what has been defiled or stolen. Korosec-Serfaty explains the consequences of this in the following terms:

> The individual lives with the holistic feeling of his coherence, but the burglary makes him realise that he has been, this time, victimised by the illusion of his coherence. He is thus made to acknowledge the vulnerability of the construction of self.
>
> (Korosec-Serfaty 1986: 336)

Because treasured objects can become intrinsically associated with self identity, burglary has a striking impact on an individual's deeply rooted sense of security and place. This is demonstrated when victims of burglary show relief when only money is stolen instead of treasured objects that have strong sentimental associations with the past, especially those which have been inherited from other family members and provide intergenerational anchors on self identity.

Finally, the loss of secrecy through the act of burglary has a fundamental impact on victims' sense of place. Three respondents from Maguire's (1982) study made the following comments:

> I shall never forget it because my privacy has been invaded. I have worked hard all my life and had my nose to the grindstone ever since and this happens. Now we can't live in peace. I have a feeling of 'mental rape'. I feel a dislocation and disruption of private concerns. I have destroyed everything they touched. I feel so extreme about it.
>
> I'll never get over the thought that a stranger has been in here while we were in bed . . . the idea that a stranger, who could be one of those horrible revolting creatures, has been mauling my things about.
>
> They had gone through all my clothes. I felt a real repulsion – everything felt dirty. I wanted to move – I had nightmares, and it still comes back even now.
>
> (Maguire 1982: 128)

As one respondent from Korosec-Serfaty's study stated:

> they've violated our privacy, those people who came here, we feel a
> bit frustrated, we think, but . . . hey, they've seen . . . seen things
> which belong to us, which are, if you like, our little secrets, that's
> nobody's business, we don't talk about them to anyone . . . that's it,
> it's this side of it, rather than what they took off with, I'd say.
>
> (Korosec-Serfaty 1986: 339)

Having a burglar rifling through personal objects, like drawers of clothes, bed
linen or beds themselves, provoke strong responses of invasion and defilement
from victims resulting in rigorous exercises in cleaning, reordering and throw-
ing out of polluted items. People who have experienced burglary tend to
'harden' the physical boundaries of their home by installing burglar alarms, fitting locks or grilles; but more importantly, perhaps, they harden their attitude
towards 'outsiders', so indicating a withdrawal or lessening of trust in neighbours and strangers in general. (See O. Newman 1972 and Coleman 1985 for
a discussion of the controversial notion of 'defensible space'.) Discouraging
burglars can involve a number of initiatives, including the installation of
security systems, avoiding high boundary fences which help the burglar conceal themselves, producing illusions of occupancy and avoiding conspicuous
displays of affluence. Other factors that discourage burglars involve, where
possible, the co-operation (or at least visibility) of neighbours, noisy dogs and
children playing in the street and so on (Cromwell et al. 1991; Bennett and
Wright 1984).

Factors like the introduction of alarms will not deter all burglars, of course,
as Cromwell et al. (1991) show.

> A professional burglar advised that he did not care whether a house
> had an alarm or not. He would go ahead and enter and begin to
> gather the goods he planned to steal. He said that after about five
> minutes the telephone would ring (the alarm company calling to verify
> the alarm). After the call, he stated that he had 5 to 15 minutes
> before someone arrived.
>
> (Cromwell et al. 1991: 29)

This was unusual though, since alarms do generally act as a deterrent and most
burglars are opportunistic. As a consequence of the increase in burglaries and
the heightened fear of the crime, the development, production and aggressive
marketing of goods and services for household security has boomed since the
late 1970s. Manufacturers now provide a wide range of defensive items including burglar alarms of various levels of sophistication, mini closed-circuit television (CCTV) systems to monitor front doors on home television sets, a

range of grilles and shutters for doors and windows, together with security boundary fencing; increasingly, more wealthy areas use security patrols (Davis 1990, 1992a, 1992b).

Awareness of the threat of burglary has also been raised in schemes like the British Neighbourhood Watch programme, which was promoted by government to encourage neighbourhood surveillance and a local representative to work with the police. There is evidence to suggest that Neighbourhood Watch schemes can help reduce crime, but on the negative side they may also stimulate fear of crime, perhaps beyond the level of actual risk.

Integrated police and community action has also been shown to be effective in combating burglary. In Wales one study has demonstrated that reductions of up to 40 per cent in burglaries could be achieved by employing Crime Prevention Officers (CPOs) to encourage target hardening, property marking, using publicity to raise awareness of the scheme (especially to potential burglars), together with direct police action including co-ordinated searches of suspected burglars and handlers, and finally, improved investigation and detection by using informers, spreading best practice and employing better forensic techniques (Stockdale and Gresham 1995).

One central problem with target hardening, however, is that people tend not to take the issue seriously until it is too late – after they have been burgled – because they do not believe that it is going to happen to them (Laycock 1989). Target hardening is particularly important after a burglary, however, as rates of repeat victimisation is a common occurrence. As D. Anderson *et al.* (1995) have shown, for example, from a study of Huddersfield, of 3,941 burglaries committed during the period of research, there were 927 suspected cases of repeat victimisation (23.5 per cent). Furthermore, the research estimated that up to 200 out of 262 repeat victimisations could have been prevented if a CPO had acted on the initial incident quickly enough. In some cases, however, nothing seems to stop offenders, as the following example suggests.

> This retired couple moved to a bungalow with a nice garden at the rear, overlooking playing fields . . . Not long after moving in they had their first burglary. Entry was made by the patio door, so they purchased a new door (stronger than the first). Entry was again made by the patio door, so they purchased an alarm. Burglars attempted to gain entry again through this door and were stopped only because they were disturbed. The couple then purchased a 'tremble' alarm connected to the patio doors. This was so sensitive that even when the glass was touched the alarm was triggered. The garage was broken into – so they built a new garage. A front window was attacked – so they changed all the windows to small top opening ones. The side door was attacked – so they purchased a new seven lever lock door.

The house is now like (to quote) Fort Knox, but the offenders, not to be outdone, stole the satellite dish from the roof!

(D. Anderson *et al.* 1995: 16–17)

Taken to its extreme point, the protection of property can, ultimately, make the street all the more frightening as people progressively turn their houses into fortresses that no longer have an aspect on the public world (Davis 1990, 1992a, 1992b). As Vergara (1994), who has researched the urban ghettos of the United States, has argued:

> Fortification has profound consequences. Where defences are aggres-sively displayed they create bizarre, shunned streetscapes of distorted survivors and ruined losers . . . A world defined by security guards and razor-ribbon wire, by streets, hallways and nights that don't belong to you . . . The time spent opening and closing so many locks and gates, connecting and disconnecting alarms, nervously looking over one's shoulder, feeding guard dogs and explaining one's business to security personal can become exhausting.
>
> (Vergara 1994: 47)

The take up of the services of CPOs tends to be highest among the most afflu-ent home owners, but this is not to suggest that they face the highest risk. Indeed, as Table 11.3 demonstrates, burglaries are heavily concentrated in par-ticular residential areas. The most problematic areas in Britain include the poorest local authority housing estates where a cycle of neighbourhood decline can establish itself (Lund 1996).

In the United States, Vergara (1995) reports on inner cities in crisis. His analysis is salient in demonstrating the potentially isolating mentality that a preoccupation with security can produce – physically barricading people from each other and engendering lack of trust and a heightened fear of crime. The consequences of this for perceptions of the sanctity of the home are clearly negative. Hardening the boundaries of home may act as a deterrent to burgla-ries therefore (B. Brown and Altman 1983), but may also harden attitudes to the outside world to such an extent that the protection of property becomes more important than the symbiotic relationship between people and things that is essential for the projection of self identity.

Conclusion

This chapter has shown that burglary can cause tremendous personal distress to householders. This distress derives both from a sense that the private space of the home has been defiled through the burglar's invasion and because of the theft of objects of value. In legal terms, objects carry specific monetary values, and a well-phrased insurance claim can command a higher financial

Table 11.3 Relative risk of burglary in England and Wales 1994

	Burglary entry	Burglary attempt	All
Low risk			
Agricultural areas	30	10	20
Better-off retirement areas	70	65	65
Modern family housing higher income areas	60	70	65
Affluent suburban housing	80	55	70
Older housing of intermediate status	70	70	70
Medium risk			
Better-off council estates	100	90	95
Older terraced housing	115	110	115
Less well-off council estates	130	175	150
High risk			
Mixed inner metropolitan areas	205	150	180
High-status non-family areas	240	200	20
Poorest council estates	255	330	285
Indexed national average	100	100	100

Source: Tilley and Webb (1994: 1).

reward than the actual value of the stolen objects. But when some objects are stolen, monetary remuneration is no compensation, because they represent a 'priceless' embodiment of our self. Burglary in this sense can 'spoil' the identity of a home because it may be possible neither to feel fully secure at home again, nor to eradicate the feeling that the house has been in some sense permanently sullied.

While this chapter has focused on the event of burglary, its main purpose has been to demonstrate in theoretical terms how the fabric of a house, its internal space and its contents come to embody the self identity of the people who live there. The shocking nature of burglary brings into sharp relief the sense of permanence which people feel about their homes. But of course, burglary is but one way in which that sense of permanence can be disrupted. Other life events, including geographical migration, social mobility, divorce, marital violence, the death of a partner or an inability to look after ourselves or our home as we become older can all have a similarly devastating impact on our perception of home (see Chapters 6, 8, 9 and 10). Other unforeseen events, such as the arrival of 'neighbours from hell' or the building of a bypass or housing estate in the near vicinity, can be equally distressing. Sometimes we spoil our own sense of home identity, temporarily at least, by moving home. Moving home is often regarded as one of the most stressful life transitions. A creative use of the theoretical ideas presented in this chapter helps to explain why. I have not, then, been concentrating on the negative impact of burglary on the home merely to alarm or depress readers. Instead, the purpose of the analysis has been to defamiliarise the home so that we can make sense of it. That analysis is necessary because it helps to explain how people *gain* deep personal attachment to their homes without, paradoxically, recognising the *process* by which that sense of attachment comes about. Further, I have tried to show how people's absolute sense of familiarity with their home may actually conceal its fundamental importance to them: its value lies below the surface until, that is, its identity is spoiled.

12

HOUSES OF DOOM

Jenny Hockey

> The house shelters day-dreaming, the house protects the dreamer,
> the house allows one to dream in peace.
>
> (Bachelard [1958] 1994: 6)

Throughout his work on the poetics of space, Bachelard returns repeatedly to the image of the house as a space of safety, a protection from external dangers, from storms on winter nights. However frail and vulnerable the individual might be, bricks and mortar provide them with a nest, a sanctuary, a place to retire to. This chapter examines Bachelard's notion of the house as a space of shelter and peace, but it does so via another kind of house, the fabric of which entraps nightmares rather than nurturing dreams. When we dare to enter the House of Doom, we learn much about the ideal home.

The House of Doom is viewed by night-time. It has flapping casements, impossibly pitched roofs and gables, and deep shadows behind dense shrubberies. Its floors creak and its draperies are rotten. The debris of interrupted meals litters table tops and vermin scuttle behind the wainscoting. Like the seductive dream shell conjured by Bachelard, the House of Doom also yields pleasure. We visit it in fairgrounds and in horror movies. We relish its capacity to thrill us. In its own way the House of Doom is an ideal home. While the show house reminds us how family life should be lived, displaying the spatiality of our required activities and social divisions in dining rooms, lounges and bathrooms, in parents' spaces and children's spaces, public rooms and private rooms (see Chapman, Chapter 4), the House of Doom allows us to safely rehearse our terror of demons which, like God, are all-seeing and inescapable – the ghosts of unknown previous occupants. While the show home persuades us that an investment of money, time and effort can ensure our security, the House of Doom confirms our direst sense of personal vulnerability. Located in fairground or carnival we confront our terrors in their proper context, as a source of fun, farce and hysteria.

However fantastically the House of Doom is represented in the liminal space of the grotesque and the carnivalesque, it sometimes breaks out of the fairground to surface within the 'real' world of news reporting. In June 1997,

147

for example, the *Hull Daily Mail* reported the existence of a 'horror house' on one of Bridlington's council estates. Under the front page headline 'Curse of the Evil Home', the paper described how the influence of the home's previous tenant, convicted killer Michelle Nicholson, had blighted the life of its current occupant, Debbie Plaxton. Debbie's partner's suicide, her own depressive illness and the rape and murder of her mother had hardened her resolve to leave the house which had 'brought her nothing but bad luck'. Evil is therefore not seen to be confined to the moment, nor to the individual who is its victim or its perpetrator. It cannot be distanced to the 'other', but acquires its own agency and settles in the ordinary bricks and mortar of the council house.

A space of one's own

This inclusion of a chapter on Houses of Doom within a collection such as this might seem to be either a morsel of bloodthirsty titillation or a passage of light relief. My argument, however, is that the House of Doom plays an important part, not only in defining the nature and boundaries of the ideal home but also – for the social scientist – in highlighting the less rational or evidently materialistic aspects of home life. Over and above the practical aspects of shelter, warmth and storage, or the social aspects of consumption and personal display, the home, as lived in on a day-to-day basis, plays an important role in identity formation. Here I am not talking about self-image-making via the choice between IKEA, Waring and Gillow or industrial salvage. Rather I am setting western patterns of home, home building and home making within the context of their cross-cultural counterparts in order to find out how ideas about home might play a part in the western experience of the self.

In his anthropology of the British, Barley (1990) highlights the peculiar centrality of the home for notions of self. He makes a comparison with the identities of Indonesian hill tribespeople which are tied up with 'the glorious ancestral houses that their ancestors derived from' and not 'the modest houses' in which they actually live. Bloch (1971) offers a parallel example from among the Merina of Madagascar. Here the tombs of ancestors are 'the most solid and best built structures which the Merina undertake and the land on which they stand is inalienable'; yet they are inhabited only after death (Bloch 1971: 112). Barley (1990) goes on to describe the puzzlement of Indonesian hill tribespeople that the English should value their homes so highly, yet spend so few of their waking hours at home because they are always out at work earning money to pay the mortgage. For these tribespeople, like the Merina, the housing of death is more important than the housing of life. Nonetheless there is a commonality here. Like the English, the Merina are prepared to pay for that which provides the core of their identity. The tomb which is never home to the live Merina still remains 'far and away the greatest enterprise a Merina ever undertakes' (Bloch 1971: 114). Bloch shows that, for the Merina, rank, attachment to a fixed social order and attachment to kin are intimately bound up with these ancestral tombs and the land upon which they are built. To settle elsewhere is to be a 'guest' or 'stranger', even across four or five generations. When it comes to the expenditure of wealth on bricks, mortar or concrete it would seem, therefore, that symbolic rather than practical concerns predominate, not only among the Merina and the hill tribespeople of Indonesia, but also among the English.

If the House of Doom is a focus for intense emotion, I would argue that this reflects the powerful parallel affective ties which link the British or western home with a sense of self. Self and home are mutually self-constituting and the notion of a deviant, haunted or somehow doom-laden home represents a profound threat to the experience of the self. Discussing Bachelard's ([1958] 1994) work on the home, Korosec-Serfaty (1984) compares the different aspects or levels of human consciousness with the regions of the house. She argues, for example, that the cellar 'corresponds to the obscure area in the consciousness of the individual, that area which participates in the collective unconsciousness', while the attic corresponds to 'the world of the conscious and the rational' (Korosec-Serfaty 1984: 306). She highlights the separation between the home's private and public spaces, pointing out that rooms such as the lounge reveal those aspects of the home owner which are socially acceptable, yet in such a way that outsiders are kept at a distance. To penetrate into the hidden spaces of cupboards, garages and cellars is to get to 'the heart of the matter', to those aspects of the home owner which are both fundamental and withheld. Cellars and attics are therefore associated with personal privacy, hidden aspects of one's autobiography, foodstuffs holed up against another season, dirt, disorder and creepy crawlies. Korosec-Serfaty (1984) argues that spaces such as these, at the lowest and uppermost boundaries of the home, help to define the limits of the self (see Chapman, Chapter 11). As I shall go on to argue, moving into a new home therefore inevitably involves entering those regions of another person's home/self which are normally kept hidden.

The interconnection of self and home is elaborated in Barley's (1990) account of the structure of the British home. Front gardens, for example, are like the human face. They are there to be looked at, but not to be sat in or hung about with washing. Similarly the front door, like the eyes and lips, is 'cosmeticised' with door furniture and heavy panelling. To venture beyond the front step, legitimately, visitors must abide by unwritten rules, depending upon who they are and why they knocked on the door. The bodily aspects of entry into the home are brought out in sexual metaphors which liken forced entry to rape. Once inside, it is again the body and its various functions which would seem to provide a model for the division of internal space. Key physical acts – eating, washing, elimination, sex – are usually carried out in rooms designated for that purpose. Eating in the bedroom is justified on the grounds of illness. Sex in the lounge or kitchen carries a frisson of danger as a 'private' act is carried out in 'public' space. However, to be found eating in space reserved for defecation – or even drinking a cup of tea while seated on the toilet – can arouse feelings of shame, rather than just embarrassment.

What this chapter argues is that the structure and use of the English home reveals much about how the self is conceptualised, and particularly about the nature of its relationships with others. While the Indonesian hill tribespeople and the Madagascan Merina both derive their sense of self from their attachment to dead ancestors, westerners attain full personhood by *separating* themselves from others, from their parents and their parental home (see Kenyon, Chapter 7) and from the members of other families. Thus to acquire a first home signals the attainment of adulthood. Moving out of shared accommodation – a bed-sit, a bed and breakfast hostel, a student house – marks one out as independent, both socially and economically and, again, in possession of full adult status. Those who share accommodation frequently feel personally undermined, if not sullied, by flatmates' dirt and disorder and resort to separate food cupboards and filling the fridge with sternly labelled items.

The potential infringement of others upon the self in this kind of living arrangement is exemplified most horrifically in the film *Shallow Grave* (1994). Here a new and unknown flatmate dies without warning, anonymously, in his locked room – a disturbing event in its own right and one that precipitates the intrusion of the other flat-dwellers into the deceased's private life. Having stolen the money which they find in his room, they dump his body after sawing off its hands to prevent identification. The flatmate who performs this operation rapidly loses his sanity, a status made evident in his retreat to the flat's attic. Socially and mentally estranged, he then invades the rooms of his other two companions at unpredictable intervals, via the holes he has drilled in the ceilings of the flat's various rooms. In a more light-hearted vein, comic television sitcoms such as *Men Behaving Badly* and *Game On* endlessly replay the joke of adults who, in failing to marry or have a family – who remain flatmates – inevitably engage in chaotic adolescent or even child-like behaviour.

While moving out of shared accommodation signals the attainment of adulthood, the move into collective living arrangements because of ill health or decrepitude – for example, into hospital or residential care – represents a threat to personhood. Repeatedly, therefore, we find bodily separation to be a key aspect of social identity in western society. Trains, for example, when they became popular in the nineteenth century, represented the threat of exposure to people of a different social class, hence the initial division of seating into three classes, one which persists in the presence of first-class carriages on all mainline trains. To gather together with other people for more than a brief interval – and to relinquish the possibility of a nightly return to the private space of the home – is an activity fraught with danger. Holidays taken with old friends or neighbours are notorious for wrecking social relationships. Cut off from retreat to the privacy of their own homes, people discover one another's 'true' natures – their 'snobbishness', their 'dirtiness' in food preparation and personal hygiene, their 'strange' timetables for eating and sleeping.

150

Hotels bring similar social problems, as evidenced in the silence of the guest-house dining room where embarrassed families crunch cornflakes in painfully close proximity. Hotel bedrooms are particularly high-risk zones and evidence of the bodily presence of previous occupants is heavily stigmatised, some hotels actually binding the cleansed toilet with a paper sash bearing words such as 'sanitised for your safety and convenience', in order to convey a sense of unsullied sterility. As Mary Douglas (1966) notes, our system of hygiene is essentially symbolic. That which we abhor as a source of pathogenic 'germs' is, more often than not, matter which has strayed from its customary place. Few of us live in sterile kitchens and bathrooms with no trace of the bodily processes of eating, washing and elimination. Yet to find food scraps or smears on cupboards and work surfaces in a new home or holiday cottage is to find 'dirt'. Similarly, even discoloration in toilets, baths and wash-hand basins raises implicit spectres of 'disease'. Hair on the head is attractive and indeed desirable. Hair discovered between hotel sheets or trapped in plug holes is repellently dirty. It is matter out of place.

The containment of the body and its processes within the private home is therefore crucial to the way in which the self is understood and experienced within Western society. It allows individuals to separate themselves from others who might compromise their claims to independent adulthood, good health, a prized social class position or a particular way of organising their leisure time – and as such is a defining characteristic of the ideal home. However, the need to separate ourselves from others, if only as a result of ageing, means moving into new homes. We leave our parents' home for our own home; we move into a new home when our children, in turn, move out. Many of us experience additional house moves during the interim period. Yet, problematically, when we engage in this kind of geographical mobility, we find ourselves exposed to spaces which have associations with other people – those who came before us.

This in part explains the attraction of newly built property, unsullied by former occupants. Nonetheless, even a new house can take on the history enacted upon the land into which its foundations are driven and to discover that one's prospective Barratt home has been built upon the site of a former graveyard, battlefield or asylum may well be sufficient grounds to deter the would-be purchaser. The ghosts of previous occupants may however be part of the attraction of pre-twentieth-century property, its price reflecting its desirability. Those long-dead people who made their home in the Georgian house, the seventeenth-century farm cottage or the Elizabethan manor house are remote, exotic beings. They represent a more idyllic, a grander or a more innocent way of life, normally accessed only indirectly via television historical dramas, yet in the purchase of such property, the aspiring home owner can appropriate the more positive aspects of their way of life.

What I am arguing, therefore, is that moving into a new home raises issues above and beyond material factors such as house size, condition or location.

We frequently deplore a previous owner's taste and rip out furnishings and decoration not on grounds of quality, but of taste (Bourdieu 1986). Equally, we expend special effort on scouring kitchens and bathrooms to remove organic waste, the invisible particles of previous owners' bodies. Whether or not we reflect on them consciously, I am arguing that practices such as cleaning and redecoration are not only matters of hygiene or aesthetics, but also the powerful symbolic acts of cleansing through which we manage our engagement with the selves of those who came before us. Without them we risk a dangerous spatial intimacy or proximity with others from whom we are separated merely by time. Moving into a new home means moving into the spaces that housed the hidden and not necessarily socially acceptable aspects of other people's lives. It is this fear, whether implicit or explicit, which animates the spectre of the House of Doom.

Pleasurable terrors

Most potently, in literary and media representations, it is those houses which offer a respectable, well-kept exterior which can turn most frighteningly upon the innocent visitor or purchaser. In other cases, we the readers or viewers may be given clear indications of the menace held by particular houses – the give-away rattling windows and dark passages – but the film's 'good' characters are frequently oblivious to either the exterior or interior decor of the immediate environment. Instead of remaining behind locked bedroom doors, vulnerable young women in night-dresses wander implausibly into dank cellars and gloomy attics, there to encounter the inevitable evidence that this is a House of Doom, haunted, infested, malevolent.

One example is to be found in Charlotte Brontë's novel *Jane Eyre*, which was first published in 1847. From Brontë's descriptions, Thornfield Hall, the home of Jane Eyre's employer, Mr Rochester, is a five-star House of Doom. On arrival Jane finds it 'a pretty place', yet gives the reader hints of its future frightening prospects:

> The steps and banisters were oak; the staircase window was high and latticed; both it and the long gallery into which the bedroom doors opened looked as if they belonged to a church rather than a house. A very chill and vault-like air pervaded the stairs and the gallery, suggesting cheerless ideas of space and solitude.
>
> (Brontë [1847] 1960: 100)

Later Jane is given a tour of the Hall and again a sense of menace is evoked:

> imperfect light entering by their narrow casements showed bedsteads of a hundred years old . . . traces of half-effaced embroideries, wrought

by fingers that for two generations had been coffin-dust. All these relics gave to the third storey of Thornfield Hall the aspect of a home of the past: a shrine of memory. I liked the hush, the gloom, the quaintness of these retreats in the day; but I by no means coveted a night's repose on one of those wide and heavy beds: shut in, some of them, with doors of oak; shaded others, with wrought English old hangings crusted with thick work, portraying effigies of strange flowers, and stranger birds, and strangest human beings – all of which would have looked strange, indeed, by the pallid gleam of moonlight.

(Brontë [1847] 1960: 108–109)

Jane's fears of nocturnal transformations are later confirmed. She wakes to hear demonic laughter at the keyhole of her room. In true gothic horror form, 'Something gurgled and moaned. Ere long, steps retreated up the gallery towards the third storey staircase' (1960 [1847]: 151). In time Jane discovers the secret of Thornfield Hall, the presence of her employer's mad wife, Bertha. That which transforms Thornfield Hall into a House of Doom is the presence of an individual whose proper role would be to make this Hall into a home. However, rather than being an angel of the hearth, Mrs Rochester is, in her husband's words, a fearful hag, a possessed woman who burns people in their beds at night, stabs them and bites the flesh from their bones. Her presence leads Rochester to describe his home in the following terms:

Thornfield Hall – this accursed place – this tent of Achan – this insolent vault, offering the ghastliness of living death to the light of the open sky – this narrow stone hell, with its one real fiend, worse than a legion of such as we imagine.

(Brontë [1847] 1960: 302)

Though Rochester and Jane fall in love, honourable Jane will have no truck with a married man, whatever his circumstances. Leaving the Rochesters to their House of Doom, she finds a new home. In her description of it, we find a marked contrast with Thornfield Hall. In the details of its simple furnishings, home and self are again compounded as Jane's virtuousness is implicitly compared with the doomed home/selves of the Rochesters:

My home, then . . . is a cottage; a little room with whitewashed walls and a sanded floor, contained four painted chairs and a table, a clock, a cupboard, with two or three plates and dishes, and a set of tea-things in delf. Above, a chamber of the same dimensions as the kitchen, with a deal bedstead and chest of drawers – small, yet too large to be filled with my scanty wardrobe.

(Brontë [1847] 1960: 360)

What makes *Jane Eyre* so compelling a novel is the suspense generated as a result of the hidden, yet highly threatening presence of Bertha Rochester within an apparently well-maintained family home. Thornfield Hall is not a mental asylum in which the presence of the insane is expected. Yet, when Jane enters her new home, she slowly encounters the ultimate horror – uncontrolled proximity to someone who is mad, bad and dangerous to know.

We relish Brontë's novel. Its carefully unfolding story-line allows us to witness Jane's vulnerability at a safe distance. In fairground Houses of Doom we experience similar pleasures. On big wheels and roller coasters we allow ourselves to be terrorised through an assault on our bodies; in Houses of Doom we invite terror through an assault on our imaginations. In both cases we believe that our excursion into danger is short-lived, that it represents no real threat. It is like the delighted fear we feel as children when tickled by our parents. Talking of jokes, Mary Douglas says:

> The joke merely affords opportunities for realising that an accepted pattern has no necessity. Its excitement lies in the suggestion that any particular ordering of experience may be arbitrary and subjective. It is frivolous in that it produces no real alternative, only an exhilarating sense of freedom from form in general.
>
> (M. Douglas 1975: 96)

To play at terror in a fairground or horror movie House of Doom is not to open up the possibility of 'real alternatives'. Our rational minds 'know' that when previous owners leave a house, all that remains is bricks and mortar. We 'know' that ghosts are either imagined or have hidden material explanations. Yet, as Douglas says of jokes, they are funny to the extent that they correspond to social experience; hence our struggle to find the humour in jokes from other cultures or historical periods. However, the excitement of fear, or our laughter as we exit from the ghost train, results from something we actually recognise – the possibility that things can go bump in the night, that our new home's atmosphere stems from something more than just its gloomy colour scheme or the shadows cast by an overgrown garden. As Carroll (1990: 166) says of the monsters of the horror genre: 'monsters are not wholly other, but derive their repulsive aspect from being, so to speak, contortions performed upon the known . . . They are not wholly unknown, and this is probably what accounts for their characteristic effect – disgust'.

The 'other', inevitably encountered in a house move, may not be a monstrous Bertha Rochester, yet in her monstrosity Bertha represents but a 'contortion' of the more ordinary, though still problematic 'others' who once inhabited our homes. Moreover, our pleasurable encounters with terror, via fairgrounds, novels and horror movies, may, in part, be explained as an attempt to expunge our unacknowledged fears by revealing them in exaggerated form. As Carroll (1990: 199) says, 'The abnormal is allowed center stage solely as a foil to the cultural order, which will ultimately be vindicated by the end of the fiction'. And the cultural order which here concerns us is our deeply embedded cultural resistance to unwanted intimate exposure to the private selves of others, made manifest in that most hidden of spaces – the private home.

At home with the 'other'

Even without venturing into the 'external' spaces of films or novels, many individuals still experience terror first hand in the safety of their own homes. The shell of the house fails to protect them from materialisations which defy rational explanation, which transgress the laws of physical matter. As a result people run out into the street in terror. They call the Samaritans. While their problems can be addressed by experts of many kinds – from structural engineers to social workers – the less that their experience is amenable to rational explanations, the more likely it is that the expert will be a member of the clergy. What follows is data derived from an interview with an Anglican minister who has developed a national, indeed international reputation as an exorcist. He describes how a policeman's family living in a house in Yorkshire began to experience considerable disturbances. While they were in bed they would hear all their furniture and belongings below in the living room being wrecked – overturned and thrown about. In response they contacted him and he came to perform an exorcism. During his visit a bolt of electricity went right through every member of the group while they were sitting in a line on the settee. The family also saw objects move about on the mantelpiece and despite the fact that the objects had been counted and everyone in the house was present, one of the objects would disappear and then be found in another room.

Significantly, in seeking explanations for these events, the minister will enquire about the home's previous occupants. Thus, in the case of the policeman's family, it was later discovered that the previous tenant had died and when her daughter was contacted it appeared there had been disturbances in the family which would explain why her mother was returning to her former home. Furthermore, her daughter described her mother as frequently wearing a long nursing coat, something which matched sightings in the house of a figure with a modern hairstyle but long old-fashioned clothes. When the former occupant's daughter provided the policeman's family with a photo of her mother, they instantly recognised their intruder.

In another case, a woman and her adult daughter were troubled by an evil smell in their house. Although they were rehoused several times, the smell kept returning. The minister could not detect the smell himself, but he saw both the mother and her daughter coughing, with tears streaming down their faces, quite overcome by it. Other members of the local council had actually experienced the smell directly. Later the minister discovered that another daughter had died in a scalding hot bath while in institutional care and he believed that the smell could well have been connected with her burns. While the home is usually seen as something which can be sealed off from intruders, representing a clear boundary between the occupant and their neighbours or other family members, hauntings such as this represent a transgression of this boundary.

Often people are driven out of their homes by the sudden intrusion of a ghost of some kind. In one case, the family raised the alarm in the middle of the night after seeing an old man. The previous tenants had also left rather hurriedly. Eventually the minister contacted a family who had lived in the house for about ten years. They reported seeing the old man by the television set, upstairs in the bedroom while they were making the beds, down in the kitchen when they were cooking and out in the passageway. The children were often disturbed by his presence in their bedrooms. Their mother 'screamed the place down' at the first intrusion, but the family eventually came to accommodate him without any fear, only a sense of nuisance.

In another case a woman feared for her mental health when she repeatedly heard bangs and crashes on the outside wall of her house. Up on the landing she experienced a feeling of despair and her sons reported an old woman who looked in on them at night. Their mother became increasingly distressed, crying over the prospect of her sons leaving home even though they were only young. Again, the minister came up with information about the previous occupants of the house. An old lady had once lived there with her adult son. When he left to marry in his thirties and broke off the close relationship he had with his mother, she became intensely depressed to the extent that she eventually tied a rope to the banisters and threw herself out of the landing window, where her body thumped down against the outside wall of the house. Every aspect of this woman's experience – the sounds she heard, her dread of losing her sons, her terrible depression – seemed to represent a merger between the selves of the home's past and present occupants. After the minister's prayers and blessings the two women separated, the present occupant receiving a visit from her earlier counterpart during a vivid dream. The older woman said: 'Thank you love I'm with the Good Lord now', thereby signalling her spatial as well as spiritual departure from the home within which she had suffered so much.

Over and above the presence of former occupants of houses, there is the possibility of evil persisting within its walls. The minister described how people might feel a 'terrible sense of menace' in a house, only to discover that previous occupants had 'dabbled in weird stuff' such as ouija boards. After a blessing performed in an attic, its damp, icy walls suddenly grew warm, causing everyone present to pull away from them. Sources of power within the home – fridges, televisions, radios – similarly take on 'human' rather than mechanical properties, switching themselves on and off regardless of whether they are plugged in. It is the fusion of home and self which informs the minister's explanation for the way bricks and mortar can take on human qualities or new occupants can sense or embody a home's former occupants. He also referred to individuals who, while never 'dabbling in the occult' or experiencing profoundly distressing events, had nonetheless 'worshipped that house, this is my house, this is my God, I'm not leaving it'. Even after death they determinedly continue to live alongside its new occupants, albeit in disembodied form.

The notion that houses can be doomed in this way represents a radical challenge to materialist understandings of the human environment. When terrifying experiences take place, concrete explanations tend to be the first response: is it the hot water pipe or the wind coming from a particular direction which produces the sound of an outsider's presence within the home? Corroboration is sought from a range of professionals – soil experts, plumbers, sanitary inspectors, local councillors or structural engineers. The minister himself used theoretical perspectives which, while spiritual in their orientation, still drew on rational principles. For example, ghosts were memories or tape-recordings from the past, holograms or stressed energy entrapped in the fabric of the home. The possibility that the home may encompass more than just its material fabric is therefore an idea which lies beyond the margins of western thought and experience. As Warner (1996: 13) argued, 'magic and fantasy have often been ascribed to the Other, to the Stranger, who is consequently characterised as primitive, barbaric, even inhuman'. In the final section of this chapter, however, we move on to examine Houses of Doom which would seem to embody much that lies beyond simple materialism.

Sites of evil

Manifestations of our home's previous occupants – as sounds, smells and apparitions – overflow the categories of rational thought. We may believe there to be an undiscovered cause within the fabric of the house; we may reflect on alternative realities, either with a sense of pleasure or disturbance. However, the terror of a supernatural invasion of Bachelard's ([1958] 1994) seductive dream shell has a material counterpart. The western home is also the site of sexual abuse, murder, dismemberment and the disposal of the human body. It may be the body of a wife or child; or that of a stranger who was somehow enticed into the privacy of someone else's home. As Goldsack (Chapter 11) notes, violent attacks are represented in the media and in police personal security literature as events which take place at the hands of strangers in dark lanes or areas of desolate urban decay. This image of personal vulnerability is more readily accepted than the idea that the much prized home offers little by way security, not only from external intrusion but also from internal attack. It is a perspective that we find difficult in relation to our own homes and supposedly loving family members; it is also one which we find hard to take on when we move into a new home. Yet there lurks the fearsome possibility that we might inadvertently make our home in a site of violence.

As already demonstrated, the haunted house can be encountered by choice, within the realm of fantasy (via the gothic novel and the fairground) or as an inescapable aspect of everyday experience – the thudding of a ghost body on an outside wall, a sickening stench of boiled flesh. The House of Horror can similarly constitute both entertainment and a planner's nightmare. The women's glossy magazine *Marie-Claire*, alongside the froth of its fashion and film pages, titillates the reader with the question 'Could you wash in the bath where a woman had been drowned by her husband or sleep at night in a flat where a man had hacked up his wife with an axe?' (December 1997). Head-lined by clippings from the tabloid press – 'Wife's body "cut up and roasted"' and 'The body in the bath' – *Marie-Claire* fleshes out the repressed nightmare of unwanted proximity to a home's previous occupants by allowing the browsing reader pleasurable access to three separate Houses of Horror.

Desperate for somewhere to live, Rob Spororno and his girlfriend agreed to take on the East End flat in which philosophy post-graduate student and former Samaritan, Nicholas Boyce, had strangled his wife, filleted her flesh and hacked up and roasted her bones. So notorious was the murder within the area that fifty local families had refused accommodation which would bring them into spatial, though not temporal, proximity to the Boyces. The fusion of the terrifying selves of these former tenants with the bricks, mortar and fit-tings of their home did not deter Rob Spororno and his girlfriend initially. Yet, as he told *Marie-Claire*'s interviewer, on moving in they found the flat to be cold, even in summer, as if the air conditioning was left on constantly. The couple's formerly harmonious relationship deteriorated and within three years they split up. Rob and friends conducted a seance in the flat during which he asked Mrs Boyce how she felt while being murdered. Suddenly he was choking and tears poured down his face. Local children evidence a more literal sense of the fusion of self and home. They still dig holes in the lawn outside the flat's front window. Mrs Boyce's left hand was never recovered and rumour has it that Boyce buried it somewhere near the flat.

Rob Sporono knowingly took up residence in a site of violence and now regards Mrs Boyce as another of the flat's current occupants. He senses her presence, asks her aloud if she's all right and 'likes to keep the place looking nice because it might make her a bit happier'. Rose Williams, however, realised the nightmare of unknowing entry into a site of violence. Only after thirteen years did she discover that a former occupant had murdered his wife in the bath, but now links the event firmly with the coldness in the downstairs bathroom, one which the children have always been unwilling to use. Meg Renou and her partner in Melbourne, Australia, similarly fell foul of the risk which every house move involves. Only after they moved in did they find out that former tenants, Suzanne Armstrong and her house-mate, were raped and stabbed to death by an unknown intruder. Afterwards, Suzanne's baby son remained alone in his cot for days until neighbours found him, alive but severely dehydrated. The current tenant, Meg Renou, reports terrifying dreams, pictures falling off walls, blood-coloured stains seeping up through carpets and a family dog who 'hates the place with a passion'.

While *Marie-Claire*'s three sets of tenants had all found ways of living along-side their nightmare predecessors, the notion persists that a site of violence retains the evil which has been enacted within it – even after the perpetrator has been brought to justice or has died. As such the building must be destroyed. Thus, Meg Renou's boss easily, though mistakenly, reassured her that the house in which Suzanne Armstrong was murdered had been bull-dozed. Similarly Jane's discovery of Thornfield Hall, the hidden resort of mad Bertha Rochester, in ruins is central to the romantic resolution of the novel, *Jane Eyre*:

> The lawn, the grounds were trodden and waste: the portal yawned void. The front was, as I had once seen it in a dream, but a shell-like wall, very high and very fragile-looking, perforated with paneless windows: no roof, no battlements, no chimneys – all had crashed in. And there was the silence of death about it: the solitude of a lone-some wild.
>
> (Brontë [1847] 1960: 427)

This destruction of bricks and mortar is a not unusual response to acts of insane violence. It underscores the peculiarly western confounding of self and home. Just as the homes within which great novels or symphonies have been composed are visited in order that the tourist, in wandering among old pieces of furniture, may somehow experience direct contact with genius, so the homes which are sites of violence offer the terrifying prospect of an encounter with evil.

When Fred and Rosemary West were finally removed from 25 Cromwell Street in Gloucester in 1994, their home yielded up the bodies of the women murdered in that house across twenty years or more. Many of the details of the couple's systematic abduction, rape, torture and murder of their victims which emerged during their trial were unprintable in the popular press. In October 1996 the *Guardian* reported: 'West's House of Horrors to bite the dust . . . the most notorious house in Britain is to be obliterated . . . during a two-week operation to destroy the last remnants of 25 Cromwell Street'. Thirty-four members of Gloucester's local council were unanimous that 'It is important to erase the physical reminder of these events' although 'It will take some time for the scars to heal'. Even the transformation of the site into a memorial garden was resisted by the victims' survivors, one of whom said, 'I'd like to see it knocked down so that no sign of it is left at all'.

Conclusion

The destruction of bricks and mortar which have housed evil may seem an obvious measure. There was no difference of opinion among the thirty-four members of Gloucester's council. But even the obliteration of the building was an insufficient measure, given the power of what was enacted upon the land, which led to real uncertainty among the councillors about what to do with the site. This uncertainty is revealing, because it shows how the destruction of the fabric of a House of Doom serves, in some sense, to validate its terrible reality. Throughout this volume we have argued that the material conditions of people's home lives are an appropriate focus for social scientists, rather than just architects and planners. In the House of Doom we find exemplified at their most intense, the cultural, social and emotional aspects of our physical surroundings. As argued throughout this chapter, the House of Doom is more than just a fun-fantasy source of pleasurable terror. It represents and articulates that which is powerfully culturally repressed, the horror of unwanted proximity to the hidden selves of others. In the responses of the unwitting inhabitants of haunted sites of violence – who run into the road or support the bull-dozing of property – we find, writ large, the imperative to separate the self from those who otherwise bring the risk of a contaminated, indeed stigmatised personal identity.

Part IV

CHANGING PERCEPTIONS
OF HOME

13

'YOU'VE GOT HIM WELL TRAINED'

The negotiation of roles in the domestic sphere

Tony Chapman

On his BBC *World Tour of Australia* shown on television in 1996, Scottish comedian and raconteur Billy Connolly told a story about a large placard, erected outside somebody's house. Resembling an estate agent's sign, it read 'For Sale: complete set of Encyclopaedia Britannica'. Beneath this headline, the banner carried the following by-line: 'Never used, *because wife knows everything*'. Its audaciousness makes the story funny. How could a man have the cheek to state so publicly that his wife is such a know-it-all? And worse, what might be the consequences of his admission that, in the domestic sphere at least, he had been so completely defeated that he had gone public on his supposed emasculation? Connolly's story demonstrates so aptly the contradictions that are inherent in domestic relationships, showing the ebb and flow of power between men and women as they bring their pre-marital expectations and experience into their shared home and try to negotiate their place within it. The man with the placard outside his home is not defeated, even if he *feels* it, because he has the courage and power to advertise his plight, and to get away with it.

The story is also useful because it highlights the point that women's know-how about all things domestic generally goes unquestioned by men and women. The assumption that women know best is accepted for a number of reasons. Most important of these is the well-documented evidence that married women generally expend much more energy and time running the home than men (see, for example, Deem 1986; Green *et al.* 1990; Oakley 1974a, 1974b). Second, women are socialised into the expectation that they will take primary responsibility for the home and must, by implication, be trained into that role (Abbott and Wallace 1997; Sharpe 1995; Griffin 1985). Third, the idea that the home is the preserve over which they are likely to have most control is relentlessly reinforced by, for example, the media in various forms including women's magazines, popular fiction, film, radio and television drama and comedy, through advertising, marketing and retail psychology (Faulkner and Arnold 1985; Falk and Campbell 1997; Corrigan 1997). Finally, the view that women know best is reinforced by women themselves: mothers and daughters, siblings, neighbours and friends all participate in the process of monitoring and supervising each other's performance as housekeepers. However subtle the process of socialising women into this role may or may not be, the end result is the same: women feel responsible for the organisation of the home and, as a consequence, come to believe that they *know* the best way that tasks should be done.

It is usually assumed that men are not interested in the home. A man's 'natural' habitat, according to the conventional wisdom, is in the public sphere and not the domestic (Hearn and Morgan 1990; D. Morgan 1992; Gamarnikow *et al.* 1983). If men are concerned with domestic issues, they are generally exercised in the public sphere – exhibiting their skills as chefs, hotel managers, politicians concerned with the family, or as grocery retailers, designers of household technology and so forth. As the dominant actors in the public arena, men have traditionally been extremely successful in gaining power and influence, and have shaped the world to a large extent to suit their needs. Although an increasing number of women have a role to play on the public stage, the public world is still drawn in the male image. But this chapter is not about the public world; instead it is about power and resistance in the domestic sphere and seeks to show how men's continuing dominance can nevertheless be circumscribed in the home.

The discussion will begin with a brief reminder of what was once known as the 'conventional' sociological view of the position of women and men in the household. Following this, it addresses the feminist critique of the nuclear family which, in broad terms, interpreted the family and home as an institution within which women experienced oppression under the system of patriarchy in general, and by their husbands in particular. The second section will include a brief discussion on what it is like to do domestic labour by testing some taken-for-granted assumptions in the academic literature about its apparently inherently dissatisfying qualities. In the third section it will be argued that both the feminist and functionalist accounts of women's and men's domestic roles and power relationships in the home are partial. The argument proceeds from the view that while women's life choices may be more constrained than men's, many writers on domestic labour have overestimated the impact of socialisation and structural factors upon women's attitudes about home life. As Hakim (1991) puts it:

> theory and research on women's work and employment seems particularly prone to an over-socialized view of women, or with structural factors so heavily weighted that choice flies out of the window . . . It is time to abandon the concept of women as so totally formed and

constrained by past patterns of economic activity and sex-role stereo-typing that they are unable to shape their own lives to any meaning-ful degree.

(Hakim 1991: 114)

In reality, women can exercise considerable control over men in the domestic sphere, even if this control may, ultimately, serve to meet what many men regard (perhaps wrongly) as their best interests. Oakley (1974a: 236) argued more than twenty-five years ago that women and men need to negotiate a new set of roles in the home if both partners are to gain advantage and pass this on to their children. That process of negotiation has been going on for some time now, I suspect, but it has yet to be properly recognised in the socio-logical literature.

Functionalist and feminist views of men's and women's roles in the household

For much of the twentieth century, it has generally been accepted that the home *is* the woman's domain – the place where women can nurture their young, satisfy the domestic and personal needs of a husband and exercise their own creative energies. In popular songs, films, novels and television pro-grammes, this view of the home has been constantly – *relentlessly* – reinforced. Even today, when women are shown to refuse conformity – such as the debauched lives of Patsi and Edina in *Absolutely Fabulous* – their effect is to produce a role model of how *not* to be.

Talcott Parsons, perhaps the most influential sociological theorist of the family in the mid-twentieth century, celebrated this view of men's and women's roles in the domestic sphere. Like many biological determinists in the fields of anthropology, ethology and eugenics (Oakley 1974a), Parsons (1954) asserted that these roles were not only natural, but also embodied 'a certain kind of mutuality and equality'. Apparently unaware of the offensive tone of his comments, Parsons elaborated upon his view of equality:

> Each is a fully responsible 'partner' with a claim to a voice in decisions, to a certain human dignity, to be 'taken seriously'. Surely the pattern of romantic love which makes this relation to the 'woman he loves' the most important single thing in a man's life, is incompatible with the view that she is an inferior creature, fit only for dependency on him.
>
> (Parsons 1954: 192)

The possible impact of this mismatch in power and status in the family that is implicit in the above quotation is made explicit when Parsons (1954: 193, added emphasis) points out that 'the *normal* married woman is debarred from

165

testing or demonstrating fundamental equality with her husband in competitive occupational achievement'. Not only did Parsons fail to provide a
critique of this unequal power relationship, but also he went some way towards
endorsing men's dominance. That said, Parsons was aware of potential strain
in the mismatch between women's aspirations and roles, but his analysis was
not sympathetic. Indeed, it led him to produce one of the most astonishing
sexist outbursts in twentieth-century sociology.

> There is . . . a good deal of direct evidence of tension in the feminine
> role. In the 'glamour girl' pattern, use of specifically feminine devices
> as an instrument of a compulsive search for power and exclusive atten-
> tion are conspicuous. Many women succumb to their dependency
> cravings through such channels as neurotic illness or compulsive
> domesticity and thereby abdicate both their responsibilities and their
> opportunities for genuine independence. Many of the attempts to
> excel in approved channels of achievement are marred by garishness
> of taste, by instability in response to fad and fashion, by a seriousness
> in community or club activities which is out of proportion to the
> intrinsic importance of the task.
>
> (Parsons 1954: 194)

It is easy to see how prejudiced men may succumb to the view that this is
what women really are like. Some, maybe most women, do from time to time
exhibit bad taste, succumb to the dictates of fad and fashion and are overtaken
by the seriousness of events in work, community or club. What Parsons failed
to point out was that men – as golfers, amateur photographers, bird watchers,
academics or whatever else – are also susceptible to flights of fancy, perversely
motivated outbursts and cravings for the latest fashion. What is more, men are
still more likely to have the spare cash and available time to exhibit such
tendencies (Deem 1986; Green *et al.* 1990).

Such ideas about women were not confined to academic debate. The com-
posers of the great jazz standards of the mid-twentieth century, for example,
portrayed women in much the same way in songs like *The Lady is a Tramp*,
Satin Doll and *Girl Talk*. This emphasis on the frivolity of women's conversation, their parochial interest in house, neighbourhood and fashion, and their
gossipy and bitchy orientation to one another can be found in countless films,
novels, shows and television comedies that ran through the 1940s, 1950s and
beyond. While there remains a highly vocal minority of mainly right-wing
commentators who promote the idea of a return to the 1950s model of the
family (Carlson 1993; P. Morgan 1995; Dennis and Erdos 1993), there is
much evidence to demonstrate that this is neither possible, nor necessarily
desirable. It is inappropriate to make universal assumptions about the benevo-
lent exercise of patriarchal power by men. On the contrary, women are more

likely to suffer violence and intimidation from men they know in their own home than in the public domain (see Chapter 11).

There are other reasons why it is not possible to return to the 1950s middle-class model of the family, including substantial and irreversible changes to the occupational structure which have led to a majority of married women working (H. Bradley 1989; Siltanen 1994; Crompton and Sanderson 1990; R. Brown 1997). Greater affluence has, in turn, resulted in higher expectations of standards of living which households could not maintain with only one partner working (see Chapter 4). Most importantly, however, are the changed expectations and motivations of women themselves which were given voice and authenticity by feminist writers and activists in the 1960s and 1970s (Abbott and Wallace 1997).

The functionalist or 'conventional' view of the family was challenged by feminist writers from the 1960s onwards, when it was shown that the home was not so much a place where women could exercise their own interests as a location within which women became the slaves of other people's needs. The home was much the same as the public world in that it represented the principal site within which women's lives were oppressed – and often endangered – by men. Radical feminists argued that men had created a 'system' of patriarchy in society – that is, an integrated web of constraints to keep women in their place – servicing the needs of men (see Walby 1986, 1990). Many of the exponents of this view suggested that women could not trust men because they would always seek advantage (see, for example, Millett 1977; Mitchell 1975; Delphy 1977, 1984; Firestone 1974; Dworkin 1981). From analyses such as these, it came to be generally accepted over time, in academic circles at least, that the experience of doing domestic labour was intrinsically devoid of personal gratification, socially demeaning, isolating and invisible, and economically unrewarded (Oakley 1974a; Malos 1980; Lewis 1986; Siltanen 1994; Deem 1986). As Barrett and Mackintosh (1980) put it: 'The daily regime in the prison . . . is long hours of working banged up in a solitary cell while the guards attend to other, more important business' (cited in Bell and Ribbens 1994: 231).

The fact that women continue to do more housework than men is not in question: Table 13.1 clearly demonstrates this. But what worries me is that the rosy view of the 1950s housewife, which was under-researched and over-laden, perhaps unconsciously, with patriarchal attitudes, has been replaced by a new feminist conventional wisdom which automatically assumes that housework is intrinsically dissatisfying and the incumbents of that labour are necessarily powerless. This is a contentious argument, of course, but when something is so obviously accepted without question in the academic literature, it is time that such an argument was reappraisal. I shall attempt this by considering, first, what it is like to do housework and assess whether or not it can give satisfaction, and second, assess the extent to which the housework role confers power on its incumbent.

Table 13.1 Hours spent on household tasks 1996

	Fathers	Mothers
Cooking, preparing meals	2.50	13.30
Cleaning	2.00	13.15
Washing and ironing	0.55	9.05
Spending exclusive time with children	5.05	8.45
Household shopping	2.50	5.50
Washing up	2.00	3.40
Driving children to school	1.45	2.55
Gardening	3.00	2.00
Sewing/mending	0.10	1.20
Other activities	2.55	1.40
Total hours of work per week	23.00	62.00

Source: Social Trends (1997: 215, Table 13.4).

What is it like to do housework?

While many feminist writers have argued that doing housework is inherently oppressive and dissatisfying, there is evidence which seems to suggest that women hang on to this role with some tenacity (Hakim 1991; Martin and Roberts 1984) and further, that women do not necessarily find domestic labour intrinsically dissatisfying (Baxter and Western 1998). Baxter and Western were uncomfortable with their finding that women gained satisfaction from housework because they believed it to be intrinsically dissatisfying. They review some explanations for this 'paradox'. First, that women's lack of power and resource, relative to men, tends to reflect more limited opportunities in other areas of life such as a career; consequently, they weigh up the pros and cons of marriage and settle for their situation as cheerfully as they can. Second, it may be the case that women are satisfied with housework because they have been socialised into this role – that 'Women who see childcare and housework as an essential part of being "good" wives and mothers are more likely to be satisfied with unequal divisions of household labour' (Baxter and Western 1998: 103). Third, their satisfaction may derive from the fact that women do fewer hours of paid employment than men – and that women who do full-time jobs are less likely to be happy doing the housework. Finally, Baxter and Western put forward the explanation that women may enjoy housework more than men. This last option they reject on the following grounds: 'This explanation seems unlikely given early studies of housework which showed women's generally negative feelings about house work tasks, in particular the sense of isolation, boredom and repetitiveness associated with most housework activities' (Baxter and Western 1998: 103). The studies cited by Baxter and Western are out of date now, including Oakley's text

The Sociology of Housework (1974) and Malos's *The Politics of Housework* (1980), which was a collection of polemical papers which did not include any substantive research findings.

Baxter and Western's (1998) study shows that women gained satisfaction from housework but do not question the idea that domestic labour is inherently dissatisfying because 'Women may deal with situations over which they feel then have little control by defining them as satisfactory' (1998: 104). It can be problematic when sociologists glean the opposite conclusions from what people tell them, as is the case here. Indeed they go as far as to argue that 'gender differences in satisfaction with housework between men and women may reflect women's greater propensity to define *objectively unsatis-factory circumstances* as satisfactory' (1998: 104–105, added emphasis). But who decides what 'objectively unsatisfactory circumstances' are? And with what do we compare them? Many paid occupations could, presumably, be defined as 'objectively unsatisfactory', such as mining, fishing and other dangerous and dirty work – and yet the people who do those jobs take pride from their work. Certainly, it is not appropriate to state that domestic work must be unpleasant just because some aspects of it could be called 'dirty work'. Indeed, as Mary Douglas argues:

> As we know it, dirt is essentially disorder. There is no such thing as absolute dirt: it exists in the eye of the beholder. If we shun dirt, it is not because of craven fear, still less dread or holy terror. Nor do our ideas about disease account for the range of our behaviour in cleaning or avoiding dirt. Dirt offends against order. Eliminating it is not a negative movement, but a positive effort to organise the environment . . . In chasing dirt, in papering, decorating, tidying we are not governed by anxiety to escape disease, but are positively re-ordering our environment, making it conform to an idea. There is nothing fearful of un-reasoning in our dirt-avoidance: it is a creative movement, an attempt to relate form to function, to make unity of experience.
>
> (M. Douglas 1966: 2)

While Douglas represents the cultural practices established for the removal of dirt as creative and integrative, it is also crucial to recognise that the task of managing dirt is stigmatised and delegated in many cultures. Everett C. Hughes (1958) argued some time ago that in the world of employment, 'dirty' work tends to be delegated to subordinates. By this he is asserting that the removal of dirt is a social process as much as a physical one and that the process of delegation involves a process of social interaction. Because the removal of dirt is generally regarded as a low-status activity, the people who do it have to adjust to their stigmatised position. That said, most occupations have some aspect of 'dirtiness' or 'deviance' attached to them. As Hughes (1958) notes:

Now every occupation is not one but several activities, some of them are the dirty work of that trade. It may be dirty in one of several ways. It may be simply physically disgusting. It may be a symbol of degradation, something that wounds one's dignity. Finally, it may be dirty work in that it in some way goes counter to the more heroic of our moral conceptions. Dirty work of some kind is found in all occupations. It is hard to imagine an occupation in which one does not appear, in certain repeated contingencies, to be practically compelled to play a role, of which he thinks he ought to be a little ashamed. Insofar as an occupation carries with it a self-conception, a notion of personal dignity, it is likely that at some point one will feel he is having to do something that is *infra dignitate*.

(quoted in Woollacott 1980: 194)

As professions have become established, so dirty aspects of their work have been delegated to others. In medicine, for example, doctors delegate the task of cleaning patients to nurses, while nurses gain assistance from trainees or auxiliaries to work in the sluice room. Whatever the occupation, people attempt to increase the 'social distance' between themselves and the dirt they deal with. This social distance can be alleviated more easily in those jobs which carry very high social status, although this is not always the case. Doctors, for example, gain social prestige from their work, and yet they still have to examine bodies. While it may be more degrading for a patient to have to submit to an anal examination, it remains the doctor who undertakes this dirty work.

Unless a household is wealthy enough to engage an employee to do the domestic cleaning, it is left mainly to women to deal with. But this does not, in itself, represent a state of complete powerlessness; instead, it has to be recognised that knowledge gleaned through cleaning and tidying can be a powerful resource for the person who does that work. Similarly, the curtailment of this service and the return of dirt to its generator is another potential opportunity for the exercise of power, as evidence in strikes among refuse collectors and grave diggers in the 1970s.

Hughes' (1958) study of apartment block janitors shows how the removal of rubbish injured the incumbent's dignity, even if he earned more money than his tenants. Yet, even though the work that janitors did was dirty, it conferred upon them a degree of power. They gained knowledge of their tenants' habits through the removal of rubbish and they could control their behaviour through the exercise of favours or withdrawal of service (see also R. Gold 1952; Garfinkel 1956; Hughes 1958).

In the case of domestic labour, power can be gleaned in two ways; first, in that it provides its incumbent with knowledge about the people who live in the house, and second, in the sense that it is possible to define the standards of order and comfort which are permissible in the household. The problem, as Martin (1984) points out, is that

> housework as the ritual creation of order also confers a form of domestic power on women which is so 'natural' and habitual that we have largely ceased to recognise its existence, though its consequences reverberate through the gender and generation tensions in the family.
>
> (Martin 1984: 20–21)

I shall return to these points later.

Tasks can, in themselves, be more or less satisfactory to different people. I do not mind ironing, but hate washing up, you might enjoy putting freshly laundered towels away in neat piles in the airing cupboard, but cannot stand cooking. But there is more to it than the intrinsic qualities of the task itself; the experience of housework is also affected by gendered expectations of who should do it, how to do it and how well, and how often the task is done. Research demonstrates quite clearly that among married couples, women do most of the cooking. For many women, especially for those who dislike cookery, the sheer routine of the task can make it become a drudge, although exceptional forms of cookery, such as the dinner party, may be a more lively and imaginative process which can be looked forward to and enjoyed (see, for example, Charles and Kerr 1988; Lupton 1996; De Vault 1991). For those men who generally do less cooking, the task may carry a novelty value. They may enjoy it because they might receive praise from their partner for doing the job – for *helping*. Their children might join in, because it *is* a novelty, and give him more praise than a mother who is used to hearing the timeless refrain 'Is it nearly ready?' Perhaps the novelty of the task makes it interesting as a problem-solving exercise, in opposition to the regular cook's experience which might be 'What on earth should I make for dinner today?'

While many household tasks are gendered in this way (although they may differ from household to household) we must be careful not to take it as read that all aspects of housework are fundamentally disempowering. While life in the suburbs can present problems for women (Greed 1994; Booth *et al.* 1996; Little *et al.* 1988) it does not follow that this is necessarily an isolating experience. Circumstances are now very different from the 1960s when sociological work on the isolated suburban housewife began to emerge (see Gavron 1968). The 1960s studies of the isolated housewife were often based in new towns and suburbs where social networks had yet to be established, where shops were distant and inaccessible because few women drove cars and there were very limited opportunities for employment (see, for example, Attfield's (1989) fascinating study of Harlow). There is now a substantial body of evidence to show that women are more mobile, have more work opportunities and develop a wide range of social networks in all kinds of communities, whether they are suburban, inner city or rural areas; or whether they are for young mothers, working women or older women (see Bell and Ribbens 1994 for a review of this literature). This is not to say that all women want to be involved in extensive social, work and childcare networks; as one woman in Ribbens' study stated: 'company doesn't bother me. I'm quite happy in my own little world. I mean I used to go out and take him to the shops and take him for walks, more so as to give him fresh air, but actually going into people's houses didn't really bother me' (in Bell and Ribbens 1994: 251–252).

Does the repetitious nature of some aspects of domestic labour make it intrinsically dissatisfying? Even though the work may pile up relentlessly, domestic labour allows for a degree of autonomy in deciding when and how the work is done compared with the level of surveillance and control that is experienced in contemporary factory or office work (Taylor 1997; Beynon 1997). Psychological studies show the central role of personal control in ameliorating the impact of stress in the work environment (Karasek and Theorell 1990). It is likely that this finding has implications for work in the home. Some domestic work tasks require the development of skills which cannot be used at work, and further, even though some domestic tasks require little skill and are repetitive, it does not necessary follow that they are intrinsically dissatisfying. Dissatisfaction is gleaned, perhaps, from the inability to escape from the work because nobody else is willing to do it. It is important now to try to explain why this might be the case.

Negotiating roles in the home

The process of negotiating a division of domestic labour is fraught with problems. This is because women and men have deeply seated gendered attitudes about home life which are difficult to eradicate. While domestic labour can give women power in the domestic sphere, they do not necessarily enjoy its exercise, nor even recognise that it is power. As Martin (1984) argues, the cause of women's sense of ambivalence to the power they hold is that it is unrecognised socially, and as a consequence, goes unrewarded:

> the world seen through the traditional housewife's eyes is a place in perpetual need of taming and tidying. This is surely the root of the supposedly 'natural' conservatism of women. We are the guardians of that vital ingredient in taken-for-granted meaning which depends on the 'rightness' of the way things are disposed in the intimate world of the home.
>
> (Martin 1984: 22)

Because domestic work takes up so much of women's time, it is hardly surprising that they believe that they have gained a monopoly over the knowledge of how it should be done. This helps to explain how men can be excluded from the process of learning *how* to do the job, because the correct method has already been determined by the woman with whom they live. It is, of course, an irrelevance if this 'knowledge' of the right way to do domestic tasks is not consistent between women.

Even if a man has lived alone and done domestic labour satisfactorily, *in his mind*, it is likely that his partner may impose her own methods and standards of work in the household because she feels that she 'knows best'. Crudely put, this can lead to one of three strategic responses from men. First, they can engage in a struggle to do things their own way – or even take control of the job completely. Second, they can conform to their wife's methodology – and do the job her way. Third, they can purposely make a mess of it, or just give up, and let her do it instead. All three of these positions create tensions for women and men.

The first route, getting fully involved, is likely to produce particular problems. The man who takes over the method and role is likely to alienate women from their right to 'not only create the basic framework of order, but [also] *police it*' (Martin 1984: 24, original emphasis). Ironically, the man who takes complete control is humiliating the woman by showing her (and by implication the public world outside the house) that he knows best. Whether the man shows off about this, adopts the role of an emasculated domestic martyr, or even exercises magnanimity in his work, the result is the same – he is demonstrating that she can't cope.

Women have a store of public insult to throw at the persistent male who keeps on 'helping', as if it is in some sense 'not natural' for a man to voluntarily and competently undertake domestic chores. This point was caught well in Alan Plater's comic television series the *Beidebecke Affair*. The principal character, Trevor Chaplain, who is hopelessly henpecked – like so many of Plater's male leads – sets about the task of making tea for his current partner, Jill Swynburne, and for an ex-girlfriend who has just come to visit:

'You've got him well trained,' says his ex-girlfriend.
'You ought to see him fetch sticks from the sea,' says Jill.

For men to be told that they are 'a treasure' or 'well trained' – a faithful servant – reinforces women's notion of personal power over domestic work, rather than giving ground to men who may be perfectly capable of doing the job. But Plater's dialogue reveals deeper insight in that it demonstrates how the ex-girlfriend is not just criticising Trevor for having become emasculated, but is also criticising Jill for *doing this to him*.

When men take to domestic work with enthusiasm, it is likely that they will react crossly when they are criticised or corrected for what their wife regards as a mistake or a misdemeanour. As a respondent from McRae's (1986) study of families within which women had better jobs than men reported:

The time we tend to argue the most is in the first ten minutes when one of us steps through the door. Particularly if I've been working all day and cooked a meal. For example, you know, cooking the meal and I'm all steamed up and then she's had a hard day, she's driven all the way from Slough or something . . . maybe I'll have done cabbage or something with the dinner and she'll say; you know, you really ought to have done potatoes with that meal. Which would be true of course because potatoes give you padding and all that sort of stuff. But I'll go: ya, ya, Hell! I've just cooked you this fantastic stew and I've got sweet corn and cabbage and you come in here and you wind me up about the fact there's no potatoes. You want potatoes – do your own damn potatoes!

(in McRae 1986: 130)

McRae shows that couples who *accepted* unusual job status differences and income mismatches generally shared housework more equally. It is interesting to note also, that because such couples were non-traditional in their attitudes about roles, they tended not to get too worried about the standards of house-work they adopted. In one case, an administrative officer married to a heating engineer had a fairly well-defined division of labour; she did the ironing and laundry, while he did most of the household repairs and gardening. The rest of the work they did together. As they commented.

The housework isn't organised. We both tend to leave it until we can't stand it any more. We do so much else we don't have time to fuss about it. I always feel I ought to do more. My wife tends to do more cooking than I do.

We do it as and when we can. It's shared out and it tends to be a blitz. We get fits of cleaning and luckily usually at the same time, although he tends to do more cleaning than I do. I don't feel it's my responsibility to keep the house clean, or to get food on the table.

(in McRae 1986: 129)

But mismatches in occupational status do not necessarily lead to men doing more domestic work. In McRae's study, when women and men clung to tradi-tional views about gender roles even though their own occupational circum-stances were different from the norm, this produced a good deal of animosity over domestic work. Similarly, the experience of unemployment can lead to men participating less in domestic work even though they have time on their hands because they 'feel' emasculated by their loss of their traditional bread-winner's role (see, for example, McKee and Bell 1983). Even among graduates, in spite of their exposure to a liberal educational environment, the evidence suggests that if a woman has a better job than her husband, he is likely to react by limiting his participation in domestic duties such as cleaning, laundry and cooking compared with men with an equal or higher status occupation (Chapman 1989: 108).

Judging from the statistics presented in Table 13.1, it can be safely assumed that few men take complete control over domestic tasks or participate equally (see also Baxter 1993; Berk 1985). The second group, those men who 'help', are likely to be the most numerous. But through their helping, by definition, they not only have to submit to women's 'right' to lay down the rules on the proper way of doing things, but also have the right to supervise and inspect the quality of the work done. This process of defining how a task should be done is, I suspect, a common way of maintaining power, but it is a dangerous strategy for women, as it gives men the opportunity to leave things half finished – or better still, let the women do the job themselves.

It is useful to take one example to illustrate this from a study by Gregson and Lowe (1994) on the division of labour among dual career families where a dispute over domestic labour has arisen between two higher education lecturers, in their thirties, with young children. While they both have full-time jobs, it is clear that the husband put in longer hours at work than his wife. This meant that she did more childcaring and housekeeping than he did, and when he did do domestic work, she reported that he did so 'under duress'. In other words, she had to make him do things by complaining at him for not doing his bit. On the surface, this looks like entirely justified action on her part because he is taking advantage of his culturally defined position as a primary breadwinner and as a consequence devotes more time to his career. The consequence of this in the long term, as both of them well know, is that his career is more likely to flourish than hers. On the surface, this case study provides a textbook example of how men avoid domestic work in order to pursue their careers. The interviewer, correctly, gleaned from the following evidence a view that the woman respondent was dissatisfied:

INTERVIEWER: Was this situation something you were happy with?
RESPONDENT: It was the cause of – I guess we'd actually started to live together in a shared house with other people. At that stage things were shared out strictly equitably and there was a lot of pressure on people to do their fair whack. So he was quite capable of doing these sorts of things. But he just has a different perception of what it is necessary to live on and he would live on a diet which I'd find totally unacceptable. He'd live on cauliflower cheese five days a week! So there was a tension to begin with about what was to be done. And I felt the burden fell on me and he didn't. But we sort of negotiated that one through in the end. And basically it came down to him being prepared to do only a certain amount. And he didn't see the necessity to do any more. Further than that I had to do myself. And in the end I have to accept that.

(in Gregson and Lowe 1994: 65)

This is a fascinating and rich account of the negotiation of roles in a marriage, from which Gregson and Lowe (1994: 67) drew the following conclusion: 'The situation here then is one of male intransigence and of female acceptance'. Drawing a conclusion of this kind requires the authors to accept, as indeed they do, some fundamental premises about the nature of housework wholly uncritically. Taking the basic elements of the quotation one by one, we can see that this man – whether we approve of his attitudes or not – has the requisite skills to do household chores, which he demonstrated in a shared house. Second, we learn, admittedly at second-hand, that he is not much bothered about what he eats – he would eat cauliflower cheese every day to save the bother of cooking. Third, it is clear that he has defined in his own mind what *he* regards as an acceptable level of household order and cleanliness. His views, as reported by his wife, are clear cut.

For the woman, who reports these facts, his position is not acceptable to her. She wants a more varied diet, and wants the house to be ordered and cleaned to a higher standard than he does. She has *defined* the appropriate standard of diet and housekeeping. If that is the case, it is surely true to say that he is intransigent about changing his ways to meet her standards. He just does not see the point in wasting time on such things. But the notion of female 'acceptance' is used in a pejorative sense: she is accepting that she has to do the extra labour to meet *her* standards – not a standard imposed upon her by him. In this case, the woman had a good salary and career, and when they had children, she solved the problem by employing a nanny and by buying all the household durables to help out with the tasks of laundry, dish washing and so on. Because her husband 'continued to refuse to participate further' she employed a cleaner.

This, I suspect, it a fairly typical story, but it requires careful interpretation. Certainly it is not easy to countenance this man's attitude because he is making his partner unhappy by sticking to his guns and refusing to do work above and beyond what he thinks is acceptable. By the same token, she is probably making him unhappy by trying to force him to live in a way which he sees as unnecessary. This, of course, assumes that he is not just playing games with his partner – that he explicitly states the limits of his interest in diet and household cleanliness, but does not actually mean it. In reality, although there is no evidence here to show this, he might very well like a more varied diet and a clean and ordered household – and he gets all this by default, by playing a stereotypical role of a man who is wholly uninterested in his home environment. Maybe he is, maybe he isn't. Certainly, though, it cannot be taken as read that this man is manipulating the situation to coerce his wife into doing all the work which he really wants to be done – just as it is not possible to assert that men in general have a lower threshold of tolerance for standards of cleanliness, diet and household order than women.

Martin (1984) may be right when she argues that women get into a mindset of controlling the home and its inhabitants by becoming 'both the household witch or priestess whose domestic rituals make the world "safe" and give it meaning, and she is also her own KGB and CIA; she patrols the boundaries of order spying out subversion, imposing rules and exercising sanctions' (Martin 1984: 24). This process of checking and monitoring, though degrading in one sense, is shown to be a powerful medium for control of men by Martin:

> She knows the minute details of all our personal habits and has the right to comment, instruct and require. She knows when daughters menstruate and sons have nocturnal ejaculations: whether anyone has been smoking or drinking: when outsiders have been brought in; what provisions have been used and when. Even without recognising it she becomes adept at fitting together all the clues that tell her exactly how the territory and resources of home have been used, even in her absence.
>
> (Martin 1984: 31)

Or so she thinks. Men and children learn strategies to undermine a mother's control over knowledge without actually challenging her certainty on all things domestic. Men might even develop strategies to buck the system; like a father wetting the children's toothbrushes after they have already gone to sleep – knowing that their mother will check up on her husband's flawed parenting skills when she comes home late. Returning to McRae's (1986) study of cross-class families, it can be shown that women often impose such high standards on housework that they believe it impossible that their husband could do the job properly – even if this tires them enormously. As one woman stated:

> It is too much. I get very tired. But a lot of it is my own fault. I'll be honest, I keep the work to myself. I've spoiled them. I find it quicker and easier, without a lot of arguments, to do it myself. And that's how it's gone. And it's wrong – I pay. I'm tired. But then, no one could do it the way I wanted it done. I'm very house proud. It's my own fault. And if they do do it, I have to sort of bite my tongue and leave it for a day or two and then do it all over again.
>
> (in McRae 1986: 137)

Or as another woman stated:

> I do every bit of it. I think it's because I'm a perfectionist: if a job's worth doing, it's worth doing well and I do not suffer fools gladly. If they don't do a job well, I'll do it over again myself. It's been my undoing really, because it's ended up with my doing everything. I get very tired really.
>
> (in McRae 1986: 137)

Women are often aware of the fact that they effectively stop their husbands from participating. As one woman, whose husband does very little in the house, said

> I think he'd do more if I weren't so bossy. The thing is, I don't think he would clean the house as conscientiously as I do. I think he'd think that he did, but I would know that he didn't. He sometimes suggests changes – suggests helping – but I guess I'm a bit old fashioned.
>
> (in McRae 1986: 138)

The power that women exercise in the household, then, ultimately serves to reinforce their sense of personal oppression. Many women feel that they have no real choice about when the work is done, so domestic labour is costly in terms of lost opportunities. Perhaps women make a rod for their own backs? When a favourite programme comes on the television, why is it that women with families so often miss the first few minutes, or perhaps only ever watch snippets while sitting on a chair arm or leaning against the jamb of the door? Arguably, it is not because they do not have the time, so much as their mind-set does not allow them to *take* the time. Men, on the other hand, are more likely to *expect* to have free time. In the domestic sphere this is reflected by their approach to housework. For example, much of men's domestic labour is occasional or seasonal, such as car maintenance, decorating, repairs or heavy gardening. These tasks can consume a great deal of time, but the fact that they are occasional means that choices can be made about when the tasks are done.

It needs to be made clear, then, that women do not just work hard because the work is there to be done. As Martin (1984) demonstrates, women constantly have to work to retain their position, especially when in the view of their charges.

> Her busy-ness can be doubly irritating to them – by its implicit insistence on the moral contrast between her 'work' and their 'leisure' and by its interference with their relaxation in the interests of keeping order intact – the order which is, of course, maintained for their sakes.
>
> (Martin 1984: 27)

Perhaps most women engage in practices such as this, such as 'putting things away' prematurely or unnecessarily, or vacuuming during *Grandstand* on a Saturday afternoon and insisting upon it that everyone on the sofa puts their legs in the air so that the machine can roar around underneath them. Such behaviour by women is explicable, although their efforts are not necessarily met with thanks or reward; indeed, a woman 'can experience her husband and children as a species of insatiable vandals, for ever intent on undoing what she has just achieved and consuming *her* time' (Martin 1984: 27, original emphasis). Martin is careful to recognise that women may not be fully aware of their power; indeed, they may perceive their role quite differently, which gives some credence to the popularity of the more radical feminist accounts discussed earlier.

> The alienating effect of her control of domestic order is normally experienced, not as evidence of her *power* but as a sign of the failure and rejection of her *love*. She can never do enough for her men folk, yet still they devote their ingenuity to escaping from her.
>
> (Martin 1984: 34, original emphasis)

Conclusion

Media images of the home usually portray men in a negative light – as crotchety or plain bad-tempered like Alf Garnett in *Till Death Us Do Part* or Victor Meldrew in *One Foot in the Grave*, who is retired from the public world and has become an impossible nuisance to his wife; or as henpecked and emasculated men like Dan, in *Roseanne*. In situation comedy, men are often seen as wholly incompetent or unwelcome in the domestic sphere and as a consequence, are consigned to the shed or garage, out of women's way, but forever under their surveillance. Ray Clarke's Mrs Batty in *Last of the Summer Wine* literally sweeps Compo from her front steps with her broom. It is necessary to brush the men away because they make a mess in the home – they undo what has just been done. Perhaps Clarke is going even further than this, and is showing that men *are* mess – as far as women are concerned – that they represent matter that is out of place. Much of this series' humour derived from women's surveillance of men: their personal appearance and hygiene, their bodged attempts at marital infidelity, their behaviour in public spaces such as the café.

Situation comedies are funny because they produce critical reflections on people's experiences of home. They play with patterns of resistance to women's control, just as in the public world of work, comic import is taken from women's resistance to the established mores of men. Where men are in control of the domestic sphere in, for example, *Men Behaving Badly*, they are shown to be hopelessly incapable. Their refrigerator is full of lager and mouldering remnants of long since forgotten food. Similarly, in *Rising Damp*, Rigsby the landlord and his male lodgers are seen to be pathetically in need of a stable relationship, however much they pretend that this is not the case.

In spite of the negative images of men at home, getting married and setting up home is a major part of the whole package of successful adulthood that men aspire to achieve. Earlier in the twentieth century, men aimed to keep a wife at home, caring for household and children while they engaged in life-long careers of full-time employment. The arrangement brought them the

Table 13.2 Domestic work of young people[a] 1996 (percentages)

	Males		Females	
	Always	*Never*	*Always*	*Never*
Cleaning own room	42	9	64	3
Making own bed	34	18	56	9
Washing own clothes	14	52	38	26
Making own meals	13	10	30	7
Household shopping	11	34	30	20
Washing up	11	21	30	7
Cleaning rest of house	8	25	28	8
Looking after children[b]	4	32	24	19
Making meals for family	3	37	22	15

Notes
[a] Aged 16–25.
[b] Not applicable for 27 per cent of males and 20 per cent of females.
Source: Social Trends (1997: 214, Table 13.3).

respect of their family, friends and neighbours and meant (in theory at least) that they were spared the bother of undertaking domestic chores (R. Roberts 1973; Dennis *et al.* 1956; Young and Willmott 1957; Gittins 1993). Things have changed. Men's paid work is much less secure than was the case, redundancy and periods of unemployment are commonplace. When work is found, it often requires a high level of flexibility but relatively little skill. Promotion prospects are more limited and remuneration is rarely sufficient to keep a wife at home and sustain family life to the standards that are now accepted as normal (R. Brown 1997; Chapter 4 in this volume).

It is, arguably, no longer socially acceptable or economically desirable for men to keep a wife at home. Women have changed and are more confident about their own role in society, have a more positive view about the opportunities for their own education, leisure and employment. Working couples, consequently, have less time to get the work of the household done and there are some indications that men are becoming more interested in getting involved in the lifetime project of bringing up children, or developing skills that cannot be used at work (McRae 1986; Pahl 1984; L. Morris 1990, 1997). While the evidence is not particularly promising (see Table 13.2), some younger men may *want* to engage in domestic life more fully than their fathers. But as this chapter has shown, the process of moving into the territory of women's traditional roles and responsibilities is less straightforward than might be expected. It is one thing for women to expect men to participate equally in the execution of household chores, but quite another to let men get on with it and do it their own way.

14

THE MEANING OF GARDENS
IN AN AGE OF RISK

Mark Bhatti

Gardening is often portrayed as an entirely innocent everyday activity, a retreat from the public world of work and politics. But as Hoyles (1991) points out, gardens convey important ideas about our relationships to our culture; politics, understood in the widest sense, permeates the history of modern English gardening. There are new interpretations, new uses and an emerging debate about the meaning of gardens in the age of increasing environmental risk. Why is there such popular interest in domestic gardening? Is it because we are collectively destroying nature, that we are trying as individuals to get closer to nature? What does the way that people think about the home and garden tell us about our relationship with nature? For those worried about the state of the planet, the garden becomes the 'nature' to be looked after and valued. By 'getting closer to nature' through the garden, could we reformulate our relationship with 'mother earth' and live more sustainably?

This chapter attempts to link debates on the sociology of the environment (Dickens 1992, 1996; Soper 1995; Redclift and Benton 1994) with the analysis of the domestic garden. In the context of deteriorating environmental conditions and the search for sustainable futures (Bhatti 1993, 1994), it is important to explore the possibilities offered by sociology for the 'greening' of the home to compliment existing analyses from environmental science. The chapter is in three sections: the first section offers a brief history of the idea of 'nature' and places the garden at centre stage within current debates about the state of the environment. The second looks at the history of garden styles and gardening today. The third section critically examines the meaning of gardens from the position of the currently dominant Modernist 'culture of nature' (A. Wilson 1992) which views the garden as an entity to be conquered. Finally, ecological approaches to the understanding of the garden and its linkages with the wider environment are considered.

Nature, the garden and sustainable futures

What is the role of the garden in mediating and shaping ideas about nature? What kinds of ideas about 'nature' will be important in sustainable futures? As Raymond Williams (1980) has observed, different conceptualisations of nature are shaped by historical circumstance. In pre-modern European society, for example, nature was regarded as a divine chain of being – connecting God to everything and everyone, but in a strict hierarchical order. Animals, trees and rocks all had a purpose and a place, and humans were seen as a part of this order. As Williams (1980) argues, nature was abstracted and personified; like God, it was all powerful – a single force shaping human development. In contemporary terms, this view is similar to New Age ecological thought (see Pepper 1996). But as M. Gold (1984) suggests, the idea of nature was about to change: 'By 1500 the dominant image of nature and the world was a living organism. By 1700 the dominant image was the machine' (M. Gold 1984: 140). This led scientists to produce mathematical models of a 'clockwork' universe. The gardens constructed by Louis XIV at Versailles between 1661 and 1690 are celebrated examples of this power of the King over his subjects, as well as domination over nature. Indeed the aristocratic English gardens of the seventeenth century were very formal affairs, as well as being ostentatious spectacles of wealth, power and 'taste'.

During the eighteenth century two visions of nature developed side by side: the scientific notion that nature is something that could be used to benefit people became dominant (K. Thomas 1983), although the pastoral view of nature remained important. This was a more romantic vision of nature as restorative, sublime and innocent; a vision that arose precisely at the time when capitalism demanded a more instrumental attitude to nature and transformed the countryside and the city in its wake (Williams 1975). From this pastoral vision arose a romantic view of nature as the embodiment of moral values which was, in turn, reflected in the image of the garden as a picturesque rural scene.

By the time that the capitalist system had become embedded in the economy and society in the nineteenth century, conceptions of nature had changed yet again. By this time it was regarded as a resource to be used for the greater glory of humankind. Here humankind sits outside nature looking on, studying evolution, seeking to control the 'laws of nature' for human advancement and profit. Yet, paradoxically, the emerging capitalist class celebrated the picturesque (sometimes referred to as 'gardenesque') as they retreated to the countryside to build their mansions while they made their fortunes in the cities (Girouard 1978). For all its subtle and appealing beauty, in those English gardens designed along the principles established by Lancelot 'Capability' Brown, Humphrey Repton and Horace Walpole, the 'gardenesque' was a false reconstruction and its effects were much the same as the formal grand design: this was still domination of nature. Both the 'scientific' and 'romantic' views of nature are still with us and in many ways are reflected in the modern garden.

Modern environmentalism and the garden

Since the 1980s there has been a rise in the number of people concerned about the environment; in some areas this has developed into protest movements as well as environmental action programmes. Modern environmentalism in many ways reflects the underlying visions of nature discussed above (see Pepper 1996). Techno-centrics or 'light greens', for example, accept that natural resources are finite, but argue that environmental problems are primarily caused by inefficient use of these resources. If society can make efficient use of environmental resources, it is argued, through human ingenuity, science and technology, then economic development can be sustainable in the long term. Thus environmental problems can be solved without any fundamental change in society. This anthropocentric or human-centred approach regards the depletion of natural resources or the destruction of nature as important only in terms of its potential impact on human activity.

An eco-centric or 'deep ecology' approach seeks to achieve more than just saving the planet for the sake of humankind; in contrast, it argues that the natural world must be saved for its own sake. This approach rejects the notion that humankind stands at the pinnacle of nature's hierarchy. Instead, humankind is subject to the same 'natural laws' as all other species of flora and fauna and must be regarded as just one part of the eco-system. All of nature is, therefore, seen as part of a 'web of relations' whereby each part is essential and makes up the whole. From this perspective, environmental problems can be overcome only through a radical shift in our personal and social priorities which in turn requires a fundamental rethink of our relationship with nature. The debate between 'light greens' and 'deep ecologists' is not simply about how best to 'care for the planet', whether to adopt this policy or that. It is a more fundamental disagreement about how humankind engages with the natural world.

In the context of that debate a new environmental discourse is emerging which seems to go beyond these two opposing perspectives. This discourse is partly about 'risk' and how it is managed, and partly about the effects that knowledge of risk has on individuals and groups; that is, the anxieties people feel about knowing that they will suffer, but not knowing what to do to avoid the dangers. As Beck (1992) argues, the risk society is also a reflexive society, that is, the presence of risk means that people have begun to question the causes of the daily threats they face. While anxieties about environmental risk may lead to fatalistic attitudes or the construction of personal barriers so that individuals do not have to confront the problems, it could be argued, in contrast to Beck, that the knowledge of 'risk' intensifies the search for local meaning and ontological security in everyday objects, in our case the garden. With increasing pollution threats, almost daily food scares and recent extreme weather conditions which may be due to climatic changes, people are becoming more aware of environmental risk, but they are also more uncertain about what to do. This confusion is, in turn, fuelled by scientific disagreements over the causes and potential effects of environmental change. One way that people can ease these anxieties, it is argued here, is to retreat to the bedrock of everyday life – the home and garden.

This chapter focuses on the garden for two reasons. First, gardens are artefactual and therefore creations of human creativity that mould nature according to individual frames of reference. Indeed a considerable amount of time, effort and money is spent by gardeners on what is mistakenly called a 'hobby', but is actually an important part of the development of social identities and home making. In this sense gardens are the work of human agency, a very personal act steeped in emotion, family history and self identity. Second, the meanings surrounding gardens are derived from social and cultural exchanges and gardens often make resonant statements about ourselves and nature. Ordinary places created by ordinary people are important loci for everyday understandings of natural processes.

The garden, therefore, allows us to examine the links between common sense or lay knowledge of nature and the environment, including everyday experiences of the natural world, and the way that environmental cultures are developing in and around the home. The home garden is important for many reasons. These can be loosely divided into the 'environmental' and the 'human', although the separation is artificial. In terms of environmental reasons, it is a place which can yield greater understanding of biological and ecological processes such as the flows of energy and the cycling of matter, food webs and chains, habitats and niches, predator–prey relationships, growth, reproduction and senescence; it is a place where people can learn the basics of reducing their impact upon the earth through collecting water in a water butt, making compost and using biological pest controls. It is a place where people can learn to care for and develop their understanding of soils and it is a place where people can begin to develop self-sufficiency through growing food (see *Town and Country Planning*, October 1995).

The movement towards environmental responsibility can be progressed through the arena of the home garden. The growth of gardening since the late 1980s presents an opportunity for lay understandings of environmental problems to become a part of everyday life. There are many reasons why people garden, however, and there exist tensions and conflicts in the way that people construct meaning through the practice of gardening. In line with a changing relationship between human beings and the concept of 'nature', we also have a rich and varied history of gardening which forms a backdrop to contemporary practices.

A nation of gardeners

The home garden is an area of 'enclosed cultivated ground' within the boundaries of the owned or rented house, where plants are grown and other materials arranged spatially. This rather formal definition belies the enormously complex history of gardens and their role in leisure/cultural activities and social change. Constantine's (1981) history of popular recreation shows how gardening achieved such a popular place in Britain and Turkington (1995) links the late-twentieth-century garden back to two dominant and contrasting styles developed in the late nineteenth century: the vernacular tradition and the English formal/gardenesque landscape.

Before the nineteenth century the enjoyment of gardens was almost exclusively a pursuit for the landed classes. By the late nineteenth century, the urban middle classes were emulating the aristocracy by moving out from the deteriorating industrial conditions of urban life to 'villas' on suburban estates (Girouard 1990). Indeed, the origins of gardening magazines can be traced back to this period. For example, the *Villa Gardener* noted in 1870 'the movement outwards from the turmoil and din of a busy city . . . to the free air of the country and the pretty villa' (quoted in Constantine 1981: 390). As the editor of *The Gardener* stated in 1867:

> It will be our special aim to make it useful to the large and increasing class of the community who previous to the development of the railway system lived in cities . . . and who occupy their hours of relaxation from the city business, with or without the aid of a common labourer, their suburban garden.
>
> (quoted in Constantine 1981: 390)

Gardening became for the middle classes more than just a leisure pursuit. It was widely assumed that gardening lifted the spirits and improved the mind and body. As one contemporary writer commented, gardening was 'the purest of human pleasures and the greatest refreshment to the spirit of man'; it 'relaxes nervous tension by contact with the peaceful and regular operations of nature' and 'new health interests are imparted to life' (quoted in Constantine 1981: 390). Gardening was often seen, then, to have an 'elevated' intellectual and moral value.

Many philanthropic Victorians asserted the value of gardening for the improvement of the moral values of the working classes. It was assumed that gardening would encourage home-centredness, thrift and family values. Gardening was also seen by some middle-class Victorians as a cure for leisure-time idleness, that is, a form of recreation requiring physical work and thus a continuation of the work ethic. To work in the garden was regarded, then, as a virtuous form of recreation – a kind of moral antidote to the corrupting vices which were thought to be endemic to the labouring classes (Constantine 1981; Turkington 1995).

While the middle classes attempted to impose their moral authority upon the working class by setting up, for example, gardening societies and shows, it was an open question whether their actions actually had much impact. There are two reasons for this: first, there always was a vernacular tradition of gardening, exemplified by the cottage garden and allotment, which contrasted sharply with the rather formal Victorian suburban style; second, as enclosures and industrialisation proceeded, fewer and fewer working people actually had access to gardens until the mid to late twentieth century.

As Hoyles (1991) shows, the 'cottage garden', or the 'wild garden' as Gertrude Jekyll defined it, has a long history going back to the early medieval period. These gardens were simply spaces attached to residences where fruit, vegetables, herbs and flowers were grown together. It seems ironic that two of the key personalities in gardening movement, William Robinson and Gertrude Jekyll, drew their inspiration from the cottage garden when challenging the rigidity of the Victorian formal garden. Their imaginative reconstruction of the common labourer's garden concealed the fact that this was originally a product of necessity in order to stave off hardship. Jekyll in particular was accused of 'bourgeois fantasy' because she did not notice the plight of the cottagers, nor the 'chicken house, rabbit hutches and earth closet' (Hoyles 1991: 225).

The second problem for Victorian reformers was that as the urban population grew and pressure on land intensified, the vast majority of people had less access to gardens. While there were exceptions in the industrial model villages of the north of England (Creese 1966), even the suburban middle classes had to think small. As Turkington (1995: 185) notes, 'The features of the . . . landscaped garden were diminished still further, until all that remained was a lawn edged by a paved path and bordered by flower beds'. This lack of space, for the working classes in particular, was largely due to the domination of the housing market by private landlords who developed terraced housing with small back yards – if any outside space existed at all (Daunton 1983b; Burnett 1986). Even so, Turkington (1995) shows how many urban working people did not lose their knack for gardening and used whatever space or means was available to continue the tradition.

During the twentieth century, access to private gardens has been gained by the majority of the population. This increase in the proportion of land given over to gardens was led by fundamental changes to patterns of urban land. One early boost to the idea of the urban or suburban garden for working people was the Garden City Movement at the turn of the century (Fishman 1977). This was followed by the building of municipal housing with gardens in most cities. Among those people who gained social mobility into the new middle classes, opportunities to gain garden space came from the development of semi-detached suburbia (Oliver et al. 1981). While there was a movement towards the provision of gardenless flats for the working classes in the 1950s and 1960s (see Brindley, Chapter 3), access to a small back garden has become a normal expectation for most families. Even flat living did not necessarily dissuade people from living without gardens, and many flat-dwellers grew indoor plants or cultivated flowers and vegetables in pots on balconies (Davidson 1988). Increased access to privately owned gardens among poorer people continues unabated. Between 1980 and 1994 garden ownership increased 3.2 per cent overall, but in categories D and E of the Registrar General's scale it has increased by 5.6 per cent and 5.3 per cent respectively (Mintel 1994). As Constantine (1981: 397) notes, 'the cultivation of a private garden [is now] within reach of a large and previously uninitiated section of society'.

Gardening today

In comparison with the rest of Europe, Britain has an unusually high number of houses with private gardens. Nearly 85 per cent of households have a garden and in 1996 there were 20.2 million private gardens in the UK. In terms of land area, private gardens make up around 3 per cent of England and Wales, approximately 1 million acres, which is considerably more than the 85,000 acres protected as nature reserve (Gilbert 1989). As the high level of home gardens shows, people in Britain are a nation of gardeners. Over half of the adult population claim gardening as a hobby (Mintel 1997b) with most being 'leisure' gardeners. Additionally, there is a hard core of 8 million horticultural hobbyists, that is, serious gardeners. In the UK gardening is the third most popular activity behind watching television, and playing games and hobbies (Mintel 1997b) and positive attitudes to gardening are spread across the social scale. Not everyone likes gardening, of course; 20 per cent of respondents from one study said that it was a chore, even though many more, 47 per cent, found gardening rewarding (Mintel 1996). Some gender differences emerge in attitudes to gardening; for example, one study showed that women found gardening harder work than men, and yet 50 per cent of women against 43 per cent of men found gardening rewarding (Mintel 1996).

While the growth in popularity of gardening is undoubtedly related to the increased access people have to gardens, other key factors can also be identified. In particular, the increasingly sophisticated and diversified gardening 'industry' has also had a significant impact. Garden centres have grown from small specialist nurseries into expanded retail operations with a 'leisure' theme; they sell a range of gardening products, and a variety of other products such as barbecues, books, garden furniture, outdoor ornamentation and so on. The political economy of the gardening industry has yet to be fully explored (see Bhatti and Church 1998), but the influence of the industry is reflected in the fact that there now exist around 2,400 gardening outlets in Britain. Most outlets are family controlled, but increasingly larger chains such as Wyevale,

Hillier, Notcutts, Jardiniere, Garden Pride and Country Gardens are expanding by taking over the smaller retailers. This industry has seen sales rise by
27 per cent between 1988 and 1993 and Britons spent around £3 billion in
1996 on gardening and related products, a figure which was projected to grow by
6 per cent in 1998 (Mintel 1997a). In 1995 31.4 million people visited garden
centres, a rise of 1.1 million on the previous year (*Observer*, 13 April 1997).

The growth of interest in gardening can also be linked to increased media
coverage and the presentation of gardening as a 'creative and artful' activity.
Gardeners are well catered for in terms of gardening magazines, newspaper
columns, television programmes and books. Despite the recession, one magazine *Practical Gardening* sold 90,000 copies of each issue in 1990 rising to
104,000 in 1994. The BBC *Gardener's World* magazine (founded in 1991)
gained a circulation of 272,000 with a readership of 1.5 million after only
three years of its initial publication. Gardening programmes on television and
radio also provide a focus for attention on gardening issues with over 8 million
people regularly watching *Gardener's World*. In addition 2,500 gardening
societies provide advice, information and support to gardeners, many of which
are affiliated to the Royal Horticultural Society, which has 177,000 members
(Hoyles 1994).

The meaning of gardens in the age of risk

The garden is significant because it is here that people have their most
immediate and sustained contact with nature. While there has been considerable sociological interest in the home as a focus of social research; as Sime
(1993: 240) has put it 'The "home garden" as a significant part of the home
and a physical "locale" for "home making" and "dwelling" has been
neglected'. The growing public interest in the garden, which is demonstrated
in Table 14.1, suggests that gardening performs important psychological as
well as social functions in people's lives. But it also represents tensions and
oppositions between, for example, men versus women (Constantine 1981;
Hoyles 1991; M. Morris 1996), consumerism versus self-reliance, science
versus intuition, chemical versus biological control, rich versus poor, sacred
versus profane (Francis and Hester 1990).

The meanings that are attached to the garden are, therefore, multifaceted
and multidimensional. It may be a retreat, a haven from work and public life
(Kaplan and Kaplan 1989). At a personal level the garden can be a setting for
creativity, a connection to personal and family history and a reflection of
one's identity (Sime 1993). In the new and emerging meanings of the garden,
it is a learning tool, a symbol of caring for nature and a natural world rendered
comprehensible. For others the garden is a 'chore' constantly needing attention with limited time and few resources. The garden can also be a signifier of
status, a very public place to show off social standing and 'taste'. Contests for
the best kept gardens can generate intense competition in the neighbourhood.

Table 14.1 Garden ownership trends 1985–1996 (adults)

	1985	1990	1993	1996	% point change 1985–1996
Any garden	84.0	85.6	84.8	83.9	−0.1
Garden containing					
Lawn	74.6	77.7	77.1	76.0	+2.0
Flowers	74.0	76.3	76.0	75.1	+1.1
Fruit	32.3	28.5	26.6	24.5	−7.8
Vegetables	34.7	25.7	22.6	19.9	−14.8
Allotments	3.4	2.3	2.5	2.2	−1.2

Source: Mintel (1997b).

The garden has also been seen as a fashion statement, with creative design and objects of 'art' prominently displayed to project a trendy lifestyle (see *Observer*, 4 May 1997). For some, the garden remains a symbol of moral authority or a reproach to those who do not conform to informal rules of respectability and produce an 'eyesore' from which others glean clues about the 'standards' of that family (Constantine 1981). The garden can also be a source of intense conflict between neighbours because of different stylistic preferences, disagreements over borders or overhanging creepers and trees. A 1997 survey highlighted the emergence of 'garden rage' whereby 21 per cent complained about neighbours' pets, 20 per cent disapproved of next door's leaves falling into their garden; and 22 per cent said that their neighbour's garden looked untidy (*DIY Week*, 16 May 1997). The cause of disputes becomes more clear from this report when it is noted that over 80 per cent of respondents believed that their garden was more tidy than their neighbours. 'Over the garden wall' arguments are so commonplace and intense that they have been featured on television series, including *Neighbours from Hell* (BBC 1998) and *Neighbours at War* (ITV 1997).

While it is difficult to generalise about the way that gardens represent meaning, Francis and Hester (1990) help to focus analysis by stating that the garden has four simultaneous features; these are the garden as an idea, as action, as a place, and as an experience. Each of these facets of gardens will be discussed briefly in turn.

First, the garden can be understood as 'an idea', Francis and Hester (1990: 2) argue, because 'The garden has long served as a way of thinking about nature and about culture and how each influences the other . . . as the balancing point between "human control" on the one hand and wild nature on the other'. Until the 'natural cottage garden' was popularised in the 1980s, the garden was generally seen as 'nature-under-control', as an ordered entity with everything neatly in its place. It was, in essence, a display of what nature *should* be and what it should look like. To illustrate this, Alexander Wilson (1992) has argued that the suburban garden reflects a particular notion of nature which is framed by a capitalist political economy and a Modernist aesthetic. This 'technologised' view of nature demands that perfection can be achieved. Wilson shows how in some arid regions of the United States, for example, dead grass is sprayed green! This is nature that is standardised, but to achieve that requires intensive management and chemicals to keep it at its best. It is possible in Britain to assemble the component parts of a garden straight from the garden centre, drawing upon expert advice from the radio or according to a particular style depicted in the popular magazines. But this 'image' of nature here is idealised, manipulated and controlled. Garden centres, in promoting this view of the perfect garden and making its achievement more easy, thereby communicate hidden messages about which 'styles' of gardening are appropriate. Thus by cultivating the garden, we also cultivate our identities. The point here is that a technologised 'culture of nature' gives rise to gardening as a practice which reinforces and maintains our destructive relationship with nature. This approach is now being challenged by a more 'ecological gardening', but it remains the dominant force.

Second, conceptualising the garden *as action* helps us to examine gardening as a process, as a creative activity for the creation of a sense of place. Gardening can be seen quite literally as a process for 'mixing with the earth', as Francis and Hester (1990: 6) note, 'We cannot dig, plan, trim, water, or harvest with detached passivity. Gardening can hardly be done without getting hands dirty and in most cases getting earth under the finger nails'. Thus caring for pot plants, or creating window boxes, is as much about gardening as growing flowers and vegetables in the ground. The psychological benefits of gardening have always been claimed by gardeners themselves, and academic research suggests that the action of gardening helps to reduce physiological and psychological aspects of stress and increases well-being (Kaplan and Kaplan 1989, 1990). This raises the issue of how 'mixing with the earth' may help us towards understanding the sense of place that people themselves create in the home through gardening, and the implications that this may have for alleviating environmental anxieties.

Third, considering the garden *as place* is perhaps the most common understanding: it is after all a physical entity. Indeed the word 'garden' comes from Hebrew meaning 'a pleasant place'. There are many types of gardens located in many places ranging from public parks, pleasure gardens and arboreta to cemeteries and botanic gardens. A garden can be created out of pot plants, window boxes and in containers. Thus window boxes on the thirteenth floor of a tower block may be 'the garden' for some households. Even so, the garden as a place helps us to raise wider issues; for example the recent rise of interest in the home garden as private space may be associated with a retreat from public parks (Hoyles 1994). However, there is evidence to suggest that it may also contribute to a sense of sharing, community and local involvement (Giraud 1990).

Fourth, the garden *as experience* involves being in the garden which can be a source of inspiration, or a place to escape and be alone. The sights, sounds and smells generate a unique personal experience, but one that can be shared across the garden wall. Research by Kaplan and Kaplan (1989) suggests that the garden as a setting is just as important as the garden as activity. Thus there is a restorative experience, whereby being in the garden is a mode of withdrawal from modern society as well as a source of fascination and discovery. Being in the garden is timeless and may be a way of connecting ourselves back to nature.

The garden is also a place of learning for adults and children. In fact this use of the garden goes back a long way, as Davidoff and Hall (1987) show in their study of nineteenth-century middle-class life: 'Gardens were used as teaching devices. Children were given small plots to inculcate patience, care, tenderness and reverence along with practical science lessons' (Davidoff and Hall 1987: 373). Many younger children now cultivate their own small piece of the garden and in the process learn about nature. The role of women as educators in the garden needs also be highlighted; indeed it is often women who are custodians of the family/garden history and pass seeds, cuttings and knowledge on to their daughters (Sime 1993).

Conclusion

The idea of the garden as a reflection of a cultural view of nature is important because the garden shapes our everyday experiences of nature and may help us to link into aspects of a new environmental culture. This link can be seen currently in the drive towards more ecological styles of gardening among local authorities, landscape designers and their contractors, in the permaculture movement, in city farms and especially in schools, where organisations such as Learning Through Landscapes promote children-centred ecological design.

In the home garden there is evidence to suggest that more and more people are challenging the conventional approach which is dependent upon pesticides and herbicides among other things, and prefer the organic 'wild garden'. Increasingly, gardeners are looking to buy organic or environmentally friendly gardening products. For example, in 1996, 39 per cent of garden fertiliser purchases were organic (Mintel 1997a). There is also a growth in the number of environmentally friendly chemical products.

While the organic tradition of gardening needs to be more thoroughly researched, interest in 'organic' or 'ecological' gardening has grown considerably in tandem with raised concern for the environment. This combination of organic gardening and environmentalism is producing interesting results and may establish new and alternative relations with nature. If the gardenesque is an ideal type of the modernist landscape, then the post-modernist landscape may increasingly become 'ecological', that is, where 'natural elements are allowed to function in a natural manner' (Gilbert 1989: 2). Purdue (1997: 14) highlights the key aspects of ecological gardening: 'organic growers see themselves as working with the ecological cycles as far as possible . . . [they] rely on local knowledge of the complex local ecosystem and uses a stock of low level interventions based on empirical evidence'.

Wilson, similarly, notes the rise of ecological gardens and gardening in the USA:

> much of the innovative work in landscape design has come from the grassroots – amateur gardeners, community activists . . . 'open space' and 'green city' campaigns: these projects represents a radical critique of modernity and its relationship with nature.
>
> (A. Wilson 1992: 108)

Research by Kaplan and Kaplan also reveals a crucial difference in attitude between 'conventional' gardeners who rely mainly on chemical remedies to control nature, and 'organic' gardeners who, 'Rather than struggling to control the garden environment . . . saw themselves as a harmonious part of a larger whole' (Kaplan and Kaplan 1990: 242).

Alternative ideas and practices are emerging, therefore, whereby the garden is not seen as space to be dominated or controlled, but 'managed' in such a way that it can function symbiotically. Given the right learning tools and familiarity with the practice of ecological gardening, we may begin to experience the garden as a reconnection with the earth. Studying the way that gardens are used, and the meanings attached to them, can highlight a way in which people learn about nature, and may lead us to identify the barriers and opportunities for developing a deeper environmental culture.

There are many meanings and uses of the garden, only a few of which have been explored here. Some of these meanings lead to instrumental uses of the garden, but alternative meanings can help to promote the role of gardening in a developing environmental culture. Indeed, meaningful and sustained environmental action usually starts from the way people actually interact with the natural world at the day-to-day level. The related dimensions of the garden which have been discussed, as *an idea* that shapes *our experiences*, and garden *as action* for the creation of a sense of *place* are key points from which to develop an environmental culture. As Francis and Hester (1990: 6) suggest, 'Through gardening we are reconnected to "mother earth" and to the larger ecology of the world in which we live'. Here the garden is seen to connect us to the earth; it is seen as a place for holistic thinking and ecological practice.

While gardening does not automatically lead to an environmental culture, as I have demonstrated through the analysis of the dominant mode of gardening which is sponsored by capital, it may be that the one place from which to develop the new environmental culture is the garden. The garden may help people to understand the plight of planet earth, but it crucially depends on the specific 'culture of nature' within which the 'garden' is embedded. As Cooper-Marcus (1990: 32) so eloquently put it: 'Our garden earth is desperately in need of care. By focusing on the simple landscape of the domestic garden we can perhaps begin to reconnect with that most complex and precious of gardens, our planet earth'.

15

DARING TO BE DIFFERENT?

Choosing an alternative to the ideal home

Tony Chapman, Jenny Hockey and Martin Wood

Through discussion of a wide range of studies, this book has critically addressed the concept of the 'ideal home'. What these studies make clear is that people's perspectives on what constitutes an ideal home are heavily circumscribed by a range of social forces. Simply put, we have strongly challenged the conventional wisdom that the home is an entirely private domain – a place where people can live their lives unfettered by external influence. On the contrary, we have demonstrated that society shapes our images and experience of home through the life course. In Chapter 4 of this volume, for example, it was argued that capital is successful in creating images of the ideal home, and that this imagery is consciously manipulated to sell not only a house, but also the accoutrements of an idealised form of family life itself, however unrealistic and unattainable this may or may not be for the incumbents who buy into the dream.

While it is the case that capitalism is extremely powerful in its attempt to shape people's ideas about what they want and how they should live, marketing directors, retail psychologists, advertising executives and the rest must, ultimately, operate within the wide 'cultural framework' of a particular society. Beneath the lustred veneer that capital has imposed globally, cultural differences between and within societies are endemic and enduring. This strength of endurance is reflected by the way that people consume goods and services in *opposition* to alien cultures, rather than just in passive acceptance of what is on offer. It is part of the way in which people distance themselves from 'foreign' others, whether they be neighbours of a different social class or ethnic origin; whether they be nation-states from another continent. As Mary Douglas (1997) has argued:

> Protest is a fundamental cultural stance. One culture accuses others, at all times. Instead of the weak notion that some choices among consumer goods are acts of defiance, I would maintain much more

strongly that consumption behaviour is continuously and pervasively inspired by cultural hostility . . . Culture itself is the result of myriads of individual choices, not primarily between commodities but between kinds of relationships. The basic choice that a rational individual has to make is the choice about what kind of society to live in.

(M. Douglas 1997: 17)

While Douglas, as an anthropologist, draws heavily on cross-cultural examples to explain patterns of cultural conservatism, it is possible to demonstrate that such conservatism also exists *within* social groups in the society. This conservatism may be tapped into by capital through its identification of niche markets – but in some cases, of course, the cultural hostility of the group to capital itself might preclude this possibility – as in the case of the 'eco-warrior' who actively avoids manufactured goods and attempts to undermine unsustainable production processes. In other words, as Douglas argues, apparently 'individualistic' choices are the product of an interaction between 'own' culture and 'other' culture, however spatially and socially distant these might be.

One approach to sociological analysis is that of symbolic interactionism (Rock 1979; Becker 1970; Meltzer and Petras 1975). While these writers often studied groups who lived unconventional or exotic lives, they demonstrate the constraining force of convention on social behaviour even in sub-cultural groups such as drug takers (Becker 1963). In the study of the domestic sphere, such an approach can help to explain how society constrains people from making, or even imagining the possibility of making radical departures from convention. An analysis of this kind would concentrate on the way that most people worry about giving the 'wrong impression' to 'significant others' – including families, neighbours and friends or other outsiders who come into the household like doctors, cleaners, midwives or social workers. The fear of being 'stigmatised' by others for behaving in a deviant manner is a powerful force in maintaining the social order (Goffman 1963).

Following in this tradition of sociological writing, Goffman argues in *The Presentation of Self in Everyday Life* (1959) that people set the scene for social encounters with the intention of letting other people see them in their 'best light'. The idea that people present a 'front' to the world which may conceal much from the observer (see Chapters 11 and 12) is an important idea because it exposes several layers of social behaviour, from that of the physical 'stage set' where the performance takes place, to the deeply embedded spoken and unspoken behaviour patterns of the actors. While the home may provide people with a site of retreat from the public gaze, it is also the stage upon which people project the most intimate image of their 'selves' to the world. The fact that they can 'control' this image to a certain extent is important, but their control is mediated by expectations about acceptable forms of decoration, furnishing, social manners, service and order.

Our awareness of the importance of establishing an appropriate stage set is highlighted when official or important visitors arrive without warning. Many households adopt emergency procedures to create the right impression for people they seek to impress and so avoid the prospect of being 'stigmatised' for their unruly lifestyle. A classic example is the doctor's home visit to a sickly child, where, in spite of the parents' obvious concern for the child in having called the doctor in the first place, they still find themselves tidying madly, up to the point where the doctor's car door bangs outside. How many times must doctors have witnessed people shoving toys or discarded clothes under a child's bed with the side of their foot? The necessity of keeping up a front like this is obviously connected to the need to give an impression of respectability, from which the doctor may impute a sense of care for the child's welfare and environment. The doctor may not see it this way and may believe that chaotic households are among the happiest ones in that the house is always in a moderate state of disorder where there is a comfortable relationship between people and things.

In order to maintain social respect, individuals also strive to match the achievements of their neighbours. To break the rules that are accepted by family, friends and neighbours is a potentially risky business; and as a consequence cultural conservatism tends to predominate. As Veblen (1934) pointed out, only those people 'with an aberrant temperament' (quoted in Coser 1977: 268) refuse conformity and dare to be different. Veblen's notion of an 'aberrant temperament' is interesting, in that he highlighted the fact that individuals who do not pull themselves back into line with social expectations will be stigmatised.

From the way that we have presented our argument, an impression might have been given that there is no escape from social control. But not everyone is equally bothered by what other people think. Indeed, this chapter is concerned with the people who resist convention and have excluded themselves from the mainstream by 'daring to be different'. What we argue, however, is that in practice an attempt to escape convention can actually narrow the opportunities for individualism and even lead to a higher degree of social control. This paradox arises from the fact that most people who do make radical departures from convention do so in the company of other like-minded individuals. Such a strategy makes sense, as it may help to protect them from the wrath or derision of the wider population. Putting up social barriers against the majority in order to behave differently often requires its members to agree a strict set of ground rules to maintain social order and cohesion; and it is through this establishment of a sub-cultural social order, that the free exercise of individualism yet again finds itself under threat.

Daring to be different

While most individuals can play with surfaces, produce variations on a theme or covertly live more exotic or terrible lives than expected behind the 'front' of conformity that they project to the world, it is only exceptional people who fundamentally challenge the social rules of conventionality. For the most part, however, those people who escape the trappings of conventional life, whether it is a voluntary choice or the result of circumstances well beyond their control, cause considerable offence (or at the very least amusement) to people in the mainstream. Undoubtedly, some people enter the world of Bohemia and throw off the surfaces of conventionality for reasons of self-publicity or as an act of resistance to irritate their neighbours. In every community, as they say, 'there is always one', like the man who erected a 20 foot model shark diving into his roof in a London suburb as an artistic gesture, or the Manchester man who has cars half buried in his garden and sticking out from the walls of his house.

Even the so-called respectable middle classes are not immune from upsets caused by the behaviour of neighbours. For example, Alan Bennett, the writer and dramatist, allowed an elderly female vagrant to live on his driveway in a stinking broken-down van for a period of years until she eventually died in it. Despite his irritation with her, Bennett (1994) felt an empathy for the woman which was not shared by his neighbours. However public his 'bizarre' living arrangements might have been, he was not deterred by 'what the neighbours might say'. Finally, there are the notorious council estate neighbours from hell with their unruly children and dogs, their intimidating or violent behaviour and their interminable noise produced at night in the process of fixing cars in their gardens or on the streets.

We are talking here about exceptional people. The majority, however, appear to submit to the pressure to conform to a model of respectability among neighbours where even the most trivial infractions can produce minor disputes or skirmishes, like the height of a hedge, the impact of a satellite dish on the status of the neighbourhood, or the ostentation of the external decoration of the house. A television series produced by the BBC offered viewers a 'fly on the wall' opportunity to watch neighbours locked in hugely costly legal battles over the height of hedges or the building line between adjacent properties. While the programme focused upon the most dramatic cases, it served to demonstrate the lengths to which some people will go to bring individuals into line in respecting the unwritten rules of respectable behaviour.

However, for many westerners, mainstream life at the turn of the twenty-first century – the noise and stress – is manageable only through systematic retreats into the 'heal breaks' currently offered by religious communities throughout Europe and advertised in *The Good Retreat Guide* (Whiteaker 1998). For others, the necessity of compliance to the norm, or the sense of being an alien in the mainstream, is an intolerable burden. This sense of alienation may lead to the finding or founding of some 'alternative' form of community that requires the establishment of a partly or wholly separate living arrangement. People who find themselves living in such alternative forms are rather like religious pilgrims. They move outside the norms or structures of everyday life to discover something which they feel to be lacking in mainstream arrangements. It may be 'freedom' or 'spirituality'; it may be commitment to a different form of family or resistance to modern technology. Once located on the periphery, such individuals find themselves in a state of 'liminality' (V. Turner 1974). In other words, they are absolved from the rules, structures and categories of the wider society. However, as Turner argues, the experience of human relations as entirely free and unstructured – a state he calls 'communitas' – has an in-built tendency to generate its own collective social system. Alternative groups therefore often form themselves into an initial state of rulelessness, or 'existential communitas', only to transform themselves subsequently into a state of 'normative communitas',

> where, under the influence of time, the need to mobilize and organize resources to keep the members of a group alive and thriving, and the necessity for social control among those members in pursuance of these and other collective goals, the original existential communitas is organised into a perduring social system.
>
> (V. Turner 1974: 169)

Total institutions

While the people who live in total institutions are often forced to do so, as is the case with prisons, mental hospitals, boarding schools and children's homes, there are individuals who, in choosing to resist the conformity of mainstream society, 'do their own thing' by submitting to the rigours and discipline of an institutional life. Even academic life, which is often thought of as 'liberal', 'individualistic' or even 'eccentric', was itself up until the middle part of the nineteenth century highly regimented in its structure and demanded considerable restraint upon its privileged members. Academics were, in principle if not in practice, quite literally 'cloistered' from the real world by living in isolation from the town in closed colleges. Cambridge University was, for example, set up in remote fenlands to avoid the distractions of metropolitan life. Rules of celibacy were still enforced on fellows at many university colleges well into the nineteenth century on the principle that the scholar must sublimate his bodily desires with his work (Clough 1982; Engel 1983).

Early Christianity provides examples of voluntary submission to even more rigorous regimes in the form of monastic life. The establishment of monasteries was preceded by the withdrawal of early Christians from society. Living as hermits in the loneliest of places, these people opted for a life of extreme asceticism. As Painter notes:

> Alone, with the absolute minimum of clothes and food, they passed their time in prayer and contemplation. All lived a life of frugality

and celibacy. Some mortified the body in more ingenious ways, as did the well-known St Simon the Stylite, who sat upon a pillar. As the recognition of Christianity as the state religion moved most Christians to compromise to some extent with the demands of the Roman world, more and more enthusiasts turned to the extremely ascetic life of the hermit.

(Painter 1953: 17)

By the fourth century, monasteries were established in embryonic form, presumably to counter the extreme vulnerability of the isolated hermit. Crudely put, two types of monastic communities emerged. In northern Egypt, Saint Anthony organised hermits into co-operative colonies where each hermit retained a separate cell for prayer and contemplation, but worked collectively to provide basic needs. Saint Anthony believed that the perfect Christian life could be attained only through solitary prayer and contemplation; Pachomius, on the other hand, emphasised the value of work. Following his teachings, Saint Basil established monasteries which encouraged the complementary ideas of work and fellowship. Saint Basil believed that his monks should live frugal lives, but not to the point of mortifying their bodies.

These distinctions remained, to a greater or lesser degree, in the many monastic orders that have been established over the last fifteen hundred years in Europe. While different monastic orders applied different rules about, for example, poverty, silence, social isolation, diet, fasting, sleep deprivation and a strict routine of work, celibacy, prayer and scholarship, all monastic orders required complete obedience. However, it would be a mistake to assume that in practice monasteries always maintained such high levels of discipline.

Anyone seeking Christian perfection could renounce the world in favour of the cloister. But what could he do if the monasteries themselves had become sinks of iniquity, no better than brothels, 'snares baited with whores' (to quote some of the charges levelled by the chroniclers)? When monasticism became corrupt, the nobly-born virgins who entered nunneries were exposed to the risk of defilement, and their brothers in monasteries to a lifetime of vainglorious brawling and drunkenness.

(Heer 1990: 40–41)

Consequently, the rules of monastic life were often reformed, especially in the eleventh and twelfth centuries when many new orders were established to meet the needs of faith and maintain discipline. In summary, while monastic life does not guarantee immunity from the scandals produced by human frailties, our example demonstrates how communities that lie outside the mainstream may offer opportunities for greater social control and certainty than in society. This point can be emphasised by drawing attention to the problems of adaptation that former military personnel experience when they rejoin 'civvy street'. The regime in military organisations requires absolute obedience to the prescribed system of authority; and in a sense, the organisation does its members' thinking for them. Consequently, when this safety net of organisation affiliation is lost, ex-servicemen and women may experience a turbulent and confusing period as they learn to exercise authority over their own actions rather than submitting to the authority of the organisation.

Religious and industrial communities

Life in total institutions is deliberately rigorous in its discipline in order to dissuade its members from acting upon personal whims which may destabilise the community. But are all closed communities socially constraining in their regimes? There were many attempts in the nineteenth and early twentieth centuries in Britain and the USA to establish communes in which individuals could live differently from the wider society. Unlike their mainstream neighbours they pursued the principles of utopian socialism and/or non-conformist religious belief. In some cases their movements endured over time. The Hutterites, for example, who fled from Switzerland in 1528, saw the society of their time as:

> carnal, corrupt, idolatrous and fun-seeking and therefore removed from God . . . Their aim was, and is, to emulate as closely as possible the life of the early Christians as related in the Acts of the Apostles, and in order to fulfil this aim they have sought to withdraw from the world.
>
> (Rigby 1974: 24)

Hutterite colonies were established on the principles of hard agricultural work from which no members of the community were exempt, including the minister and colony steward. While it is claimed that the Hutterite colonies were organised on egalitarian principles, they were profoundly patriarchal, meaning that only men could participate in reaching majority decisions that affected communal life (Hostetler 1997; Janzen 1990). Other religious communities, such as the Shakers, often turned their backs on the outside world in the belief that isolation was necessary to achieve their ascetic principles of self-denial, hard work and adherence to their faith (Stein 1992; Brewer 1986).

Not all communes in the nineteenth and early twentieth centuries were established on the basis of absolute religious devotion, although religion remained important in most cases for the legitimation of authority. Emanuel Swedenborg, Annie Besant, Rudolf Steiner and William Blake lent their support to the notion of living a perfect life on earth (rather than waiting until the next life). Blake believed that 'God is Man and exists in us and we in him' and sought to 'build Jerusalem in England's green and pleasant land' (quoted in Rigby 1974: 29). The Owenites were among the most successful in establishing communes on 'egalitarian' principles:

> separate interests and individual family arrangements with private property are essential parts of the existing irrational system. They must be abandoned with the system . . . I know that society may be formed so as to exist without crime, without poverty, with health greatly improved, with little, if any, misery, and with intelligence and happiness increased a hundred-fold; and no obstacle whatsoever inter-venes at this moment except ignorance, to prevent such a state of society from being universal.
>
> (quoted in Rigby 1974: 34–35)

In most cases, the establishment of industrial communities, or model villages, cannot be defined as egalitarian in any sense. Instead, they were the products of paternalistic ventures in improving the working classes. Certainly, the efforts of Salt, Cadbury, Leverhulme and Rowntree, for example, were well meaning – but the imposition of their will on the lives of their workers was often oppressive (Creese 1966; Girouard 1989). In most model industrial villages of this type, the philanthropic owners were deeply concerned about the moral education of the workers and their families. They built chapels, schools and adult education institutes together with community buildings to engender moral attitudes, but they built no dance halls, pubs or gin palaces in order to discourage debauchery and drunkenness. Leverhulme, for example, strongly encouraged his workers and their families to till the soil in the gardens he generously provided, hoping that this would take their minds off bodily pleasures. Leverhulme was intrusive to the extent of instructing wives to stop their husbands from sleeping with their mouths open (Creese 1966).

While some industrial communities were established on egalitarian prin-ciples, they were characterised by their adherence to patriarchal power rela-tionships which demand that women undertake all domestic duties. There are, however, examples of communities where there have been attempts to tackle the burden of domestic work on women. For example, in the nineteenth century a number of co-operative housekeeping experiments were established. Although they were small in number, including only about fifteen experiments in Britain between 1874 and 1925, they represent an important attempt to challenge the conventional wisdom about the organisation of the household. The origins of communities such as these can be found early in the nineteenth century with the establishment of seven Owenite communities in England, Scotland and Ireland between 1821 and 1825 (Pearson 1988). It was intended that the first of these communities, established at Clerkenwell in London, would provide opportunities for 250 working-class families, although only 21 families actually joined. The aim, according to an *Economist* report of 1822, was for women to undertake domestic tasks collectively and thereby

201

save time to enable 'females either to be profitably employed, or to command a considerable portion of leisure for rational pursuits and innocent recreations' (Pearson 1988: 4). While men were not expected to take part in domestic duties, the Owenites provided well-equipped kitchens to reduce women's labour. In one community, Manea Fen in the Isle of Ely, which was established during 1839–41, prospective members were told that 'The food will be cooked by a scientific apparatus; thus saving an immense labour for the females . . . Machinery, which has hitherto been for the benefit of the rich, will be adopted in the colony for lessening labour' (Pearson 1988: 4).

In spite of the good intentions of the Owenites, the projects were not popular among working-class women. For the remainder of the nineteenth century, a range of approaches to communal domestic work were attempted, but these were mainly concerned with the work of working-class women, since the middle classes were able to employ servants to undertake the bulk of domestic work. In the twentieth century, however, there were attempts to provide communal domestic arrangements for middle-class women, especially in the new Garden Suburbs.

Designed by M.H. Baillie Scott, Waterlow Court, opened in Hampstead Garden Suburb in 1909, is a cloistered quadrangle of fifty flats set around a central lawn. Designed for unmarried professional women, the flats were served by a central dining room, common room and kitchen. Although each flat had a cooker and scullery, it was not assumed that these professional women would undertake their own domestic duties and a servant's hall and annex were added. The example is a useful one as it demonstrates the opportunity for single women to live communally at a time when there was a clear expectation that marriage was the only acceptable route for the respectable woman (Zimmeck 1986). As one columnist stated, 'The way ladies live after working hours is of more importance than the question of how or where or when they work'; she went on to suggest that women who were not married were likely to become careless in their living conditions and suggested that the single woman may fall 'below her natural birthright of a lady; and her companions know it' (Pearson 1988: 109). While there were many twentieth-century attempts at creating opportunities for communal living for women, or communised domestic work for working-class families, these fell into decline as the provision of better designed households, serviced with mains water, electricity or gas, eased the work of married women.

Self-actualisation in communes

From the eighteenth to the early twentieth centuries, most communitarian movements were based on the principle that individuals who wished to step outside the dominant or mainstream society must be willing to subordinate themselves to the interests of their chosen community – the most successful of which owed their longevity to the acceptance of the legitimacy of religious doctrine. By contrast, in the twentieth century, the notion of the commune as a retreat for people wishing to exercise unconstrained individualism became more popular. This might seem be a radical departure from earlier forms of retreat which rejected societies which were seen to be unprincipled or without discipline.

Aldous Huxley championed the view that society limited the individual's scope for self-actualisation. He argued that in a world of 'overpopulation and over organisation . . . a fully human life of multiple relationships [has become] almost impossible' (quoted in Rigby 1974: 30). Huxley sought to achieve his mystical aim of discovering his inner self or the 'Divine Ground' or 'Ultimate Reality' through the use of hallucinogenic drugs. In this sense, Huxley antici-pated the development of a new approach to communal life which developed in the 1960s. Rigby explains the principles of later communes:

> For many of them, drug experiences are defined in pantheistic terms, and the goals of drug-taking are expressed in terms of expanding the consciousness in order to attain that level of awareness whereby the individual becomes one with the divine . . . the purpose of life is not to conquer the material world but is rather to conquer the ego and to discover one's true self. Moreover, many trippers claim to have become aware through their drug experiences, of the essential unity of all things, of the universal link that is immanent throughout all things, especially between the brotherhood of man.
>
> (Rigby 1974: 30)

These dual aims of achieving contact with the inner self while also attaining notions of universality were commonly expressed in mystical terms by the commune dwellers of the 1960s and 1970s in Britain and North America and formed the basis upon which many young anarchists attempted to escape from the conformist restraints of the mainstream. Without the unifying discipline of faith, however, communes tended to have fairly short lives. One of the main stumbling blocks for such groups was their attempt to rid the commune of the ties between kin and replace them with genuinely egalitarian and open relationships. One of Rigby's respondents reflects this view:

> The nuclear family is a repressive and horrible institution . . . where there are only two people, then misunderstandings can arise, you only get a restricted view of each other – in a commune there are others there to give an 'objective' account of their perceptions, clear the air, and so enable you to become more fully aware of each other as humans, clear up the misconceptions that develop through distorted perceptions.
>
> (quoted in Rigby 1974: 266–267)

The strong belief in achieving full awareness of the self and each other is a central thread in many attempts to establish communal life at this time, but ultimately, the two aims created real tensions. Rigby demonstrates that there were many ways in which these strains could manifest themselves.

> The propensity for secular communities to be split by dissensions has usually been heightened by the fact that a large proportion of the members of such communities have been attracted to such experiments as believers in individual freedom and liberty, ends which they have sought to attain through communal living. Such people, who have traditionally found the constraints of life in conventional society irksome, would be unlikely to accept without question the demands of the communal leaders.
>
> (Rigby 1974: 283)

The notion of 'leadership' itself led to the collapse of many communes. Rigby provides examples of leaders (often owners of the property) who demanded, for example, complete sexual freedom; this demand was soon enough discovered to be an excuse to sleep with all the women under his roof. As one woman wrote of her hippie community experience in the United States:

> The talk of love is profuse but the quality of relationship is otherwise. The hip man like his straight counterpart is nothing more, nothing less, than a predator . . . the idea of sexual liberation for the woman means she is not so much free to fuck but free to get fucked over.
>
> (Rigby 1974: 285)

Communes disestablished themselves for other reasons, of course, including arguments over property, over money, work (or laziness), of the degree of openness of the group which may involve outsiders taking advantage of the permanent members and so on. The decline of communes was well under way by the middle of the 1970s as the hard economic realities of post-oil crisis recession took hold of the Western world. There remain some vestiges of New Age idealism, of course, best represented in Britain with New Age Travellers.

Non-communal alternatives

If we look outside these more organised or collective forms within which people 'dare to be different', what scope is there for attaining the opportunity to live in truly alternative domestic and community environment? In Britain it has remained difficult for individuals or groups to simply set up house and home on marginal land due to the long established and rigorous control over land use and the constraints of high land prices. Nomadic lifestyles, such as that chosen by Gypsies, are therefore highly constrained by policies which prohibit the use of waste land for living accommodation, however temporary (Okely 1983). Unlike the United States, Canada or Australia, it has rarely been possible for people in Britain to establish anything resembling a frontier mentality in their approach to settling or building. One notable exception is the plotlands movement during the recession of the 1930s, when land prices fell so low that individuals and families could buy small plots for as little as £3 (King 1984; Ward 1985). The building of these unplanned and makeshift suburbs, which were established all over Essex, in the Thames Valley, the Weald of Kent and Sussex, was 'deplored by all right-thinking (i.e. well housed) people and has been outlawed by post-war planning legislation' (Ward 1989: 32). For the people who lived there it was a different story:

> Such housing was not, however, despised by its inhabitants, who were often poor families from the East End of London, and wherever a policy of benign neglect has been adopted by planning authorities the properties have been endlessly improved by their owners and are gratefully lived in today by their grandchildren.
>
> (Ward 1989: 32)

Ironically, some of the most famous plotland sites are now revered by the architectural aesthetes who may once have sought their removal on the grounds that they represented a blot on the natural landscape. Indeed, some plotland sites are now protected as conservation areas. If there ever was a truly post-modern juxtaposition it is that of the architectural critic showering praise on a sham of clapboard and corrugated iron houses with brightly painted picket fences, quirky chimney pots and flower-laden open-fronted porches.

There are, in fact, many examples of resistance to the dictates of conventional planning and design in Britain and the rest of Europe which provide alternative opportunities of housing. For example, in Almere, to the north-west of Amsterdam, the houses built as part of competitions to design alternative housing in 1982 and 1985 continue to form thriving communities. Designed to be cost-efficient, temporary and energy-saving, they include a red steel tower house, a wooden hut on stilts and a tiny house with polystyrene walls and neo-classical detailing (*Observer*, 22 February 1998). It is not possible here to explore such innovations extensively; we can, however, look in more detail at the example of community self-build schemes.

There have been over a hundred schemes developed by community self-build groups in the UK since 1990. Their very existence points to the possibility of alternatives, not just for the very wealthy, but also for the marginalised and the disadvantaged. Unlike conventional groups of self-builders, who collectively raise the finance necessary to develop a site and then build for ownership, community self-build schemes enable groups of people who are unemployed or on a limited income to build homes which they are then able to rent or partly own (Broome and Richardson 1991).

The first scheme of this nature was developed by a group drawn from the council house waiting list in Lewisham, south London, between 1979 and 1981. This was a pioneering initiative utilising the revolutionary construction approach formulated by the architect, Walter Segal. The approach lends itself to self-build because the construction technique is relatively simple and people with no building experience can swiftly gain the necessary skills. Houses are built around structural frames which stand above the ground on 'spot foundations', eliminating the costly, messy and time-consuming process of levelling the site and digging conventional foundations. Roofs are attached immediately after the frames have been raised and before the walls have been filled in. This means that the rest of the construction can take place under cover. Unlike traditional self-build groups, there were no penalties to ensure that everyone 'pulled their weight' because Segal claimed that the less you tried to control the group members, the more likely that good will would be engendered. As Segal commented:

> They were told that I would not interfere with the internal arrangements. I let them make their own decisions . . . What I found astonishing with these people was the direct personal friendly contact that I had with them and which they had among themselves. And quite beyond that the tapping of their own ideas – countless small variations and innovations, and additions were made by them.
>
> (quoted in Ward 1988: 53)

There was a second equally successful Lewisham scheme but very few other schemes like this got off the ground in the 1980s. The reasons for this are complex. Until the Walter Segal Self Build Trust was established in 1988 and the Community Self Build Agency in 1989, there was little knowledge about the possibilities. Indeed, there was considerable scepticism among the planning fraternity about alternative construction techniques which often stemmed from their earlier experiences with system building and prefabricated timber framed schemes.

While the current level of activity suggests that many of these problems have been overcome, much of the idealism that characterised early schemes has now gone. As Turner (1974) notes, the spontaneous good will or 'communitas' which characterises the initial phase of alternative movements frequently gives way to 'normative communitas', the production of ground rules and differentiated social roles. Thus, the roots of this new realism may be seen in the organisation of the Zenzele Self-Build Scheme in Bristol. In this project, the emphasis was upon a 'clear chain of command' and on 'compliance with rules'. The project was initiated to provide incentives and work experience, to enable young people to acquire their own accommodation and take pride in it, and to 'demonstrate that a home of one's own is a possibility for even the most disadvantaged members of society' (National Federation of

Housing Associations 1988). The accounts of the Zenzele scheme do not mention participant involvement in design issues; in fact, the size and layout of the flats were deliberately kept 'as simple as possible' in order to ensure that there would be no arguments over who got what when the flats were allocated (National Federation of Housing Associations 1988).

The actual level of involvement, beyond basic construction work, often depends upon the way that a scheme has been initiated. If the initiative has come from an authority external to the group, then it is likely to be 'directed', while in those initiatives that are self-determined – such as short-life housing co-operatives, squatters or an existing community group – the degree of involvement appears to be much greater. The Fusions Jameen Self-Build Co-operative, for example, is a group of young African-Caribbean men and women in Lewisham which established themselves when a short arrangement with the local authority came to an end. As Barrymore James, a member of the group, explained:

> We knew that Lewisham was looking into alternative forms of housing for the growing number of single people on its waiting list, and that one of the options was self-building. At the same time the local secondary [housing] co-op CHISEL was promoting self-build using the Walter Segal method and had come up with schemes whereby you didn't need to have a lot of money or earning a lot to be able to do it.
> (Walter Segal Self Build Trust 1993)

Fusions Jameen designed their homes with their architects, Architype, and the project has been described as an outstanding and innovative example of projects which attempt to take account of the specific cultural needs of a minority ethnic group (North Housing Trust 1993). While it is the case that members of self-build schemes often end up 'falling out' with each over the allocation of houses, about the level of financial commitment, the effort that has been expended and so forth, self-building does offer opportunities to the less well off. Undoubtedly, getting a house that is better or bigger than would otherwise be available and being in some way remunerated for the labour undertaken is the key motivating factor for most individuals involved in self-building schemes. But the opportunity to collaborate in the design process presents participants with some options to think critically about the domestic sphere and thereby change the way it is structured.

Conclusion

People who dare to be different are in the minority, often celebrating that status and defending it from the constant pressure to 'conform' to the mainstream, or, in some cases – like 'deep green' activists – adopt a more evangelical stance, and try to bring the rest of the population into ecological line.

For the majority, however, notions of the ideal home are circumscribed by capital, state and civil society, their family, neighbours and friends. People's conceptions of home and the pattern of life that it affords are also shaped by the life course itself, the rigours of which force us into patterns of behaviour that might at one time have seemed impossibly mundane and restrictive. The birth of a child, for example, changes attitudes towards the home completely. Whereas once a couple might spend a Saturday afternoon sipping coffee in a sophisticated café while enjoying animated discussion of the latest fashion in interior design – they find themselves only months later, living in Bedlam caused by the baby they believed they could fit into their existing lifestyle. At the other end of the life course, as Hockey (Chapter 9) has shown, decisions about the management of our own homes can be taken from us altogether, as we are put into the care of others in the old people's home.

Establishing alternatives is difficult for most people, then, because they are too busy snatching opportunities to play between long bouts of work, to conceive of some kind of radically different lifestyle. That is not to say that people do not dream of a change. Perhaps about three-quarters of the population do this every week as they queue for their Lottery ticket on a Saturday afternoon. Just because most people do conform to conventional lifestyles, it does not follow that their lives lack meaning or interest. Some writers arrogantly make an immediate association between suburban living and banality (for critical discussions of suburban life see, for example, Silverstone 1997; Carey 1992; Oliver et al. 1981). That is, of course, both offensive and unfair; most of the writers who have contributed to this book live in the suburbs! A more positive gloss on the situation can be found in the writings of C. Wright Mills, whose shrewd sociological imagination led him to point out that:

> Each day [people] sell little pieces of themselves in order to try to buy them back each night and week-end with the coin of fun. With amusement, with love, with movies, with vicarious intimacy, they pull themselves into some sort of whole again, and now they are different.
>
> (Mills 1951: 237)

More recently, other writers demonstrate that people make 'escape attempts' from the mainstream, but not at the cost of losing the respect of significant others (Cohen and Taylor 1992). While it may be the case then, that most people are 'culturally conservative', they have a good reason for being so: they have not got the resources to do much else.

Those people who join together with a vision of a better community and 'dare to be different' face all manner of unanticipated pressures to conform, as this chapter has shown. Some such groups survive across the centuries, but that is a product of their cohesive system of rules, together with the sublimation of personal interest to collective beliefs. The excessive levels of social integration of those communities that are led by charismatics can produce serious problems too, of course, as was demonstrated to be the case in the Waco massacre in the United States, or the periodic incidents of mass suicide in closed religious communities.

Absolute individualists are the real exception, like Albert Dryden, who shot dead Harry Collinson, a Derwentside District Council planning officer in front of television cameras because he sought to protect his ramshackle and illegally erected property from demolition. Little can be done about the determined odd-balls, the people who do not just dare to be different, but celebrate their individuality, while driving everyone else crazy in the process, like a cunning individualist in North Yorkshire who has built a swimming pool on wheels to avoid requiring planning permission (R. Brown 1997). And yet, even these individualistic people, in a contradictory kind of way, serve to reinforce the belief among the rest of us that order in the community allows us to be ourselves. While we may not be able to control 'outsiders', they at least confirm our belief that *order* – irritating and confining though it may be from time to time – is preferable to chaos because it lets us get on with our lives.

BIBLIOGRAPHY

Abbott, P. and Wallace, C. (1997) *An Introduction to Sociology: Feminist Perspectives*, 2nd edn, London: Routledge.

Abrahams, R. (1983) *The Man of Words in the West Indies*, Baltimore, MD: Johns Hopkins University Press.

Adams, S. (1993) 'A gendered history of the social management of death and dying in Foleshill, Coventry, during the inter-war years', in D. Clark (ed.) *The Sociology of Death*, Oxford: Blackwell/Sociological Review.

Adorno, T. (1991) *The Culture Industry: Selected Essays on Mass Culture*, London: Routledge.

Ahlberg, J. and Ahlberg, A. (1977) *Burglar Bill*, London: Heinemann.

Ainley, P. (1991) *Young People Leaving Home*, London: Cassell.

Allan, G. and Crow, G. (eds) (1989) *Home and Family: Creating the Domestic Sphere*, London: Macmillan.

Allen, I., Hogg, D. and Peace, S. (1992) *Elderly People: Choice, Participation and Satisfaction*, London: Policy Studies Institute.

Anderson, D., Chenery, S. and Pease, K. (1995) 'Biting back: tackling repeat burglary and car crime', Police Research Group: Crime Detection and Prevention Series no. 58, London: Home Office.

Anderson, S., Grove-Smith, C., Kinsey, R. and Wood, J. (1990) *The Edinburgh Crime Survey*, Edinburgh: Scottish Office.

Appadurai, A. (1996) *Modernity at Large: Cultural Dimensions of Globalization*, Minneapolis: University of Minnesota Press.

Aries, P. (1981) *The Hour of Our Death*, Harmondsworth: Penguin.

Arnold, E. and Barr, L. (1985) 'Housework and the appliance of science', in W. Faulkner (ed.) *Smothered by Invention: Technology and Women's Lives*, London: Pluto.

Attfield, J. (1989) 'Inside pram town: a case study of Harlow home interiors 1951–61', in J. Attfield and P. Kirkham (eds) *A View from the Interior: Feminism, Women and Design*, London: Women's Press.

Bachelard, G. (1969) *The Poetics of Space*, Boston, MA: Beacon Press.

Bachelard, G. ([1958] 1994) *The Poetics of Space*, Boston, MA: Beacon Press.

Bailin, M. (1994) *The Sickroom in Victorian Fiction: The Art of Being Ill*, Cambridge: Cambridge University Press.

Balchin, P. (1995) *Housing Policy: An Introduction*, 3rd edn, London: Routledge.

Banham, R. (1960) *Theory and Design in the First Machine Age*, London: Butterworth.

Barbey, G. (1993) 'Spatial analysis and the experience of time: identifying the dimensions of home', in E.G. Arias (ed.) *The Meaning and Use of Housing: International Perspectives, Approaches and their Applications*, Aldershot: Avebury.

Barker, D. and Allen, S. (1976) *Dependency and Exploitation in Work and Marriage*, London: Longman.

Barley, N. (1990) *Native Land*, Harmondsworth: Penguin.

Barrett, M. and Mackintosh, M. (1980) *The Antisocial Family*, London: Verso.

Bartram, M. (1985) *The Pre-Raphaelite Camera*, London: Weidenfeld and Nicolson.

Bauman, Z. (1988) *Freedom*, Milton Keynes: Open University Press.

Bauman, Z. (1991) *Modernity and Ambivalence*, Oxford: Polity.

Baxter, J. (1993) *Work at Home: The Domestic Division of Labour*, St Lucia: University of Queensland Press.

Baxter, J. and Western, M. (1998) 'Satisfaction with housework: examining the paradox', *Sociology*, 32, 1: 101–120.

Beck, U. (1992) *Risk Society: Towards a New Modernity*, London: Sage.

Becker, H. (1963) *Outsiders: Studies in the Sociology of Deviance*, Glencoe, IL: Free Press.

Becker, H. (1970) *Sociological Work: Method and Substance*, Chicago: Chicago University Press.

Bell, C. and Newby, H. (1976) 'Husbands and wives: the deferential dialectic', in D. Barker and S. Allen (eds) *Dependency and Exploitation in Work and Marriage*, London: Longman.

Bell, L. and Ribbens, J. (1994) 'Isolated housewives and complex maternal worlds – the significance of social contacts between women with young children in industrial societies', *Sociological Review*, 42, 2: 227–262.

Bennett, A. (1994) *Writing Home*, London: Faber and Faber.

Bennett, T. and Wright, R. (1984) *Burglars on Burglary: Prevention and the Offender*, Aldershot: Gower.

Berk, S. (1985) *The Gender Factory: The Apportionment of Work in American Households*, New York: Plenum.

Berthelot, J. and Gaumé, M. (1982) *Kaz Antiyé Jan Moun Ka Rété. Caribbean Popular Dwelling*. Paris: Editions Caribéennes.

Besson, J. (1993) 'Reputation and respectability reconsidered: a new perspective on Afro-Caribbean peasant women', in J. Momsen (ed.) *Women and Change in the Caribbean*, London: James Currey.

Beynon, H. (1997) 'The changing practices of work', in R. Brown (ed.) *The Changing Shape of Work*, London: Macmillan.

Bhatti, M. (1993) 'Housing, post modernity and sustainability: towards the greening of housing studies', paper presented to the Housing Studies Association Conference, 14–15 April, University of Reading.

Bhatti, M. (1994) 'Environmental futures and the housing question', in M. Bhatti, J. Brooke and M. Gibson (eds) *Housing and the Environment: A New Agenda*, Coventry: Chartered Institute of Housing.

Bhatti, M. and Church, A. (1998) 'Gardening and leisure in the age of risk', mimeo, University of Brighton.

Bloch, M. (1971) *Placing the Dead*, London: Seminar Press.

Bond, J. and Coleman, P. (1990) *Ageing in Society*, London: Sage.

Bond, J., Coleman, P. and Peace, S. (1993) *Ageing in Society*, 2nd edn, London: Sage.

Booth, C., Darke, J. and Yeandle, S. (1996) *Changing Places: Women's Lives in the City*, London: Paul Chapman.

Borsay, P. (ed.) (1990) *The Eighteenth Century Town: A Reader in English Urban History: 1688–1820*, London: Longman.

Bourdieu, P. (1973) 'The Berber House', in M. Douglas (ed.) *Rules and Meanings*, Harmondsworth: Penguin.

Bourdieu, P. (1986) *Distinction: A Social Critique of Judgements of Taste*, London: Routledge.

Bowlby, J. (1990) *Charles Darwin: A Biography*, London: Hutchinson.

Bradley, H. (1989) *Men's Work, Women's Work: A Sociological History of the Sexual Division of Labour in Employment*, Oxford: Polity.

Bradley, I. (1997) *Abide with Me: The World of Victorian Hymns*, London: SCM Press.

Brewer, P. (1986) *Shaker Communities, Shaker Lives*, Hanover, NH: University Press of New England.

Briggs, A. (1968) *Victorian Cities*, Harmondsworth: Penguin.

Briggs, A. (1990) *Victorian Things*, Harmondsworth: Penguin.

Brindle, D. (1997) 'Rise in single households takes toll on wedding bells', *Guardian*, 30 January.

Brindley, T. (1989) 'Social theory and architectural innovation in housing design', paper presented to IAPS Symposium, Housing and Neighbourhoods, Aivkarleby, Sweden.

Brontë, C. ([1847] 1960) *Jane Eyre*, New York: New American Library.

Broome, J. and Richardson, B. (1991) *The Self Build Book*, London: Green Books.

Brown, B. and Altman, A. (1983) 'Territoriality, defensible space and residential burglary: an environmental analysis', *Journal of Environmental Psychology*, 3: 203–220.

Brown, J. (1997) 'Self-build housing and individualism', unpublished dissertation, School of Social Science, University of Teesside.

Brown, R. (ed.) (1997) *The Changing Shape of Work*, London: Macmillan.

Burbidge, M. (1981) *An Investigation of Difficult to Let Housing*, 3 vols, London: HMSO.

Burnett, J. (1986) *A Social History of British Housing 1815–1985*, 2nd edn, London: Methuen.

Butler, A., Oldman, C. and Greve, J. (1983) *Sheltered Housing for the Elderly*, London: Allen and Unwin.

Butler, T. and Savage, M. (1995) *Social Change and the Middle Classes*, London: UCL Press.

Byetheway, W. (1982) 'Living under an umbrella: problems of identity in sheltered housing', in A. Warnes (ed.) *Geographical Perspectives on the Elderly*, London: Wiley.

Byron, M. (1994) *Post-War Caribbean Migration to Britain: The Unfinished Cycle*, Research in Ethnic Relations Series, Aldershot: Avebury.

Carey, J. (1992) *The Intellectuals and the Masses: Pride and Prejudice Among the Literary Intelligentsia, 1880–1939*, London: Faber and Faber.

Carlson, A. (1993) 'Liberty, order and the family', in J. Davies (ed.) *The Family: Is it Just Another Life-style Choice?*, London: Institute of Economic Affairs.

Carroll, N. (1990) *The Philosophy of Horror*, New York: Routledge.

Casteras, S. (1987) *Images of Victorian Womanhood in English Art*, Rutherford, NJ: Fairleigh Dickinson University Press.

Chapman, D. (1955) *The Home and Social Status*, London: Routledge and Kegan Paul.

Chapman, T. (1989) 'Just the ticket? The careers of graduate men and women three years after leaving college', Higher Education and Labour Market Working Paper no. 6, London: Council for National Academic Awards.

Chapman, T. (1995) 'Stage sets for ideal lives', *New Statesman and Society*, 9 April.

Chapman, T. (1996) 'Energy conservation in a cold climate', *Policy Studies*, 17, 4: 299–314.

Chapman, T. (1999) 'The Ideal Home Exhibition: an analysis of the constraints and conventions on consumer choice in British homes', in J. Hearn and S. Roseneil (eds) *Consuming Cultures*, London: Macmillan.

Chapman, T. and Lucas, R. (1998) 'A place for a body to live: portrayals of body privacy and communion in contemporary show homes', mimeo, British Sociological Association Annual Conference, Edinburgh, April.

Charles, N. and Kerr, M. (1988) *Women, Food and Families*, Manchester: Manchester University Press.

Cheal, D. (1987) 'Showing them you love them: gift giving and the dialectic of intimacy', *Sociological Review*, 35, 1: 150–169.

Clark, D. (1993) *The Future of Palliative Care*, Buckingham: Open University Press.

Clayton-Payne, A. (1988) *Victorian Flower Gardens*, London: Weidenfeld and Nicolson.

Clifton-Taylor, A. (1984) *Another Six English Towns*, London: BBC Books.

Clough, C. (ed.) (1982) *Profession, Vocation and Culture in Later Medieval England*, Liverpool: Liverpool University Press.

Cohen, A. (1994) *Self Consciousness: An Alternative Anthropology of Identity*, London: Routledge.

Cohen, S. and Taylor, L. (1992) *Escape Attempts: The Theory and Practice of Resistance to Everyday Life*, 2nd edn, London: Routledge.

Coleman, A. (1985) *Utopia on Trial: Vision and Reality in Planned Housing*, London: Hilary Shipman.

Constantine, S. (1981) 'Amateur gardening and popular recreation in the 19th and 20th centuries', *Journal of Social History*, 14, 3: 389–403.

Cooper, C. (1976) 'The house as a symbol of self', in H.M. Proshansky, W.H. Ittleson and L.G. Rivlin (eds) *Environmental Psychology: People and their Physical Settings*, New York: Holt, Rinehart and Winston.

Cooper-Marcus, C. (1990) 'The garden as metaphor', in M. Francis and R. Hester (eds) *The Meaning of Gardens*, Cambridge, MA: MIT Press.

Corrigan, P. (1997) *The Sociology of Consumption*, London: Sage.

Coser, L. (1977) *Masters of Sociological Thought: Ideas in Historical and Social Context*, New York: Harcourt Brace Jovanovich.

Couper, M. and Brindley, T. (1975) 'Housing classes and housing values', *Sociological Review*, 23, 3: 563–576.

Cowan, R. (1989) *More Work for Mother: The Ironies of Household Technology from the Open Hearth to the Microwave*, London: Free Association.

Cowling, M. (1989) *The Artist as Anthropologist: The Representation of Type and Character in Victorian Art*, Cambridge: Cambridge University Press.

Crawford, D. (ed.) (1975) *A Decade of British Housing, 1963–1973*, London: Architectural Press.

Creese, W. (1966) *The Search for Environment: The Garden City Before and After*, New Haven, CT: Yale University Press.

Crompton, R. and Sanderson, K. (1990) *Gendered Jobs and Social Change*, London: Unwin/Hyman.

Cromwell, P., Olson, J. and Avary, D. (1991) *Breaking and Entering: an Ethnographic Analysis of Burglary*, Newbury Park, CA: Sage.

Crouch, C. and Ward, C. (1988) *The Allotment, its Landscape and Culture*, London: Faber and Faber.

Cruickshank, D. and Burton, N. (1990) *Life in the Georgian City*, London: Viking.

Csikszentmihalyi, M. and Rochberg-Halton, E. (1981) *The Meaning of Things: Domestic Symbols and the Self*, London: Cambridge University Press.

Currie, E. (1988) 'Two visions of community crime prevention', in T. Hope and M. Shaw (eds) *Communities and Crime Reduction*, London: HMSO.

Curtis, W. (1987) *Modern Architecture since 1900*, 2nd edn, Oxford: Phaidon.

Darke, J. (1996) 'The Englishwoman's castle, or, don't you just love being in control?', in C. Booth, J. Darke and S. Yeandle (eds) *Changing Places: Women's Lives in the City*, London: Paul Chapman.

Daunton, M. (1983a) 'Public place and private space: the Victorian city and working class household', in D. Fraser and A. Sutcliffe (eds) *The Pursuit of Urban History*, London: Edward Arnold.

Daunton, M. (1983b) *House and Home in the Victorian City: Working Class Housing 1850–1914*, London: Edward Arnold.

Davidoff, L. and Hall, L. (1987) *Family Fortunes: Men and Women of the English Middle Class, 1780–1850*, London: Hutchinson.

Davidoff, L., L'Esperance, J. and Newby, H. (1983) 'Landscape with figures: home and community in English society', in A. Oakley and J. Mitchell (eds) *The Rights and Wrongs of Women*, Harmondsworth: Penguin.

Davidson, J. (1988) *How Green is Your City?*, London: Bedford Square Press.

Davis, M. (1990) *City of Quartz: Excavating the Future of Los Angeles*, London: Verso.

Davis, M. (1992a) *Beyond Blade Runner: Urban Control, the Ecology of Fear*, Westfield, NJ: Open Magazine Pamphlets.

Davis, M. (1992b) 'Fortress Los Angeles: the militization of urban space', in M. Sorkin (ed.) *Variations on a Theme Park*, New York: Hill and Wang.

Dawson, A. (1990) 'Ageing and change in the pit villages of North East England', unpublished PhD thesis, University of Essex.

Deem, R. (1986) *All Work and No Play? A Study of Women and Leisure*, Milton Keynes: Open University Press.

Delphy, C. (1977) *The Main Enemy*, London: Women's Research and Resource Centre.

Delphy, C. (1984) *Close to Home: A Materialist Analysis of Women's Oppression*, London: Hutchinson.

Dennis, N. and Erdos, G. (1993) *Families Without Fatherhood*, 2nd edn, London: Institute of Economic Affairs.

Dennis, R., Henriques, F. and Slaughter, C. (1956) *Coal is Our Life*, London: Eyre and Spottiswoode.

Department for Education and Employment (1995) *Education Statistics for the United Kingdom 1995*, London: HMSO.

Department of the Environment (1994) *English House Condition Survey 1991*, London: HMSO.

Department of the Environment (1995) *Projections of Households in England*, London: HMSO.

Department of the Environment (1997) *Housing and Construction Statistics*, London: HMSO.

Design Bulletins (1974) *Housing the Elderly*, Lancaster: MTP Construction.

Desmond, A. and Moore, J. (1992) *Darwin*, Harmondsworth: Penguin.

Després, C. (1993) 'A hybrid strategy in a study of shared housing', in E.G. Arias (ed.) *The Meaning and Use of Housing*, Aldershot: Avebury.

De Vault, M. (1991) *Feeding the Family: The Social Organisation of Caring as Gendered Work*, Chicago: Chicago University Press.

Dickens, P. (1992) *Society and Nature: Towards a Green Social Theory*, London: Harvester.

Dickens, P. (1996) *Reconstructing Nature: Alienation, Emancipation and the Division of Labour*, London: Routledge.

Dittmar, H. (1992) *The Social Psychology of Material Possessions*, Hemel Hempstead: Harvester/Wheatsheaf.

Dobash, R. and Dobash, R. (1980) *Violence Against Wives*, New York: Free Press.

Dobash, R. and Dobash, R. (1981) 'Community responses to violence against wives: charivari, abstract justice and patriarchy', *Social Problems*, 28, 5: 563–581.

Dobash, R. and Dobash, R. (1992) *Women, Violence and Social Change*, London: Routledge.

Douglas, J. (1970) 'Deviance and respectability: the social construction of moral meanings', in J. Douglas (ed.) *Deviance and Respectability: The Social Construction of Moral Meanings*, London: Basic Books.

Douglas, M. (1966) *Purity and Danger: An Analysis of Concepts of Pollution and Taboo*, London: Routledge and Kegan Paul.

Douglas, M. (ed.)(1973) *Rules and Meanings: An Anthropology of Everyday Knowledge*, Harmondsworth: Penguin.

Douglas, M. (1975) *Implicit Meanings*, London: Routledge and Kegan Paul.

Douglas, M. (1997) 'In defence of shopping', in P. Falk and C. Campbell (eds) *The Shopping Experience*, London: Sage.

Dunleavy, P. (1981) *The Politics of Mass Housing in Britain, 1945–1975*, Oxford: Clarendon Press.

Dworkin, A. (1981) *Pornography: Men Possessing Women*, London: Women's Press.

Edwards, S. (1986) 'The real risks of violence behind closed doors', *New Law Journal*, 136: 1191–1193.

Edwards, S. (1989) *Policing 'Domestic' Violence: Women, the Law and the State*, London: Sage.

Engel, A. (1983) *From Clergyman to Don: The Rise of the Academic Profession in Nineteenth Century Oxford*, Oxford: Oxford University Press.

Engels, F. ([1845] 1969) *The Condition of the Working Class in England in 1844*, St Albans: Granada.

Fairhurst, E. (1997) 'Recalling life: analytical issues in the use of "memories"', in A. Jamieson, S. Harper and C. Victor (eds) *Critical Approaches to Ageing and Later Life*, Buckingham: Open University Press.

Falk, P. (1994) *The Consuming Body*, London: Sage.

Falk, P. and Campbell, C. (eds) (1997) *The Shopping Experience*, London: Sage.

Faludi, S. (1991) *Backlash: The Undeclared War Against American Women*, London: Chatto and Windus.

Faulkner, W. and Arnold, E. (eds) (1985) *Smothered by Invention: Technology and Women's Lives*, London: Women's Press.

Featherstone, M. (1991) *Consumer Culture and Postmodernism*, London: Sage.

Featherstone, M., Hepworth, M. and Turner, B. (eds) (1991) *The Body, Social Process and Cultural Theory*, London: Sage.

Finch, J. (1983) *Married to the Job: Wives' Incorporation in Men's Work*, London: Allen and Unwin.

Finch, J. and Hayes, L. (1994) 'Inheritance, death and the concept of home', *Sociology*, 28, 2: 417–435.

Finnimore, B. (1989) *Houses from the Factory: System Building and the Welfare State, 1942–74*, London: Rivers Oram.

Firestone, S. (1974) *The Dialectics of Sex: The Case for Feminist Revolution*, New York: Morrow.

Fishman, R. (1977) *Urban Utopias in the Twentieth Century*, New York: Basic Books.

Ford, J., Kempson, E. and Wilson, M. (1995) *Mortgage Arrears and Possessions: Perspectives from Borrowers, Lenders and the Courts*, London: HMSO/Department of the Environment.

Forrest, R. and Murie, A. (1988) *Selling the Welfare State: The Privatisation of Public Housing*, London: Routledge.

Forty, A. (1986) *Objects of Desire: Design and Society 1750–1980*, London: Thames and Hudson.

Forty, A. and Moss, H. (1980) 'A housing style for troubled consumers: the success of the pseudo vernacular', *Architectural Review*, 167: 73–78.

Fox, K. (1985) *Metropolitan America: Urban Life and Urban Policy in the USA*, London: Macmillan.

Frampton, K. (1985) *Modern Architecture: A Critical History*, 2nd edn, London: Thames and Hudson.

Francis, M. and Hester, R. (eds) (1990) *The Meaning of Gardens*, Cambridge, MA: MIT Press.

Frykman, J. and Löfgren, O. (1983) *Culture Builders: A Historical Anthropology of Middle-class Life*, New Brunswick, NJ: Rutgers University Press.

Gamarnikow, E., Morgan, D., Purvis, J. and Taylorson, D. (1983) *The Public and the Private*, London: Heinemann.

Garfinkel, H. (1956) 'Conditions of successful degradation ceremonies', *American Journal of Sociology*, 61, 3: 420–424.

Gauldie, E. (1974) *Cruel Habitations: A History of Working Class Housing, 1780–1918*, London: Allen and Unwin.

Gavron, H. (1968) *The Captive Wife*, Harmondsworth: Penguin.

Giddens, A. (1991) *Modernity and Self Identity: Self and Society in the Late Modern Age*, Oxford: Polity.

Gilbert, O. (1989) *Ecology of Urban Habitats*, London: Chapman Hall.

Giraud, D. (1990) 'Shared backyard gardening', in M. Francis and R. Hester (eds) *The Meaning of Gardens*, Cambridge, MA: MIT Press.

Girouard, M. (1978) *Life in the English Country House*, Harmondsworth: Penguin.

Girouard, M. (1989) *Cities and People: A Social and Architectural History*, New Haven: Yale University Press.

Girouard, M. (1990) *The English Town*, New Haven: Yale University Press.

Gittins, D. (1993) *The Family in Question*, 2nd edn, Basingstoke: Macmillan.

Glendinning, M. and Muthesius, S. (1994) *Tower Block: Modern Public Housing in England, Scotland, Wales and Northern Ireland*, London: Yale University Press.

Goffman, E. (1963) *Stigma: Notes on the Management of a Spoiled Personality*, Harmondsworth: Penguin.

Goffman, E. (1969) *The Presentation of Self in Everyday Life*, Harmondsworth: Penguin.

Goffman, E. (1974) *Asylums*, Harmondsworth: Penguin.

Gold, M. (1984) 'A history of nature', in D. Massey and J. Allen (eds) *Geography Matters!*, Cambridge: Cambridge University Press.

Gold, R. (1952) 'Janitors versus tenants: a status–income dilemma', *American Journal of Sociology*, 57, 1: 486–493.

Goldsack, L. and Ridley, L. (1998) *An Evaluation of the Zero Tolerance Campaign in Cleveland: The Final Report*, Middlesbrough: School of Social Sciences, University of Teesside.

Gore, P. (1993) 'From undertaker to funeral director: development of funeral firms in east Kent', unpublished MPhil thesis, University of Kent.

Greed, C.H. (1994) *Women and Planning: Creating Gendered Realities*, London: Routledge.

Green, E., Hebron, S. and Woodward, D. (1990) *Women's Leisure, What Leisure?*, London: Macmillan.

Greenhalgh, P. (ed.) (1990) *Modernism in Design*, London: Reaktion.

Greenwood, W. ([1933] 1969) *Love on the Dole*, Harmondsworth: Penguin.

Gregson, N. and Lowe, M. (1994) 'Waged domestic labour and the renegotiation of the domestic division of labour within dual career households', *Sociology*, 28, 1: 55–78.

Grier, K. (1988) *Culture and Comfort: People, Parlours and Upholstery: 1850–1930*, Rochester, NY: The Strong Museum.

Griffin, C. (1985) *Typical Girls?*, London: Routledge.

Guiliani, M.V. (1991) 'Towards an analysis of mental representations of attachment to the home', *Journal of Architectural and Planning Research*, 8, 2: 133–146.

Gullestad, M. (1993) 'Home decoration as popular culture: constructing homes, genders and classes in Norway', in T. del Valle (ed.) *Gendered Anthropology*, London: Routledge.

Hackney, R. (1990) *The Good, The Bad and The Ugly: Cities in Crisis*, London: Muller.

Hakim, C. (1991) 'Grateful slaves and self-made women: fact and fantasy in women's work orientations', *European Journal of Sociology*, 7, 2: 101–121.

Hakim, C. (1993) 'Five feminist myths about women's employment', *British Journal of Sociology*, 46, 3: 429–455.

Halsey, A.H. (1978) *Change in British Society*, Oxford: Oxford University Press.

Halttunen, K. (1982) *Confidence Men and Painted Women: A Study of Middle Class Culture in America, 1830–1870*, New Haven: Yale University Press.

Hamnett, C. (1984) 'Housing the two nations: socio-tenurial polarisation in England and Wales, 1961–1981', *Urban Studies*, 43: 389–405.

Hanmer, J. and Saunders, S. (1983) 'Blowing the cover of the proactive male: a community study of violence to women', in E. Gamarnikow, D. Morgan, J. Purvis and D. Taylorson (eds) *The Public and the Private*, London: Heinemann.

Hannerz, U. (1992) *Cultural Complexity*, New York: Columbia University Press.

Hardy, D. and Ward, C. (1984) *Arcadia for All: The Legacy of a Makeshift Landscape*, London: Mansell.

Hart, N. (1976) *When Marriage Fails: A Study in Status Passage*, London: Tavistock.

Hayden, D. (1984) *Redesigning the American Dream: The Future of Housing, Work and Family Life*, London: Norton.

Hayward, D.G. (1975) 'Home as an environmental and psychological concept', *Landscape*, 20, 1: 2–9.

Heal, K. and Laycock, G. (1988) *Communities and Crime Prevention*, London: HMSO.

Hearn, J. and Morgan, D. (1990) *Men, Masculinities and Social Theory*, London: Unwin Hyman.

Heatherington, P. and May, T. (1988) 'Middle England's mad, bad dream in bricks and mortar', *Guardian*, 27 January.

Heer, F. (1990) *The Medieval World: Europe from 1100-1350*, London: Weidenfeld and Nicholson.

Heise, L., Pitanguy, J. and Germain, A. (1994) *Violence Against Women: The Hidden Health Burden*, World Bank Discussion Papers 255, Geneva: World Books.

Heller, A. (1984) *Everyday Life*, London: Routledge and Kegan Paul.

Hepworth, M. (1995) '"Wrinkles of vice and wrinkles of virtue": the moral interpretation of ageing', in C. Hummel and C.J. Lalive D-Epinay (eds) *Images of Ageing in Western Societies*, University of Geneva: Centre for Interdisciplinary Gerontology.

Higgins, J. (1989) 'Homes and institutions', in G. Allan and G. Crow (eds) *Home and Family: Creating the Domestic Sphere*, London: Macmillan.

Hill, C. (1969) *Reformation to Industrial Revolution: 1530–1780*, Harmondsworth: Penguin.

Hobsbawm, E. (1969) *Industry and Empire: From 1750 to the Present Day*, Harmondsworth: Penguin.

Hockey, J. (1990) *Experiences of Death: An Anthropological Account*, Edinburgh: Edinburgh University Press.

Hole, W. and Attenburrow, J. (1966) *Houses and People: A Review of User Studies at the Building Research Station*, London: HMSO.

Holme, A. (1985) *Housing and Young Families in East London*, London: Routledge and Kegan Paul.

Home Office (1987) *Violent Crime: Police Advice for Women on How to Reduce the Risks*, London: HMSO.

Home Office (1991) *Practical Ways to Crack Crime*, 4th edn, London, HMSO.

Hope, T. and Shaw, M. (1988) *Communities and Crime Reduction*, London: HMSO.

Horkheimer, M. (1972) *Critical Theory: Selected Essays*, London: Continuum.

Hostetler, J. (1997) *Hutterite Society*, Baltimore, MD: Johns Hopkins University Press.

Hough, M. (1985) *Taking Account of Crime: Key Findings from the Second British Crimes Survey*, London: HMSO.

Hough, M. and Mayhew, P. (1983) *The British Crime Survey*, London: HMSO.

Hoyle, C. (1998) *Negotiating Domestic Violence: Criminal Justice and Victims*, Oxford: Oxford University Press.

Hoyles, M. (1991) *The Story of Gardening*, London: Pluto Journeyman.

Hoyles, M. (1994) 'Lost connections and new directions: the private garden and the public park', *The Future of Urban Parks and Open Spaces Working Paper no. 6*, London: Comedia/Demos.

HRH Prince of Wales (1989) *A Vision of Britain: A Personal View of Architecture*, London: Doubleday.

Hughes, E.C. (1958) *Men and their Work*, Glencoe, IL: Free Press.

Hughes, E.C. (1964) 'Good people and dirty work', in H.S. Becker (ed.) *The Other Side*, New York: Free Press.

Hunt, P. (1989) 'Gender and the construction of home life', in G. Allan and G. Crow (eds) *Home and Family: Creating the Domestic Sphere*, London: Macmillan.

Jalland, P. (1996) *Death in the Victorian Family*, Oxford: Oxford University Press.

James, A. (1983) 'The structure and experience of childhood and adolescence: an anthropological approach to socialisation', unpublished PhD thesis, University of Durham.

Janzen, W. (1990) *Limits on Liberty: The Experience of Mennonite, Hutterite and Doukhobor Communities in Canada*, Toronto: University of Toronto Press.

Jencks, C. (1977) *The Language of Post-Modern Architecture*, New York: Rizzoli.

Jenkins, R. (1996) *Social Identity*, London: Routledge.

Jin, J.H. (1993) 'Home as an expression of identity', in M. Bulos and N. Teymur (eds) *Housing: Design, Research, Education*, Aldershot: Avebury.

Johnston, L. (1992) *The Rebirth of Private Policing*, London: Routledge.

Johnston, R. (1980) *City and Society*, Harmondsworth: Penguin.

Jones, G. (1995) *Leaving Home*, Buckingham: Open University Press.

Kaplan, R. and Kaplan, S. (1989) *The Experience of Nature: A Psychological Perspective*, New York: Cambridge University Press.

Kaplan, R. and Kaplan, S. (1990) 'Restorative experience: the healing power of nearby nature', in M. Francis and R. Hester (eds) *The Meaning of Gardens*, Cambridge, MA: MIT Press.

Karasek, R.A. and Theorell, T. (1990) *Healthy Work*, New York: Basic Books.

Kellner, D. (1982) 'Critical theory and consumption', *Theory, Culture and Society*, 1: 2.

Kellner, D. (1989) *Critical Theory: Marxism and Modernity*, Oxford: Blackwell.

Kemp, P. (1989) 'The demunicipalisation of rented housing', in M. Benton and C. Ungerson, *Social Policy Review 1988–9*, London: Longman.

Kent, S. (1990) *Domestic Architecture and the Use of Space: An Inter-Disciplinary Study*, Cambridge: Cambridge University Press.

King, A. (1984) *The Bungalow*, London: Routledge.

Knevitt, C. (1985) *Space on Earth*, London: Thames Methuen.

Korosec-Serfaty, P. (1984) 'The home from attic to cellar', *Journal of Environmental Psychology*, 4: 303–321.

Korosec-Serfaty, P. (1986) 'Dwelling and the experience of burglary', *Journal of Environmental Psychology*, 6: 329–344.

Krier, L. (ed.) (1978) *Rational Architecture*, Brussels: Archives de l'Architecture Moderne.

Kron, J. (1983) *Home Psych: The Social Psychology of Home Decoration*, New York: Clarkson N. Potter.

Laermans, R. (1993) 'Learning to consume: early department stores and the shaping of the modern consumer culture', *Theory Culture and Society*, 10, 4: 79–102.

Lakoff, G. and Johnson, M. (1980) *Metaphors We Live By*, Chicago: University of Chicago Press.

Lambert, J., Paris, C. and Blackaby, B. (1978) *Housing Policy and the State: Allocation, Access and Control*, London: Macmillan.

Lawrence, R. (ed.) (1987) *Housing, Dwellings and Homes: Design Theory, Research and Practice*, London: Wiley.

Laycock, G. (1985) 'Property marking: a deterrent to domestic burglary?', Crime Prevention Unit Paper no. 3, London: Home Office.

Laycock, G. (1989) 'An evaluation of domestic security surveys', Crime Prevention Unit Paper no. 18, London: Home Office.

Le Corbusier (1967) *The Radiant City*, London: Faber & Faber (first English translation of La Ville Radieuse, Paris, 1933).

Lee, D. and Turner, B. (1996) *Conflicts about Class*, London: Longman.

Lee, T. (1990) 'Moving house and home', in S. Fischer and C.L. Cooper (eds) *On the Move: The Psychology of Change of Transition*, New York: Wiley.

Lewis, J. (ed.) (1986) *Women's Experience of Home and Family: 1850–1940*, Oxford: Blackwell.

Litman, V. (1969) 'The cottage and the temple: Melville's symbolic use of architecture', *American Quarterly*, 21, 3: 630–638.

Little, J., Peake, L. and Richardson, P. (1988) *Women in Cities: Gender and the Urban Environment*, London: Macmillan.

Lodziak, C. (1995) *Manipulating Needs: Capitalism and Culture*, London: Pluto.

Lund, B. (1996) *Housing Problems and Housing Policy*, London: Longman.

Lupton, D. (1996) *Food, the Body and the Self*, London: Sage.

McDowell, L. (1983) 'Towards an understanding of the gender divisions of urban space', *Environment and Planning D: Society and Space*, 1: 59–72.

McKean, C. (1987) *The Scottish Thirties*, Edinburgh: Scottish Academic Press.

McKee, L. and Bell, C. (1983) 'Marital and family relations in times of male unemployment', in B. Roberts, R. Finnegan and D. Gallie (eds) *New Approaches to Economic Life*, Manchester: Manchester University Press.

McRae, S. (1986) *Cross Class Families: A Study of Wives' Occupational Superiority*, Oxford: Clarendon Press.

Madigan, R. and Munro, M. (1991) 'Gender, house and "home": social meanings and domestic architecture in Britain', *Journal of Architecture and Planning Research*, 8, 2: 116–132.

Maguire, M. (1982) *Burglary in a Dwelling: The Offence, the Offender and the Victim*, London: Heinemann.

Maguire, M. (1994) 'Crime statistics, patterns and trends: changing perceptions and their implications', in M. Maguire, R. Morgan and R. Reiner (eds) *Oxford Handbook of Criminology*, 2nd edn, Oxford: Clarendon Press.

Malos, E. (ed.) (1980) *The Politics of Housework*, London: Allison and Busby.

Marcuse, H. (1964) *One Dimensional Man*, Boston, MA: Beacon Press.

Marshall, J. and Willox, L. (1986) *The Victorian House*, London: Sidgwick and Jackson.

Martin, B. (1984) 'Mother wouldn't like it! Housework as magic', *Theory, Culture and Society*, 2, 2: 19–36.

Martin, J. and Roberts, C. (1984) *Women and Employment: A Lifetime Perspective*, London: HMSO.

Mason, J. (1989) 'Restructuring the public and the private: the home and marriage in later life', in G. Allan and G. Crow (eds) *Home and Family: Creating the Domestic Sphere*, London: Macmillan.

Matrix (1984) *Making Space: Women in the Man-made Environment*, London: Pluto.

Mauss, M. (1954) *The Gift*, Glencoe, IL: Free Press.

Meltzer, B. and Petras, J. (1975) *Symbolic Interactionism: Genesis, Varieties and Criticisms*, London: Routledge and Kegan Paul.

Mennell, S. (1985) *All Manners of Food: Eating and Taste in England and France from the Middle Ages to the Present*, Oxford: Basil Blackwell.

Middlesbrough Safer Cities (no date) *Your Safety: A Matter of Our Concern*, Middlesbrough: Middlesbrough Borough Council.

Middleton, L. (1983) 'Friendship and isolation: two sides of sheltered housing', in D. Jerrome (ed.) *Ageing in Modern Society*, London: Croom Helm.

Miller, D. (1987) *Material Culture and Mass Consumption*, Oxford: Blackwell.

Millett, K. (1977) *Sexual Politics*, London: Virago.

Mills, C.W. (1951) *White Collar: The American Middle Classes*, New York: Oxford University Press.

Mills, F. (1985) *Determinants and Consequences of the Migration Culture of St.Kitts-Nevis*, Washington, DC: Hemispheric Migration Project, Georgetown University and Intergovernmental Committee on Migration.

Mintel (1992) 'Women and gardening', Retail Intelligence Report, London: Mintel International.

Mintel (1994) 'Specialist garden centres', Retail Intelligence Report, London: Mintel International.

Mintel (1996) 'Specialist garden centres', Retail Intelligence Report, London: Mintel International.

Mintel (1997a) 'Specialist garden centres', Retail Intelligence Report, London: Mintel International.

Mintel (1997b) 'Gardening review', Marketing Intelligence, London: Mintel International.

Mintz, S. (1974) *Caribbean Transformations*, Chicago: Aldine.

Mintz, S. (1985) 'From plantations to peasantries in the Caribbean', in S. Mintz and S. Price (eds) *Caribbean Contours*, Baltimore, MD: Johns Hopkins University Press.

Mirlees-Black, B., Mayhew, P. and Percy, A. (1996) *The 1996 British Crime Survey*, London: HMSO.

Mitchell, K. (1975) *Psychoanalysis and Feminism*, Harmondsworth: Penguin.

Momsen, J. (1987) 'Land settlement as an imposed solution', in J. Besson and J. Momsen (eds) *Land and Development in the Caribbean*, London: Macmillan.

Mooney, J. (1993) *The North London Domestic Violence Survey*, London: Middlesex University.

Moore, B. (1984) *Privacy: Studies in Social and Cultural History*, New York: Sharpe.

Morgan, D. (1992) *Discovering Men*, London: Routledge.

Morgan, P. (1995) *Farewell to the Family? Public Policy and Family Breakdown in Britain and the USA*, London: Institute of Economic Affairs.

Morris, A. (1994) *History of Urban Form: Before the Industrial Revolution*, London: Longman.

Morris, J. and Winn, M. (1990) *Housing and Social Inequality*, London: Hilary Shipman.

Morris, L. (1990) *The Workings of the Household*, Cambridge: Polity.

Morris, L. (1997) 'Economic change and domestic life', in *The Changing Shape of Work*, London: Macmillan.

Morris, M. (1996) '"Tha'll be like a blush rose when tha' grows up my little lass": English cultural and gendered identity in the Secret Garden', *Environment and Planning D: Society and Space*, 14, 1: 59–70.

Morris, R. and Rodger, R. (eds) (1993) *The Victorian City: A Reader in British Urban History: 1820–1914*, London: Longman.

Mosse, G. (1985) *Nationalism and Sexuality*, New York: Howard Fertig.

Munro, M. and Madigan, R. (1993) 'Privacy in the private sphere', *Housing Studies*, 8, 1: 29–45.

Muthesius, S. (1982) *The English Terraced House*, London: Yale University Press.

National Federation of Housing Associations (1988) *Building Your Future: Self-Build Housing Initiatives for the Unemployed*, London: National Federation of Housing Associations.

Newman, K. (1988) *Falling from Grace: The Experience of Downward Mobility in the American Middle Class*, New York: Free Press.

Newman, O. (1972) *Defensible Space: Crime Prevention through Urban Design*, New York: Collier.

North Housing Trust (1993) *Accommodating Diversity: The Design of Housing for Minority Ethnic, Religious and Cultural Groups*, London: National Federation of Housing Associations.

Nuttgens, P. (1989) *The Home Front: Housing the People 1840–1990*, London: BBC Books.

Oakley, A. (1974a) *Housewife*, Harmondsworth: Penguin.

Oakley, A. (1974b) *The Sociology of Housework*, London: Martin Robertson.

Oc, T. and Tiesdell, S. (1997) *Safer City Centres: Reviving the Public Realm*, London: Paul Chapman.

Okely, J. (1983) *The Traveller-Gypsies*, Cambridge: Cambridge University Press.

Oldman, C. (1986) 'Housing policies for older people', in P. Malpass (ed.) *Housing Crisis*, London: Croom Helm.

Oliver, P., Davis, I. and Bentley, I. (1981) *Dunroamin: The Suburban Semi and its Enemies*, London: Pimlico.

Olwig, K. (1990) 'The struggle for respectability: Methodism and Afro-Caribbean culture on 19th century Nevis', *Nieuwe West-Indische Gids*, 64, 3–4: 93–114.

Olwig, K. (1993) *Global Culture, Island Identity: Studies in Anthropology and History*, Reading: Harwood Academic.

Olwig, K. (1995) 'Cultural complexity after freedom: Nevis and beyond', in K. Olwig (ed.) *Small Islands, Large Questions: Society, Culture and Resistance in the Post-Emancipation Caribbean*, London: Frank Cass.

Olwig, K. (1997) 'Cultural sites: sustaining a home in a deterioralized world', in K. Olwig and K. Hastrup (eds) *Siting Culture: The Shifting Anthropological Object*, London: Routledge.

Orwell, G. (1933) *Down and Out in Paris and London*, Harmondsworth: Penguin.

Pahl, R. (1984) *Divisions of Labour*, Oxford: Blackwell.

Painter, K. (1991) 'Wife rape, marriage and the law', Research Report, Manchester: Faculty of Economic and Social Science, University of Manchester.

Painter, S. (1953) *A History of the Middle Age: 284–1500*, London: Macmillan.

Parker Morris (1961) *Homes for Today and Tomorrow*, London: HMSO.

Parsons, T. (1954) *Essays in Sociological Theory*, New York: Free Press.

Payne, G. (1987a) *Mobility and Change in Modern Society*, London: Macmillan.

Payne, G. (1987b) *Employment and Unemployment*, London: Macmillan.

Pearson, L. (1988) *The Architectural and Social History of Cooperative Living*, London: Macmillan.

Pepper, D. (1996) *Modern Environmentalism: An Introduction*, London: Routledge.

Pevsner, N. (1975) *Pioneers of Modern Design: From Morris to Walter Gropius*, Harmondsworth: Penguin.

Pevsner, N. (1985) *The Buildings of England: County Durham*, Harmondsworth: Penguin.

Philpott, S. (1973) *West Indian Migration: The Montserrat Case*, London: Athlone.

Pollan, M. (1997) *A Place of My Own: The Education of an Amateur Builder*, London: Bloomsbury.

Porritt, J. (1986) *Seeing Green*, Oxford: Blackwell.

Porter, R. (1990) *English Society in the Eighteenth Century*, Harmondsworth: Penguin.

Power, A. (1987) *Property Before People: The Management of Twentieth Century Council Housing*, Hemel Hempstead: Allen and Unwin.

Pratt, G. (1981) 'The house as an expression of social worlds', in J. Duncan (ed.) *Housing and Identity: Cross Cultural Perspectives*, London: Croom Helm.

Purdue, D. (1997) 'Backyard biodiversity: a sociology of seed saving in the south west', mimeo, British Sociological Association Annual Conference, York, April.

Rapoport, A. (1969) *House Form and Culture*, Englewood Cliffs, NJ: Prentice Hall.

Rapoport, A. (1981) 'Identity and environment', in J.S. Duncan (ed.) *Housing and Identity: Cross Cultural Perspectives*, London: Croom Helm.

Rapport, N. and Dawson, A. (1999) 'Identity and movement: a polemic', in N. Rapport and A. Dawson (eds) *Migrants of Identity – Perceptions of Home in a World in Movement*, Oxford: Berg.

Ravetz, A. (1974a) *Model Estate: Planned Housing at Quarry Hill, Leeds*, London: Croom Helm.

Ravetz, A. (1974b) 'From working class tenement to modern flat', in A. Sutcliffe (ed.) *Multi-Storey Living: The British Working Class Experience*, London: Croom Helm.

Ravetz, A. (ed.) (1995) *The Place of Home: English Domestic Environments 1914–2000*, London: Spon.

Redclift, M. and Benton, T. (1994) *Social Theory and the Global Environment*, London: Routledge.

Reed, M. (1984) *The Georgian Triumph: 1700–1830*, London: Paladin.

Reid, I. (1981) *Social Class Differences in Britain*, 2nd edn, London: Grant McIntyre.

Rex, J. and Moore, R. (1967) *Race, Community and Conflict: A Study of Sparkbrook*, Oxford: Oxford University Press.

Richardson, B. (1983) *Caribbean Migrants*, Knoxville: University of Tennessee Press.

Riessman, C. (1990) *Divorce Talk: Women and Men Make Sense of Personal Relationships*, New Brunswick, NJ: Rutgers University Press.

Rigby, A. (1974) *Alternative Realities: A Study of Communes and their Members*, London: Routledge.

Ritzer, G. (1996) *The McDonaldization of Society*, Thousand Oaks, CA: Pine Forge Press.

Rivers, T., Cruickshank, D., Darley, G. and Pawley, M. (1992) *The Name of the Room: A History of the British House and Home*, London: BBC Books.

Roberts, M. (1991) *Living in a Man-made World: Gender Assumptions in Modern Housing Design*, London: Routledge.

Roberts, R. (1973) *The Classic Slum: Salford Life in the First Quarter of the Century*, Harmondsworth: Penguin.

Robson, B. (1969) *Urban Analysis*, Cambridge: Cambridge University Press.

Rock, P. (1979) *The Making of Symbolic Interactionism*, London: Macmillan.

Rowan, D. (1998) 'Home alone', *Guardian*, 20 January.

Rowe, P. (1972) 'A question of architecture, a matter of style', *Architectural Design*, August: 466.

Rowe, P. (1993) *Modernity and Housing*, Cambridge, MA: MIT Press.

Saunders, P. (1990) *A Nation of Home Owners*, London: Unwin Hyman.

Saunders, P. and Williams, P. (1988) 'The constitution of the home: towards a research agenda', *Housing Studies*, 3, 2: 81–93.

Schwartz Cowan, R. (1989) *More Work for Mother*, London: Free Association.

Scoffham, E. (1984) *The Shape of British Housing*, Harlow: George Godwin.

Sharpe, S. (1995) *Just Like a Girl*, 2nd edn, Harmondsworth: Penguin.

Sherman, M. (ed.) (1946) *The Daily Mail Ideal Home Book 1946–1947*, London: Daily Mail Ideal Home Publications.

Sherwood, R. (1978) *Modern Housing Prototypes*, Cambridge, MA: MIT Press.

Shorter, E. (1979) *The Making of the Modern Family*, London: Fontana/Collins.

Siltanen, J. (1994) *Locating Gender: Occupational Segregation, Wages and Domestic Responsibilities*, London: UCL Press.

Silverstone, R. (ed.) (1997) *Visions of Suburbia*, London: Routledge.

Sime, J. (1993) 'What makes a house a home: the garden?', in M. Bulos and N. Teymur (eds) *Housing: Design, Research, Education*, Aldershot: Avebury.

Sixsmith, J. (1986) 'The meaning of home: an exploratory study of environmental experience', *Journal of Environmental Psychology*, 6: 281–298.

Sixsmith, J. and Sixsmith, A. (1990) 'Places in transition: the impact of life events in the experience of home', in T. Putnam and C. Newman (eds) *Household Choices*, London: Fortune.

Soper, K. (1995) *What is Nature? Culture, Politics and the Non-Human*, Oxford: Blackwell.

Spence, J. and Holland, P. (1991) *Family Snaps: The Meanings of Domestic Photography*, London: Virago.

Stanko, E. (1985) *Intimate Intrusions: Women's Experiences of Male Violence*, London: Routledge and Kegan Paul.

Stanko, E. (1990) 'When precaution is normal: a feminist critique of crime prevention', in L. Gelsthorpe and A. Morris (eds) *Feminist Perspectives on Criminology*, Oxford: Oxford University Press.

Stein, S. (1992) *The Shaker Experience in America: A History of the United Society of Believers*, New Haven: Yale University Press.

Stockdale, J. and Gresham, P. (1995) 'Combating burglary: an evaluation of three strategies', Police Research Group Crime Detection and Prevention Series Paper no. 59, London: Home Office.

Straus, M. and Gelles, R. (1986) 'Social change and change in family violence from 1975 to 1985 as revealed by two national studies', *Journal of Marriage and the Family*, 48: 465–480.

Sudjic, D. (1993) 'The taste cycle', *Guardian*, 24 August.

Suzy Lamplugh Trust (no date) *A Guide to Safe Travel*, London: Suzy Lamplugh Trust.

Taylor, S. (1997) 'Empowerment or degradation? Total quality management and the service sector', in R. Brown (ed.) *The Changing Shape of Work*, London: Macmillan.

Thomas, D. (1954) *Under Milk Wood*, London: Dent.

Thomas, K. (1983) *Man and the Natural World: Changing Attitudes in England 1500–1800*, London: Allen Lane.

Thomas-Hope, E. (1978) 'The establishment of a migration tradition: British West Indian movements to the Hispanic Caribbean in the century after emancipation', in C.G. Clarke (ed.) *Caribbean Social Relations*, Liverpool: Centre for Latin American Studies.

Thomas-Hope, E. (1992) *Explanation in Caribbean Migration*, London: Macmillan.

Thomas-Hope, E. (1995) 'Island systems and the paradox of freedom: migration in the post-emancipation Leeward Islands', in K. Fog Olwig (ed.) *Small Islands, Large Questions: Society, Culture and Resistance in the Post-Emancipation Caribbean*, London: Frank Cass.

Thompson, F. (1982) *The Rise of Suburbia*, Leicester: Leicester University Press.

Tilley, N. and Webb, J. (1994) 'Burglary reduction: findings from safer city schemes', Police Research Group Crime Prevention Unit Series no. 51, London: Home Office.

Tinker, A. (1984) *Staying Put: Helping Elderly People*, London: HMSO.

Tivers, J. (1988) 'Women with young children: constraints on activities in the urban environment', in J. Little, L. Peake and P. Richardson (eds) *Women in Cities: Gender and the Urban Environment*, London: Macmillan.

Tosh, J. (1996) '"New men"? The bourgeois cult of home', *History Today*, 46, 12: 9–15.

Turkington, R. (1995) 'Gardens and external space', in A. Ravetz (ed.) *The Place of Home*, London: Spon.

Turner, J. (1976) *Housing by People: Towards Autonomy in Built Environments*, London: Marion Boyars.

Turner, V. (1974) *Dramas, Fields and Metaphors: Symbolic Action in Human Society*, Ithaca, NY: Cornell University Press.

Tytler, G. (1982) *Physiognomy in the European Novel: Faces and Fortunes*, Princeton, NJ: Princeton University Press.

Valins, M. (1988) *Housing for Elderly People*, London: Architectural Press.

Veblen, T. (1934) *The Theory of the Leisure Class*, New York: Modern Library.

Vergara, C. (1994) 'Fortress mentality', *New Statesman and Society*, 4 February.

Vergara, C. (1995) *The New American Ghetto*, New Brunswick, NJ: Rutgers University Press.

Wajcman, J. (1992) 'Domestic technology: labour saving or enslaving', in G. Kirkup and L. Keller (eds) *Inventing Women: Science, Technology and Gender*, Oxford: Polity.

Walby, S. (1986) *Patriarchy at Work*, Oxford: Polity.

Walby, S. (1990) *Theorising Patriarchy*, Oxford: Blackwell.

Walker, J. and McNicol, L. (1994) *Evaluating the Police Response to Domestic Violence*, Newcastle: University of Newcastle.

Walklate, S. (1991) 'Victims, crime prevention and social control', in R. Reiner and M. Cross (eds) *Beyond Law and Order*, London: Macmillan.

Walmsley, D. and Lewis, G. (1993) *People and Environment*, 2nd edn, Harlow: Longman.

Walter Segal Self Build Trust (1993) *You Build: A Guide to Building Your Own Home*, London: Walter Segal Self Build Trust.

Ward, C. (1985) *When We Build Again*, London: Pluto.

Ward, C. (1988) 'Why not everywhere?', *Town and Country Planning*, July/August: 52–54.

Ward, C. (1989) *Welcome Thinner City: Urban Survival in the 1990s*, London: Bedford Square Press.

Warde, A. (1994) 'Consumption, identity formation and uncertainty', *Sociology*, 28, 4: 877–898.

Warner, M. (1996) *The Inner Eye*, London: South Bank Centre.

Watson, S. (1986) 'Housing and the family', *International Journal of Urban and Regional Research*, 10, 1: 8–28.

Wekerle, G., Peterson, R. and Morley, D. (eds) (1980) *New Space for Women*, Boulder, CO: Westview.

Wheelock, J. (1990) *Husbands at Home*, London: Routledge.

Whiteaker, S. (1998) *The Good Retreat Guide*, London: Rider.

Willcocks, D., Peace, S. and Kellaher, L. (1987) *Private Lives in Public Places*, London: Tavistock.

Williams, R. (1975) *The Country and the City*, St Albans: Paladin.

Williams, R. (1980) *Problems in Materialism and Culture*, London: Verso.

Willmott, P. and Young, M. (1960) *Family and Class in a London Suburb*, London: Routledge and Kegan Paul.

Wilson, A. (1992) *The Culture of Nature: North American Landscapes from Disney to the Exxon Valdez*, Oxford: Blackwell.

Wilson, E. (1985) *Adorned in Dreams: Fashion and Modernity*, London: Virago.

Wilson, P. (1969) 'Reputation and respectability: a suggestion for Caribbean ethnology', *Man* 4(1): 70–84.

Wilson, P. (1973) *Crab Antics: The Social Anthropology of English-Speaking Negro Societies of the Caribbean*, New Haven, CT: Yale University Press.

Wilson, P. (1974) *Oscar: An Inquiry into the Nature of Sanity?* Prospect Heights, IL: Waveland Press.

Winn, D. (1986) *Men on Divorce: Conversations with Denise Winn*, London: Piatkus.

Wood, C. (1978) *Dictionary of Victorian Painting*, Woodbridge: Antique Collectors' Club.

Woollacott, J. (1980) 'Dirty and deviant work', in G. Esland and G. Salaman (eds) *The Politics of Work and Occupations*, Milton Keynes: Open University Press.

Worsdall, F. (1979) *The Tenement: A Way of Life*, Edinburgh: Chambers.

Wright, R. and Decker, S. (1994) *Burglars on the Job: Streetlife and Residential Break-ins*, Boston, MA: Northeastern University Press.

Yorke, F. (1934) *The Modern House*, London: Architectural Press.

Yorke, F. (1944) *The Modern House in England*, 2nd edn, Cheam: Architectural Press.

Young, M. and Willmott, P. (1957) *Family and Kinship in East London*, London: Routledge and Kegan Paul.

Zedner, L. (1994) 'Victims', in M. Maguire (ed.) *Oxford Handbook of Criminology*, Oxford: Clarendon Press.

Zimmeck, M. (1986) 'Jobs for the girls: the expansion of clerical work for women, 1850–1914', in A. John (ed.) *Unequal Opportunities: Women's Employment in England 1800–1918*, Oxford: Blackwell.

INDEX